The Ultimate Medical
Consultant Interview Guide

Published by *RAR Medical Services Limited*
www.medicalconsultantinterview.co.uk

The Ultimate Medical Consultant Interview Guide

Dr. Ranjna Garg
Ms. Shalini Patni
Dr. Anjum Gandhi
Dr. Anil K Agarwal

OXBRIDGE
MEDICAL SOCIETY

About the Authors

Dr Ranjna Garg: Author

Ranjna has over 25 years of clinical teaching and research experience. She is currently based as Consultant Endocrinologist at the Princess Alexandra Hospital. She is a PACES examiner. She has taught hundreds of junior doctors and prepared them through postgraduate examinations MRCP, PACES and job interviews including consultant interviews. She also teaches at the Leicester University. She has authored number of publications in peer reviewed journal, and written/edited books. In her spare time, she enjoys photography, make candles and runs marathons.

Miss Shalini Patni: Author

Shalini has over 25 years of clinical, teaching and research experience in Obstetrics and Gynaecology and is based University Hospitals Birmingham (UHB) NHS Foundation Trust. She is the Honorary Senior Clinical Lecturer at University of Birmingham and is actively involved in teaching and assessment of medical students. She is the Regional lead for Ultrasound for Obstetrics and Gynaecology specialist trainees at West Midlands Heath Education England. Shalini has taught and mentored several senior specialty trainees many are now consultants.

Dr Anil K Agarwal: Author

Anil has over 25 years of experience in clinical teaching and research. He is currently the lead of stroke services at the Basildon and Thurrock University hospital. He has authored number of publications in peer reviewed journals. He is also MRCP(PACES) examiner and enjoys gardening and hiking.

Dr. Anjum Gandhi

Anjum has over 25 years of clinical, teaching and research experience in paediatrics. He is currently the Clinical Director for Children's Services at University Hospital Birmingham and holds an honorary consultant contract in paediatric cardiology at Birmingham Children's hospital. He has published widely in peer reviewed journals Anjum is also a contributor to the cardiology chapters of the new edition of Manual of Advanced Paediatric Life support (APLS).

About the Editor
Dr Rohan Agarwal

Rohan is the Co-founder of UniAdmissions and graduated in Medicine from Gonville and Caius College, Cambridge. He has tutored and supported hundreds of successful Oxbridge and medical applicants in past 5 years. He has authored more than fifty books on admissions tests and interviews for admissions to prestigious courses in the United Kingdom and Europe.

Foreword

Congratulations on taking the first step to your Medical Consultant Interview prepar[...]
for an interview then that means the hospital is interested in what you had to say i[...]
interview is not a place to recount all of this information; it is a place to showcase[...]
integrity, and your ability to offer the services you have trained so far.

Interviews require dedicated preparation - don't leave things to chance! Consultant in[...]
formulaic and you can predict the vast majority of questions that you're likely to be asked. Unsurprisingly,
so can everyone else. Thus, you do yourself a great disservice if you don't have comprehensive answers
prepared for these questions. Ensure you've done your research on the interview format, the pros/cons of
multitude of questions and you have answers lined up for the common interview questions, e.g. *"Why this
trust?"* and *"Why you should get this job?"* etc.

Most people will research their job and field comprehensively. However, they fail to prepare answers for
commonly asked questions. Its very common for applicants to misunderstand questions leading to responses
that lack structure and flow. This is where this book is most useful – it gives you examples of good and bad
responses with commentary on what makes it a good/bad response.

Ultimately, with fierce competition, there is no guarantee for success. Whilst there will undoubtedly be
conflicting demands on your time – remember that a small amount of preparation has the potential to literally
change your life. Don't take it lightly – work hard, put in the hours and do yourself justice.

Dr Ranjna Garg

THE BASICS

What is a Medical Consultant Interview?

A medical consultant interview is a formal discussion between interviewer and interviewee. This is normally the *final* step in the consultant application process. Traditionally, interviews last around 30-45 minutes. Usually, this will also include a short presentation. Topic is usually given to the interviewee beforehand. This could either be something very topical or an issue that the organisation is facing and they are looking at fresh approach. Your pre-interview visit (see later) can provide pointers to the challenges faced by the organisation. Always enquire about the time allotted for the presentation and prepare a presentation which does not exceed the expected time.

Why is there an Interview?

Consultant post is a demanding job, being a mix of clinical and managerial work requiring excellent communication skills. It requires great team working ability and the skills to get out of muddy water at times. Consultant interviews are for long term appointments (except for locum/fixed term contracts). Trust are aiming to appoint someone that can contribute clinically as well as in work within the established framework, support the organisation, takes initiatives to develop new services/newer methods of working and above all, is a good team player.

The interview process is designed to identify candidates that would be best suited for such demanding jobs by assess multiple qualities e.g. your motivation to the job you have applied, your clinical skills, communication skills, team working and leadership skills etc.

Whilst the interview is not testing your knowledge and skills about a specific subject, it helps to have a good knowledge base. The interview process will assess candidates on their abilities and mindset to manage team, provide clinical care. participate in research and can contributes to the teaching in the best efficient manner.

Trusts recognise that the interviews can be stressful and may utilise this to assess candidates' reactions to stress; to see if they can cope with the pressure. It is a process where the candidates are judged on their quick thinking, logical approach, and ability to formulate a comprehensive, coherent, structured response. The interview is not about tricking you. It's about testing your abilities to harp on your existing knowledge and use it to come up with solutions in tricky situation (dealing with a difficult colleague). The interview is also about assessing your abilities to see if you can come up with plausible solutions, in situations of conflict, even if you don't know the answer. Another aspect which the employer is keen to assess is your interest in the department and the Trust. Information obtained during the pre-interview visit is key to be prepared for this.

Following sections covers the basics of the consultant interview preparation and process that you should be aware of.

Preparing for Your Consultant Interview?

Many applicants will jump straight to the questions part of this book and attempt to learn the "good answers" by rote. Whilst this is psychologically comforting, it is of minimal value in actually preparing you for the interview. Use this book as guidance. Develop the skills to construct logical and structured answers so that you are familiar with the format. Cramming for your interview by rote learning the answers provided in this book will make your responses clichéd.

Before you get to the stage of "interview", you need to get some basics discussed below.

Top Tip! Preparation is the key. Plan ahead and plan well.

THE APPLICATION PROCESS

Search the job you want

Most of the Consultant jobs are now advertised on NHS jobs (www.jobs.nhs.uk). Other sources to look out for are BMJ careers advise, hospital doctor journal, www.reed.co.uk etc. Some trusts also advertise on their own websites. The job advert on the website may be detailed or may just advise you to visit the trust website and search within medical jobs. The NHS jobs site usually includes details of the job, essential and desirable criteria for job, a job description and link to apply (which may open the application page or take you to the trust's website). You will need to register and create a log in. You can set up email alert for specific attributes e.g. adult, substantive, Colorectal surgeon, within 20 miles of Manchester.

Weigh pros and cons of following when searching for the job:

> Teaching University hospital Vs non-teaching hospital
> Large city Vs district general hospital
> Reputation of the hospital/department/colleague
> Research facilities available/not available
> Single site Vs split site
> All hospital Vs mix of Hospital and Community Vs all community based
> Distance you are willing to travel and time it takes to travel between home to hospital (unless you are willing to relocate)
> Career progression prospects: College tutor, director of education, CD etc

Plan and Do your Research: Job

Start off by finding out exactly about the job advertised? What is expected from the incumbent? What is the department like? What is the trust like? You can do this by reading carefully the job description and person specification (criteria for short listing). These are Two documents that are most useful in the application process. It is always good to contact any person known to you who is working in the same department at the trust. Some common things to search:

> Is this a locum, fixed term or substantive post? If fixed term or locum, check if a substantive post is being created (not so for maternity cover)
> Is this a replacement post (due to retirement/resignation)? If due to resignation, it is worth exploring why the previous incumbent left the organisation.
> Are there any specific requirements from the organisation: A specific service they are looking for. It is no point applying to a bariatric surgeon job when your CV is full of Liver transplant work and lacks bariatric surgery work. Tailor your CV according to the job you want/can do.
> Is there a local candidate? Is he/she applying? If not, why? Do not be put off by the internal candidate. Internal candidates may have an edge over others as they are already in the loop and know many of the potential interviewers. But this could be a double-edged sword and they might get too comfortable and not do so well in interview (despite being the preferred candidate). This is where the role of the collegiate/lay person becomes even more important. If there is an internal candidate, do as best as you can. Even if you are not successful, you will have some interview practice and the feedback will only make you better!
> Does the job offer something that matches your interest (job/personal): This is one of the most vital aspect while you research around the job you are thinking to apply for. Does the job description fit in with your clinical interest /expertise? Is there a scope for you to develop the service? If the service already exists, would you fit in with the existing team (you could explore this in your pre- interview visit). If the service you want to offer does not currently exists, then you can sell yourself as the one to introduce a new service. If latter you need to be prepared with reasons why the new service should be introduced i.e. is there a national driver, is it a KPI, does it attract specialized commissioning etc.
> Does this job fit in with your personal life? Don't forget you will be doing this job for next 15 -30 years. It may be that you are planning a family or already have one. Good to check the area, house prices, schools, and other facilities.

Applying for the job you want

To be able to do best at an interview, it is vital to set the scene which gets started by selecting/choosing the 'right' job and then filling the relevant application form which will allow you to get short-listed. The application form should describe you in the best possible way bringing out all your strengths that will allow you to stand from the other co-applicants. This will only be possible when your 'heart is in that job.'

You will be doing this job for life (unless you decide to change). So, check and ensure that this is the job you want, the job has something in it for you. Consider your own personal development, career progression and your own aspirations.

This is the most important document which any trust is obliged to enclose with the application pack. This will detail the roles and responsibilities and skills required for the job. It is essential that you read this very carefully as it helps you in identifying if the job fits with your skills and interests before you start thinking of applying for a job.

It will not only lay the essential duties the job demands of you which are otherwise called Direct Clinical Care (DCC) but also should include time for supporting professional activities or SPA. It is fundamental that you carefully read this to understand that how many hours the job is advertised for and how those hours are split between DCC and SPA.

Job Description also contains a wealth of information about the trust and the department you wish to apply for. This includes the population it serves, demographics of that population, services it provides and services it excels in. It will often have details about trust management structure. It should also include similarly the details of your department, the consultant working within that department, and services they provide. Look at the special interest of the consultant already in post and check/explore further at pre-interview visit. This way, you can tailor your application to the needs of the department. It is no point offering service that is already provided by someone else!

Personal Specification Form

The personal specification is a description of the qualifications, skills, experience, knowledge and other attributes which a candidate must possess to be eligible for applying for that job. It forms a basis of selection criteria for short-listing process. It is usually split into 'Essential' and 'Desirable' Criteria. The Essential criteria list the minimum attributes which a prospective applicant **must** possess and often are a combination of qualifications and possession of license to practice in the country. The Desirable criteria is the list of other attributes which the employer is looking for, to be able to identify the suitable candidate complementing both the existing team and the service.

It is absolutely essential to read these carefully and these attributes are listed in your application form as and when asked for. It is also very useful that you list them when you are writing your CV so that it is tailored for the job. Carefully listed attributes make you stand out and help the employer in short listing you and equally any other attributes from desirable list helps you having an edge from other co-applicants.

Completing the Application

Most organisations now accept electronic applications. Once you have decided on a job you want to apply, you can add this to your favourite. If the job application is within the NHS online jobs, the first application may take time as you need to add all information (your demographics, training details, rotation etc) but subsequent application/s become easier. Having said that, please ensure that you individualise each application (based on job description). It is no point selling yourself as Paediatric Diabetes expert if the trust is looking for the Paediatric Cystic fibrosis expert.

For job application on the trust website, you need to complete the application form on the trust website (needs creating a log in and setting up a password) which may sound cumbersome but not as daunting as it seems (unless this is your first application). You can copy and paste from NHS jobs online application/CV, if you have one. Remember to tailor your application to the job based on requirements as set out in the job description/criteria for shortlisting without offering falsifying information!).

When completing the application form, make note of:
➤ Complete all sections
➤ Match your experience with the job description: give evidence if possible
➤ You are not writing a bible: keep is short, simple and precise but keep interesting
➤ Read it, print it, check for typos and let someone else check it as well before submitting.

Can JD change before or after job offer is made, how?

The Job description is written with careful assessment of the service needs and any vision for future expansion. It therefore is usually followed. However, this can be changed due to a valid reason. Any major change has to be communicated formally with the applicants and may need the job to be re-advertised. If there arises a need for change after the job-offer is made then this has to be with mutual discussion and agreement between the employing trust and the candidate. This does not take away your statutory rights. Job description are usually approved by the relevant royal colleges. Any changes in JD will require reapproval unless this is done with mutual consent.

Curriculum Vitae (CV)

The job application is online now so you will be applying by filling an application form. It is stil important to have CV as the information in CV could form the backbone of your application. The Curriculum vitae is a written overview of yourself describing your qualifications, training, work experience, other attributes like presentations and publications, experience in audit and research and any other achievements and hobbies or interests. In other words, it is an auto-biography for the purposes of job-seeking.

The important aspect of writing a CV is that it should allow you to stand out from the crowd! This means that it should be short and succinct but still should have all the vital details necessary for that job. One good example is the CV requirements for other industries for e.g. finance, where they specify it to be one side of A4!

It is best to break the details into meaningful headings like Education and Qualifications, Clinical, Academic, Management and Personal. It is good to use one formatting style all the way through. Make sure you have corrected the spellings and run a spell check. Proof read it few times or even ask someone as fresh eyes to do a final check for you. The author has found several grammatical and spelling mistakes in the CV's which are hurriedly written. This does not leave a good impression and depicts the candidate as one with who does not have an eye for attention to detail. Give details of the clinical work, past experience in senior role, publications or authorships of any kind. Don't forget to include your pastime as well as career ambitions.

You MUST always **tailor** the CV to the person specification to allow any other detail to be extracted which has not been either asked on the application form or is required to select from other applicants. For example, mention of the first page the job title you are applying for. The common mistake is to use a generic CV for any/all jobs. This often portrays you as either not interested or laid back! Beware that 'ONE size does not fit ALL'

Making your CV fit for purpose is essential. E.g., if the job being advertised has significant teaching commitments, highlight these and putting these early on in the CV whereas if the job is more clinical oriented than your clinical work (wards, clinic, theatre etc) should be emphasized.

List of Referees: Must be recent or within last two years. If this is your first application, one of the referees must be your educational supervisor or training programme director. For applicant already doing either a locum job or switching job, your referee must be your line manager (clinical director/service line lead of your department).

Your CV should have following headings/subheadings: Modify CV as needed (based on job and the job description advertised for the job. You may want to add or removes some details as necessary:

➢ Personal details: name, address and contact details (telephone and email). There is no need to provide your twitter handle or Instagram account details and how many followers you have!
➢ Qualifications: with year and University
➢ Current appointment(s) and Employment history: in chronological order (most recent first)
➢ Clinical experience: if your job has more than one component, give all of them.
➢ Relevant courses and training
➢ Presentations/Publications
➢ Audit and service improvement
➢ Management experience and responsibilities
➢ Teaching experience
➢ Leadership, strategic, policy experience
➢ References

Submission check list

It is prudent to ensure that you have enclosed all the documents as requested. There is usually quite useful information in the covering letter to help you with this. Alternatively, some trusts also provide you with a list of documents required along with the application pack. The commonly asked documents include:

➢ UpToDate CV
➢ License to practice: GMC Registration
➢ Proof of identity, for e.g. your passport, driving license, utility bills
➢ CRB clearance
➢ Equal opportunity form

Short Listing Process

This is the first step towards your interview process following submission of your application. This is usually done by a panel of consultants with similar interest as yourself along with the clinical director or service lead. The process is objective and fair and often based on a scoring system devised by the service lead in conjunction with Human Resources (HR). All the applications are anonymised by the HR to allow no bias and prejudice before circulating to the above panel. Each application is then scored on an agreed scoring system which takes account of the essential and desirable criteria. The applicants which score above an agreed score are then invited for the interview.

The above process is just one example and this may vary depending on the number of applicants. Usually for any job on an average 3-4 candidates are invited for the interview.

THE PRE-INTERVIEW VISIT

So, once you are short-listed and invited for the interview, you are already many steps ahead of the co-applicants who unfortunately were not successful. Your chance is now as good as any other short-listed candidate. This is therefore an opportunity to do all what you can to GET the job and shine above the other candidates invited for the interview.

One of the most important steps towards a successful interview is the pre-interview visit. This is the visit made to the trust before the actual interview. The purpose of this visit is to know your job in more detail but more importantly to meet the key people to understand what actually they are looking in the prospective candidate. Equally it is to know the internal politics within the trust and your department. Regarding the trust you may like to know how is the trust faring financially, is it meeting its targets, what is the latest CQC and Monitor rating, is it looking for a 'merger', key priorities of the trust over next 3-5 years, trust's relationship with its commissioners. Equally how is your department's position and how has it fared towards cost saving targets.

It is more or less an essential visit and even if you live far you may make it for example by visiting the trust the day before the interview and thus avoiding making 2 journeys. Some trusts organise a 'meet and greet' arrangement where the key people and the shortlisted candidate are all invited to attend. The latter also may provide an opportunity to be able to meet other candidates.

Arrange Pre-Interview Visit

The next step is to find out who are the key people to meet and how to arrange those meetings? Normally in your short-listing letter you will be provided with the names of all the members of the consultant interview panel. It is advisable to meet all of them in most circumstances. You may consider to not meet with the Royal college representative as their role is more to provide an opinion on the job description and the appointability of the candidate in terms of appropriate training to match the person specifications. Equally the chairman of the interview panel is mostly tasked with the operational aspect rather than have a say in the candidate selection.

Along with meeting the relevant members of the interview panel, you should also try and meet other people who may have information that will help you for the interview. For example, consultant from the speciality, business managers, theatre, delivery suite managers, governance and safety leads, matrons, senior nurse/midwives.

Depending on the job you have applied for, you may also like to meet consultant from other specialties, service user representatives if applicable. You may like to attend MDT meetings again depending on the job and similarly trust board meetings especially if there is also a managerial component with the job.

The suggested list of people advisable to visit/meet includes:

➤ Panel Members: CEO or representative, Medical Director, Clinical/Divisional Director, Consultants, university representative (for academic jobs), any nurse/midwife manager as listed.
➤ Non-Panel Members: Other consultants, especially who have similar interest or provide similar service, nurse /midwife manager, head of midwifery, theatre/delivery suite manager, business manager.

> **Top tip:** Your question should be probing and not merely gathering information that you can gleam from other sources. Don't ask question for sake of asking. Asking a question about the direction the trust is taking may portray you in bad light if the trust recently announced plans for merger in the board meeting.

What to ask?

It is good to have some structure and format in mind as though the information you will gather will help you towards the interview questions, equally bear in mind that the other person you are meeting with is also making their impression about you and 'First impression always counts.'

The questions you will ask each individual will obviously depend on their role within the trust. They should broadly:

➢ Obtain a clear picture of the role and the team's expectations towards the prospective candidate
➢ Discover the strengths and weaknesses of the trust and its plans for development and reforms
➢ Gauge the hierarchy within the trust and the place of the department you have applied for
➢ Understand the trust's financial position and the contribution the department you have applied for
➢ Get to know the trust's goals and targets for both short and medium term and identifying any opportunities for your development and career.

It may be that some of the above listed may not be there at the panel for e.g. Clinical Director, CEO or Medical Director. It is always wise to see them simply to be able to get better understanding of the service and prospective team. If you are unable to see them then ask if someone else is available at that level. Clinical Director will be able to expand more on your role within the department, to know if there are any immediate problems and how your appointment may help make a difference, impact on the service if there is a move towards a merger or STP or any other competition.

Equally you may/should meet other members of the team from the department as this may provide you with the opportunity to ask questions more focused on the job and the team you are hoping to join. Some examples can be:

➢ What are they looking for in the new colleague?
➢ Is this a new or replacement post?
➢ What are the department's priorities over short and medium term?
➢ What are the key areas in which department needs to improve?
➢ What are the opportunities for non-clinical roles: education, research, governance?
➢ Would there be opportunity to develop your special interest?
➢ What are the strengths and weaknesses of the team?

You may also like to find out the working relationships between the multi-disciplinary teams like with midwives, nurses, administrative staff. If applicable it may be helpful to also meet any trainees current or ex to gauge the working relationships and working environment in general and what do the juniors think of the department and trust as a whole.

In summary. this visit is mainly to allow you to have some idea of the questions you may be asked at the interview and equally give you ample time to prepare those answers well to be able to reply in a short succinct manner but with substance. This cannot be truer for some difficult questions like: trust may have a recent poor rating at CQC, negative publicity for some clinical or non-clinical issue, financial deficits, mergers, part of STP's etc.

What to take: your CV

It is essential to take several copies of your up-to-date CV. It is also worth taking copies of your application form. Many of those of whom you will meet may not have your application form and if one is ready to hand it may make them comfortable and may make a positive impression about you. Equally if CV is not asked as part of the application form it is another opportunity to sell yourself by providing additional information about yourself which may give you an edge over other candidates. It is advisable to take a rather brief or truncated CV mapped to the essential and desirable aspects of person specification.

It is often asked if it is appropriate to take some notes while at the meeting. In actual fact we would recommend you to do so. This works 2 ways. It gives you an opportunity to have some information listed upon which you can reflect later rather than relying on your memory. Equally it creates a positive impression about you that you are focused and taking it all seriously. If you like to write all the questions you want to ask at the meeting then that's fine so long as you don't come across as an interviewer! Be careful what you ask.

How to make that lasting first impression

It is essential to grab this opportunity as 'First impression is often the last impression'! Arrive ahead of the appointment time "DON'T BE LATE!" Present yourself well. You are selling yourself and sell yourself well. Interview/selection process starts with the pre-interview visit. Some tips towards this are as listed:

- ➤ Dress smartly and formally
- ➤ Engage both with your mind and body language
- ➤ LISTEN, do not interrupt
- ➤ Do your Homework well. This should include:
  - o Thorough reading of the job description and the background information enclosed in the application pack
  - o Go through the trust website: read success stories, patients' comments, friends and family reports, any other announcement? Any controversy? Media stories?
  - o Department website
  - o Trust board reports and briefings
  - o External Reports: CQC, Specialist Commissioning bodies, College Visits, Network visits, NHS LA.
  - o Ratings from independent organizations: Kings Fund, Dr Foster
     Focused reports as relevant to your department

Most of these are available through either public websites or trust websites.

What to avoid?

It is best to avoid humour, making jokes as it may cause more harm especially if nerves make them appear rather otherwise. Make sure you acknowledge what is said but don't start giving your own views unless asked for. Equally do not appear to come across as you are going to make everything right!

A strong candidate would have done a reality check to:

- ➤ Ensure their experience matches the job description and CV is aligned with the person specification.
- ➤ Ensure the references are lined up by contacting the referees in advance.
- ➤ Ensure comes across as interested in the job.
- ➤ Ensure you do not criticise others, your previous or current hospital/colleagues
- ➤ Ensure you don't engage in a controversial discussion. You never know which side other people are!
- ➤ Do not ask questions for sake of asking
- ➤ Do not appear arrogant.

> Top Tip: Keep your CV up-to-date – add or remove in things as you go!

INTERVIEW DAY

Who are the Interviewers?

Depending on the trust, most consultant interviews can be conducted by a host of different people:

- ➢ Clinical Director of the speciality
- ➢ Medical Director of the trust or a representative
- ➢ Chief executive or a representative
- ➢ Clinical lead of the department
- ➢ One or two consultant(s) from the department you will be joining
- ➢ Other speciality consultant: for mixed jobs or if there is potential interaction with other speciality (e.g. an anaesthetist for the post of consultant Ophthalmologist)
- ➢ A college representative: Usually starts off the interview and ensure that your training/experience matches the job advertised for: this is not mandatory for a foundation trust.
- ➢ A senior nurse/matron or nurse lead
- ➢ Lay person or patient representative/Non-Exec Member of trust board.
- ➢ Human resources representative

The appointment panel for locum appointments could be short and may consist of a Consultant/CD/clinical lead and HR person only.

When will be the Interview?

Substantive consultant interviews usually follow 2 to 4 weeks after the closing date for the applications. Sometimes the interview date is included in the job advert itself. This allows sufficient time to plan a pre-interview visit, research the job and prepare for the interview.

Where is the Interview?

The interview will almost always take place at the trust you've applied to. Logistically, it's worth booking an overnight hotel nearer to the venue, if you're travelling from far away. Very rarely, interviews can be held via Skype - this normally only applies to international candidates or for UK candidates in extreme circumstances.

Can I Change the Interview Date?

It's generally not a good idea to change your interview date unless you absolutely have to and have a strong reason to do so, e.g. Family Bereavement. Rescheduling your interview for your friend's birthday or a sports match is unlikely to go down well!

If you do need to reschedule, give the trust as much notice as possible and offer some alternative dates. Be aware that you may be putting yourself at a disadvantage by doing of this as your interview will likely be delayed or the invite to the interview may get withdrawn. Remember, there may be other candidates and it is not a good idea to start on a wrong foot by requesting to change the interview date for a trivial reason.

> **Top Tip!** Practise structuring arguments in your head so that you can present them in a logical and easy-to-follow way. This will show that you have previously thought carefully about the topic in hand.

How long do I need to prepare for?

You will often hear the phrase *"You can't prepare enough for consultant interviews"* – this couldn't be further from the truth. You need to prepare comprehensively to be able to answer all questions arguably above and beyond an average answer. Usually no answer is right or wrong! It also requires good communication skills. Thus, it's a generally a very good idea to start interview preparations as soon as you've applied for your job (although even earlier is better!). Don't leave your interview preparation until you've actually been invited to one as that won't give you enough time to shine on the day. The dictum is 'Practice, practice and practice!!'

Interview preparation starts in the last 2 -3 years of your specialist training (see below). You should focus on building your CV at that stage. Having a strong CV is always a good start. Work on communication skills and being aware of changing practices/policies ensures that you are able to structure your answer based on fact. Finally, develop confidence by constant practicing to ensure that you can communicate your thought process/answers in an assertive way (without appearing to be forceful). By practising and rehearsing you will not fumble and overcome nervousness.

Remember, consultant interviews test a wide variety of skills that – you can't cram for, e.g. communication, analytical skills etc. Start preparing small amounts early on and increase this time the closer you get to your interview. Planning and practice will take you to perfection.

Some tips for the senior trainees

Preparation for the consultant interview starts in last two or penultimate year of your training as Specialist registrar. This is the time when you need to ensure:

➤ Your clinical work is meticulous. You need your Consultants as your referees.
➤ You are engaged in e-Portfolio and are ready for your penultimate year assessment.
➤ You are appearing/preparing/passed relevant exit exam.
➤ Start working on your CV (see below). Ensure that you have included what makes you "saleable"
   o Remember an expert in a niche subject may sound good but the demand may be less, unless this is what the specific trust is looking for. On the other hand, being too generic takes away the uniqueness from you and you appear less employable as there may be too many like you.
   o It is always good to have 'Quality Improvement Projects (QIP)' in your CV, which are a testament to your ability to see where is the scope of improving any service and to be able to understand 'How to bring a Change'.
➤ Try, if you don't already have, some publications (preferably in indexed journals). Getting a quality audit/QIP is a good way to start.
➤ Ask your Consultant if you could attend some management meetings to get to understand how management works. Managers may have different ideas than consultants and it would be a good experience to see how your consultants dealt with the conflict in meetings. it is good to attend Governance and risk review meetings to get a feel of what happens when an incident happens and how to do fact finding and provide feedback.

Interview Planning

Congratulations on securing your invitation for Consultant interview! Getting this far is in itself a great accomplishment. Consultant interviews can be a daunting prospect, but with the right preparation, there is every reason to be confident that you can present yourself in the best possible way.

This guide is aimed at giving you a comprehensive walkthrough of the entire interview process - from the very basics of your initial preparation to the moment you walk out of the interview room. The book also include links where more information is useful for candidates in preparation.

You are almost guaranteed to be asked certain questions at your interview, e.g. "Why this job or why should you get this job?" So, it's well worth preparing answers for these frequently asked questions. However, it's critical that you don't simply recite pre-prepared answers as this will appear unnatural and, therefore, rehearsed.

Technique: Getting better

Now is the time to focus on learning the basics of interview technique and understanding the core healthcare topics that you'll be expected to know about. Once you're happy with this, go through the questions + answers in this book – don't try to rote learn answers. Instead, try to understand what makes each answer good/bad and then use this to come up with your own unique answer. Don't be afraid of using other resources, e.g. YouTube videos on medical ethics, google etc.

When you've got this down, practice answering questions in front of a mirror and consider recording yourself to iron out any body language issues. Record yourself and listen. Avoid repeating the question (unless you want to clarify).

Practice with People

It's of paramount importance that you practice with a real person before your first interview. Whilst you might be able to provide fantastic answers to common questions with no one observing you, this may not be the case with the added pressure of a mock interviewer. Practice interviews are best with someone you do not know very well - even easy questions may be harder to articulate out loud and on the spot to a stranger. During your practice, try to eliminate hesitant words like "Errrr…." and "Ummm…" as these will make you appear less confident. Ask for feedback on the speed, volume, and tone of your voice.

What Should I Wear?

When it comes to interviews, it's best to dress sharply and smartly. This normally means a full suit for men and either a full suit or smart shirt + skirt for women.

Things to avoid:

➤ Excessively shiny or intricate jewellery
➤ Bold and controversial dress colours, e.g. orange ties
➤ Excessive amounts of makeup – it's not a beauty pageant
➤ Flashy nails or eyelashes
➤ Unnecessarily large bags – leave your overnight bags at a hotel.
➤ Large broaches, tie pins, trademark symbols.

Things to do:

➤ Carry an extra pair of contact lenses or glasses if appropriate with cases/solutions.
➤ Turn your phone off completely – you don't want any distractions
➤ Polish your shoes

Body Language

First impressions last; body language contributes to a significant part of this. However, don't make the mistake of obsessing over body language at the expense of the quality answers you give.

Most people will only need to make some minor adjustments to remove some "bad habits", so don't worry about body language till fairly late in your preparation.

Once you're confident that you know the relevant material and have good answers prepared for common questions, allow your body language to show that you have what it takes to be a consultant by conveying maturity and confidence.

Posture

- ➤ When walking into the room, walk in with your head held high and back straight.
- ➤ When sitting down, look alert and sit up straight.
- ➤ Avoid crossing your arms – this can appear to be defensive.
- ➤ Don't slouch- instead, lean forward slightly to show that you're engaged with the interview.
- ➤ If there is a table, then ensure you sit around four to six inches away.
  - ❖ Too close and you'll appear like you're invading the interviewers' space
  - ❖ Too far and you'll appear too casual

Eyes

- ➤ Good eye contact is a sign of confidence and good communication skills.
- ➤ Look at the interviewer when they are speaking to you and when you are speaking.
- ➤ If there are multiple interviewers, look at the interviewer who is speaking to you or asked you the question. However, make sure you do look around at the other interviewers to acknowledge them.

Hands

- ➤ At the start, offer a handshake, if convenient or accept if offered: make sure you don't have sweaty or cold hands.
- ➤ A firm handshake is generally preferable to a limp one.
- ➤ During the interview, keep your hands still unless you are using them to illustrate your point.
- ➤ Avoid excessive hand movements – your hands should go no higher than your neck.
- ➤ If you fidget when you're nervous, hold your hands firmly together in your lap to stop this from happening.

Humour or Not!

Interview is a serious matter so why are we even thinking about humour – surely it is a no-no. However, humour judicially used can lighten the atmosphere and help establish a better and more human rapport with the panel. Laughter is an icebreaker and can have a feel-good effect. Humour, well-used can allow you to stand out of the crowd and create a positive impression as a likeable person. Equally inappropriately used it can present you as crude and unprofessional. Certainly, a consultant interview is not the place for poorly timed jokes or one-liners.

A particularly relevant place to mix humour in your answer is when being asked to discuss your weaknesses or when you are asked to talk about a particularly challenging situation and how you managed it. In an interview quoted to the authors *"I was asked about my weaknesses I mentioned a couple and then told the panel that if they were interested in acquiring an in-depth knowledge on this subject, I was happy to put them in touch with my wife who will happily provide them with a long comprehensive list of my inadequacies"*. This generated a real burst of good-natured laughter from the panel, and I could feel the panel visibly becoming more relaxed.

Use humour in your job interview only if you can do it with ease and it comes naturally to you. Avoid using jokes and focus on presenting the funny side of genuine real-life experiences, if the questions asked allow you to. Most importantly practice this with your family or friends to confirm that your answers are funny and professional before using them in the interview.

WHAT ARE INTERVIEWERS LOOKING FOR?

Many applicants think that the most 'obvious' thing interviewers are looking for is excellent factual knowledge. This simply isn't true.

Interview is a two-way interaction. You are being judged on a number of attributes. The interviewers are not just looking to judge if you have the right skills for the job but are trying to get a more wholesome picture of you as a person and as a professional. How you handle yourself during the interview, what kind of a person you project yourself as and whether you have the right team-working attributes are all actively looked for. Personally, having sat on the panel for a number of consultants interviews the kind of things I specifically look for include:

➢ Body language – are you relaxed, confident and professional with good eye contact and a smile or are you fidgety, uncomfortable and nervous.
➢ Do I have your full attention and do you actually listen to and answer the question asked or you offer a prepared, memorised answer instead?
➢ Have you made the effort of fully understanding the team and organisation you want to be part of.
➢ Do you have desirable attributes such as openness, honesty, flexibility and adaptability and do you present yourself as a team player.

Interviewers are looking for an applicant that is best suited to contribute to the trust in multitude of the way. They are looking for your motivation to take up **this** job. You will be assessed on your team working abilities, your skills, they need to know your personal attributes and would like to see if you are fit to do the job (clinical, personal levels). Having an excellent depth of knowledge may help you perform better during an interview- you're very unlikely to be chosen based solely on your knowledge. Remember, all the candidates that have applied for the job have the minimum qualification i.e. CCT in the area. To choose one out of many, you need to shine in some areas and sell yourself. Remember that the ultimate aim of this long selection process is to choose candidates that are competent, safe and would contribute to the trust in some way (education, research, clinical work etc). Some must have attribute for any clinician at any level are given below. An ability to demonstrate these in your answer will get you some brownie points.

Diligence

Medicine is a very demanding profession and will require hard work throughout your whole career. Interviewers are looking not only for your ability to work hard (diligence) but also for an understanding that there will be times where you will have a responsibility to prioritise your clinical work over other personal and social concerns (conscientiousness).

Professional Integrity

Medicine is a profession where lives could be at risk if something goes wrong. Being honest and having strong moral principles is critical for doctors. The public trusts the medical profession and this can only be maintained if there is complete honesty between both parties. Interviewers need to see that you are an honest person, can accept your mistakes and are learn from them.

Empathy

Empathy is the ability to recognise and relate to other peoples' emotional needs. It is important that you understand and respond to how others may be feeling, more so as a consultant as there may be conflict between different team members but you have to deal with implications. The easiest way to demonstrate this is by recalling situations from your experience. However, it's important not to exaggerate how much an incident has affected you - experienced interviewers will quickly pick up on anything that doesn't sound sincere.

Resilience to Stress

There is no denying the fact that being a consultant can be stressful due to the pressure you'll be put under. Interviewers are likely to explore your resilience to stress. You should be able to demonstrate that you have a way of dealing with it in a healthy manner. Interviewers are looking to see if you are able to make logical decisions when put under pressure. Pursuing interests outside of medicine, such as sport, music or drama is often a good way of de-stressing and gives you an opportunity to talk about your extra-curricular interests as well as team-working skills.

Scientific Aptitude

The buck stops with the consultant. Being a consultant is a responsibility. Your training has made you a skilled person to take on the consultant post. You may be probed on that including your commitment to the speciality/area you should be able to offer something, in addition, to make yourself stand out. The easiest way to do this is by referencing examples of where you have gone beyond the confines of your duties as clinician e.g. and audit that you excelled, a team event that went down very well, a prestigious award or a paper in a journal with high impact factor.

Self-Awareness

You need to show that you have the maturity required to deal with complex issues that you will face as a consultant. Firstly, it's important to be able to recognise your own strengths and weaknesses. In addition, you need to be able to recognise and reflect on your mistakes so that you can learn from them for the future. A person with good self-awareness can work on their weakness to avoid mistakes from happening again. Questions like, "What are your strengths?" or "What is your biggest weakness?" are common and fantastic opportunities to let your maturity and personal insight shine through.

Teamwork and Leadership

Working as a consultant requires working in a multidisciplinary team (MDT). You need to be able to show that you're a team player. One of the best ways of doing this is by giving examples from your recent past, during training or even extracurricular activities, e.g. sports, music etc.

Realistic Expectations

Interviewers are looking for individuals that are committed to the organisation and have a realistic idea and skills to deal with life as a consultant. This is why it's extremely important to display your motivation to take the job you are being interviewed for, during the interview. A common way to do this is to reflect on your training, your experience and have examples ready of common challenges that you will likely face. Examples include:
- Long hours and stress (on calls)
- Repetitiveness. A career in medicine can sometimes demand great patience. Doing the same operation day-in-day-out, seeing the same diseases, sitting through endless clinics.
- The balance between being empathetic, yet remaining objective
- **Ethical dilemmas** – these will be discussed in detail in the 'Medical Ethics' section

> **Top Tip!** Use mnemonics CAMP: Clinical, Academic, Management and Personal
> This can be used in many aspects when answering questions.

Interviewer Styles

Although interviewers have wildly different styles, it is helpful to remember that none of them are trying to catch you out. They are there to help you. You may come across an interviewer that is very polite and 'noddy' while others may have a 'poker face'. Do not be put off by their expressions or reactions. Sometimes what you thought was a negative facial response to your reply may just be a twitch. Contrastingly, a very helpful appearing interviewer may lull you into a false sense of security. Rarely, you may get an interviewer who likes playing 'Devil's advocate' and will challenge your every statement. In these cases, it's important not to take things personally and avoid getting worked up.

You don't know what type of interviewer you will get so it's important to practice mock interviews with as many people as possible so that you're prepared for a wider variety of interviewer styles. You can book one to one or small group interview practice by visiting www.medicalconsultantinterview.co.uk

Most interviews are panel style interview where you are met and questioned by a group of people. Two new styles are emerging as follows:

OSCE style

Interview is split into different sections, Candidate goes through a 'carousel' where they are quizzed on different aspects; this is mostly like a parallel interview split into 3 or 4 segments. The segments could either include –

➤ CV section where the candidates are expected to go through their experiences.
➤ Clinical scenario to discuss and advise.
➤ Checking competencies on clinical work.
➤ Situational judgement: difficult situation such a difficult colleague: testing conflict resolution/team working skills
➤ Problem solving.
➤ General interview
➤ Personal attributes: weaknesses, interests/pastime
➤ Academic: research and audit/QIP/teaching/publications
➤ The candidate might be given a paper to read and then will need to make a critical review of the paper. The paper could be sent beforehand or it may be given on the spot with a short time to read before the candidate is quizzed on it.

Value based interview

Similar to OSCE style but with a format that is based on trust values; it would therefore be very useful to be aware of the Trust values – most of the time these are available on the Trust website.

Some of the questions are testing your skills on conflict resolution team working spirit, managerial – whether you are able to implement a change, whether you respect colleagues and patients, whether you are following good medical practice. Some of the examples that this situation could cover would be as follows:

- *"Tell me about a time when you didn't feel the service your team offer to others (patient, customers, other departments) was as good as it should be; What did you do to improve it".*
- *"Give an example of a time when you felt proud of the service that you offered"*
- *"Give us an example of a time when you had to implement a change which impacted on your team or department, what resistance you came across and how you overcame it".*
- *"Give an example of a time when the team you were responsible for made a mistake".*
- *"Tell us about a time when you challenged someone in your team who was not behaving respectfully towards others".*
- *"Tell us about a time when you successfully motivated and engaged your team in working together to achieve a shared goal"*

COMMUNICATING YOUR ANSWERS

Many good candidates do not get the job offer as they don't spend enough time preparing for their interviews. A common reason is that they feel that they "already know what to say". Whilst this may be true, it is not always **what** you say but **how** you say it. Interviews are a great test of your communication skills and should be taken seriously. A good way to ensure you consistently deliver effective answers is to adhere to the principles below:

Keep it Short

In general, most your responses should be approximately one to two minutes long. They should convey the important information but be focussed on the question and avoid rambling. Remember, you are providing a direct response to the question, not writing an English essay! With practice, you should be able to identify the main issues being asked, plan a **structured** response, and communicate them succinctly. It is important to practice your answers to common questions, e.g. *"Why this job? This trust? Why should you get this job? Why should we offer this job to you? Etc"* so that you can start to get a feel for what is the correct response duration.

Some questions may require more time, e.g. questions that ask you to compare and contrast or questions with ethical dilemmas where you need to present both sides of the argument, summate and end by presenting your **balanced** opinion/views.

Focus on Yourself: Do not undersell yourself!

It's not uncommon for candidates to go off on a tangent and start describing, for example, the many hurdles their team faced. Remember, interviews are all about you - your skills, ability, and motivation (to take the job in the specific organisation). Thus, it's important that you spend as much time talking about yourself rather than others (unless absolutely necessary). Many candidates find it difficult to do this because they are afraid of being interpreted as 'arrogant' or 'a show-off'. Whilst this is definitely something to be aware of, it's important you do yourself justice and upsell yourself. **Believe in thyself.**

Understand the question

Consultant interviews are set with bar set at higher levels. You are not going to be asked "tell me about revalidation or clinical governance" or about "a topic" or asked to discuss "this or that NHS issue/change". You need to be able to bring the relevant NHS issues/topic in your answer. It is advisable to have a set agenda for interviews to try to bring in some common but important issues e.g. clinical governance, good medical practice, NHS scandals, trust's values, team working, MDT.

It is possible to do this if you understand the question and develop the skills to "drop in" key elements of the care into your answer. An example to incorporate "Clinical governance" is given below where this is "brought in" in different manner but adds value to the response.

Question: Tell us why you should get this job? (truncated response is given)

"I have the right skills and the training to get the consultant post. During my training, I was the <u>clinical governance</u> trainee's representative. This gave me the opportunity to understand various issues surrounding clinical governance and how can we make care provision robust to ensure delivery of the safe care. I have developed on this further and attended root cause analysis training so can contribute to use my experience in Datix/RCA and ensure our care in the trust is governance safe"

Above question on why one should get the job can be handled in many ways. Here the candidate is selling the skills as CG lead, involvement from early training days (showing long experience/better understanding of the concepts).

Question: tell us about a mistake you learned from?

"I am a safe clinician and I ensure I follow guidelines and NICE recommendation. Yet mistakes happen. I remember one such time where I was consenting a patient for an Endoscopy. I checked the patients name and consented the patients correctly. As I was about to leave the patient and submit the form, I noticed the date of birth which was different in the patients' record I had. There were two patients with similar name. I corrected the patient's record, consented the right p-atient, discussed this with the senior nurse in charge. As the error was identified and corrected with no harm to the patient, no further action was taken. I learned from this and now I always check the name, date of birth as well as the hospital number/NHS number. This way I ensure that the care I provide is <u>governance</u> robust. It is essential to learn from mistakes"

You may be asked follow on questions on this.

Question: Tell us about something you did in a job that made you feel proud?

"Audit is an important building block of <u>clinical governance</u>. This help us identify our deficiency or means to improve efficiency. I participated and led a QIP where we looked at the high incidence of caesarean sections in multiparous woman. We looked at the previous 2 years C-section rates and analyse this data to discover that there was a disparity with high C-Section in diabetic patient. This was because of limited input from the diabetes team due to shortage of diabetes nurse. As a result of this we were able to get extra DSN support and reduce our C-Section rates. I feel very proud of this as awareness of the governance and with a simple audit we were able to improve patient care and with better <u>CEMACH</u> outcome."

NB: see how the candidate has sneaked in a major obstetrical initiative (for follow on questions) in the answer.

Answer the Question

This cannot be stressed enough – there are few things more frustrating than candidates that ignore the interviewer's questions. Remember, you need to **answer the question**; **don't answer the topic**. If a question consists of two parts – remember to answer both, e.g. *'Should we legalise euthanasia? Why?'*

Ending the Interview

At the end of the interview, the interviewers are likely to ask you if you have any questions for them. You should have gleaned enough information from reading the job description, pre-interview visit, trust website, read information available in public domain and other sources e.g. google your future colleagues, see what they have published, what is their areas of interest etc. Unless the question is crucial, this may not be the right time to ask questions as it will show your ignorance and you appear unresearched/unprepared. Don't be perturbed that you do not have a question to ask.

DEALING WITH UNEXPECTED QUESTIONS

Although you can normally predict at least 90% of questions that you're likely to get asked, there will be some questions that you won't have prepared for. These assess your ability to handle difficult situations to see how you react to pressure and how you deal with the unknown.

Though completely abstract questions are rare in traditional consultant interviews, even the best preparation, you may come across a question e.g. a new policy/strategy being considered or a new NHS initiative that you have overlooked. Author was once caught on "new Vs follow up ratio" and *mis*understood the question initially as an education issue (for GPs) leading to more referral to acute trust (hence skewing the new/old ratio in clinic until the penny dropped few seconds later and the author steered the response in correct direction, successfully to secure the job offer! A high degree of perceptiveness is required and you must be astute enough to spot "subtle smile or glances without getting nervous"

In a rare situation, when you are asked a question that you don't have a clue about, do not panic. Pause and think. Have you come across something similar during your training/previous job? Have you read something about it? Can you see/apply your knowledge/skill? Can you use these to start a discussion?

Good applicants will endeavour to engage with the topic and try to link in their knowledge to the question, e.g. *"I have not come across this before but it seems that…"*. Weaker applicants would be perturbed by the question or not consider it seriously, e.g. *"I don't know."*

Consider the example: *"Is there a cure for multiple sclerosis?"*

You may not have read about this specific topic. However, you may know about neurological deficit and the plaques.

"As far as I know, there is no specific cure for multiple sclerosis though there are trials on vaccines/interferon that limit the progression/delay progression of this"

Of course, this relies on you having a certain level of knowledge. If you really have no clue at all and have not come across anything about this topic then it is better to acknowledge the gap in your knowledge.

"Unfortunately, I have limited information about this topic but it is an interesting question. I did read about new treatment in a recent BMJ but I'm unable to confirm the fact. I will endeavour to look this up."

Dealing with difficult questions like this gives you the opportunity to show that you are a motivated and enthusiastic person and not afraid to go back to the basics if required. This approach is better than not saying anything at all.

STRUCTURING YOUR ANSWERS

You can approach questions in your interviews by using a simple framework:

Figure 1: Structuring answer to the interview question

A good trick is to try and tick off each of these in an answer where applicable. This is a good way to ensure that you are not spending too long talking about one thing and so leaving yourself no time to talk about other things. There is little point in reeling off a list of unrelated facts when that would leave no time to show how your experiences apply.

It is better to demonstrate good knowledge and then move on to describe how insights from your work/past experience/training have also influenced you to give a more well-rounded answer. It is worth practising answering questions using this framework.

For example, consider: '*What do you think is the greatest challenge of being a Consultant?*'

What knowledge can I apply?

I know that the Consultants have very responsible task and the buck stops with them. I know they suddenly progress from a position of little responsibility as a training doctor to one of great responsibility. I know the structure of medical specialist training, which I might be able to work into the answer.

What experiences can I use?

I remember seeing my Consultants looking very busy and carrying out meetings, teachings assessments etc. I remember one Consultant explaining that she is always rushing between clinics, wards meetings. I remember seeing my own consultant and how hard she worked, how much she was able to change within the organisation.

What positive qualities can I display?

I can show a realistic understanding of the challenges of being a consultant. I can show a diligent and conscientious attitude towards the challenge of hard work and long hours. I can show an ability to handle stress and excellent communication skills with different team members.

How can I give a balanced answer?

You should recognise that there are multiple factors that make Consultant job a challenge in order to balance the answer. You can go through a thought process like this in a few seconds and continue to think about it as you begin to answer the question. Thus, your answer may be along the lines of:

"There are different factors that are challenging for a Consultant. The responsibility for patients' life, serious decision making and its impact is quite draining. Though Consultants are used to hard work from training times, this may still require a step up and even more sacrifices to be made in terms of a social life. During my SpR training, I remember a Consultant telling me that the thing she found most challenging was the sudden jump in responsibility and expectations between being a trainee doctor and being a consultant. It was this that she and her peers found most daunting."

You have to be very picky about what you include in your answer to ensure giving a well-rounded answer without blabbering. For the same question, another response could focus on striking a work-life balance as being most challenging:

"Whilst doing my training as SpR, I saw my consultant working long hours and busy in various activities e.g. ward round, clinics, admin, on-call, teaching etc. This meant that the consultants are very busy and have deadlines to meet with pressure for great clinical work. All this can potentially impact on the work-life balance. Thus, I think striking a good work-life balance could be challenging albeit possible with forward planning."

Consider:
➢ *Be realistic*
➢ *Be honest*
➢ *Choose real life examples*
➢ *Recognise your strengths and sell them well (don't be shy!)*
➢ *Recognise your limitations and improvise*
➢ *Explain what have you learned*
➢ *Bring in a positive spin towards the end*
➢ *Be perceptive to the interviewers' reaction without panicking*
➢ *Answer the question*

Top Tip! Read! If you're genuinely interested in this job then you should prepare for this interview well. Read about the job, departments, challenges the organisation is facing and think about solutions, if possible. Make notes that you can access quickly, just in case you need to (whilst seated in the waiting room)!

Step One: Do your Research

Start off by finding more about the job you would be expected to do. Then try to establish what topics are frequently asked. Some questions are asked invariably e.g. going through your CV. Use the job description to help you guide the experience you need to emphasize on. Don't rely on hearsay.

Step Two: Acquire the pre-requisite Knowledge

Once you have an idea about what is expected in the interview, you can start to tailor your preparation. For example, if the trust has a glowing CQC report, try to bring this out somewhere (governance, patient experience, audit, QIP, team working etc). Similarly, for a trust with poor CQC rating, give it a positive spin as this can be used as an example to improve CQC rating with better (governance, patient experience, audit, QIP, team working). It is important to develop the abilities to use same attributes in positive and negative manner and have the knowledge to use them effectively. Nevertheless, it's important to ensure you're familiar with the commonly asked questions. Again, don't spend extensive time trying to rote learn answers to common questions - this is not particularly helpful and is likely to be counter-productive.

Step Three: Practice with People

It's essential that you practice with real person in advance. You need to practice giving succinct yet comprehensive answers as well as creating a strong first impression. See if your consultant would help.

If there's another friend or colleague that's in similar position, it would be worth considering that you could help each other and work together. Share resources, have practice sessions together and give each other constructive criticism. Even if you do only a couple of times a week, when you're both free, it can really help to just sit down with someone and discuss an issue such as organ donation – each take a different stance, set a timer and see how you get on. Try not to be intimidated and try to stay calm. Five minutes might sound like a relatively short period of time, but it should be enough to get the most important points across.

Situational Questions on dealing with difficult colleague/doctors/nurse

Many candidates find the Mnemonic *INSIST* helpful when structuring their answers in "dealing with difficult situation":

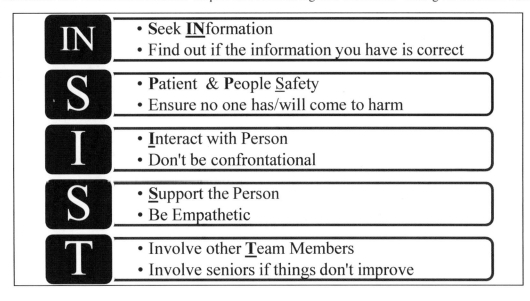

IN	• Seek **IN**formation • Find out if the information you have is correct
S	• Patient & People **S**afety • Ensure no one has/will come to harm
I	• **I**nteract with Person • Don't be confrontational
S	• **S**upport the Person • Be Empathetic
T	• Involve other **T**eam Members • Involve seniors if things don't improve

Figure 2: Confident Approach to the Consultant Interview

The STARR Framework

You may be asked questions where you need to give examples, e.g. *"Tell me about a time when you showed leadership?"*

It's very useful to **prepare examples in advance** for these types of questions as it's very difficult to generate them on the spot. Try to **prepare at least three examples** that you can use to answer a variety of questions. Generally, more complex examples can be used to demonstrate multiple skills, e.g. communication, leadership, team-working, etc. In the initial stages, it's helpful to use a framework to structure your answers, e.g. the STARR Framework shown below:

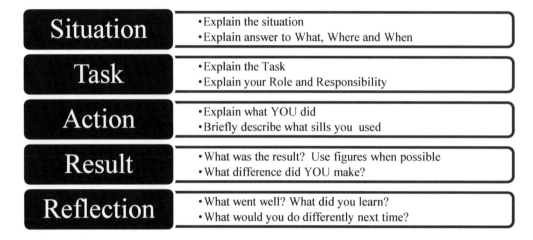

Figure 3: STARR Framework

Answering Consultant Interview Questions

Consultant interviews are more scientifically rigorous and demanding than the traditional style interviews. They are much more likely to focus on candidate's ability to demonstrate the qualities required to carry out the day to day working of the consultant creating a risk-free efficient environment.

In general, you'll be **tackling a question with follow up smaller sub-questions** to guide the answer from the start to a conclusion. The main question may seem difficult, impossible or random at first, but take a deep breath and start discussing different ideas that you have for breaking the question down into manageable pieces.

The questions are designed to be difficult to give you the chance to **show your full intellectual potential**. This is your chance to show your creativity, analytical skills, intellectual flexibility, problem-solving skills, and your go-getter attitude. Don't waste it by letting your nerves overtake or from a fear of messing up or appearing very timid.

Ultimately, the **Medical Consultant Interview process** is meant to reflect the day-to-day working of a consultant. These are led by a senior clinicians/manager and they're testing what you're like under pressure and whether you can hold intelligent, well-thought-out conversations on topics you won't be totally familiar with. Remember, it's not about the right answer, but your thought process and ideas.

MEDICAL CONSULTANT INTERVIEWS ARE **NOT** ONLY ABOUT YOUR KNOWLEDGE

THEY ARE ALSO ABOUT WHAT YOU CAN DO
WITH THE KNOWLEDGE YOU ALREADY POSSES

General Advice

➤ Apply the knowledge you have acquired during your training/work and from your wider reading to unfamiliar scenarios.

➤ **Stand your ground if you are confident in your argument**- even if your interviewers disagree with you. They may deliberately play the devil's advocate to see if you are able to defend your argument.

➤ However, if you are making an argument that is clearly wrong and are being told so by the interviewers (verbally, body language) - then concede your mistake and revise your viewpoint. Do not stubbornly carry on arguing a point that is clearly not.

➤ Remember, making mistakes is no bad thing. The important point is that you address the mistake head on and adapt the statement with their assistance where necessary.

➤ They have seen your application so they already have a feel for you. Play your strong points and give a positive spin to your weaknesses.

Communicating your answers

You have learned (see above) about structuring your question, you have the knowledge/skills to come this far. All you have to do now is convince the panel that you are the right person to take the job. The most important thing to do when communicating your answers is to **think out loud**. This will allow the interviewer to understand your thought processes. You should never give up on a question to show that you won't be perturbed at the first sign of hardship as a consultant and to stay positive and **demonstrate your engagement with the process**.

Listen carefully and make sure that you have understood the question correctly. If in doubt politely ask the interviewer to repeat the question. It is okay to take a moment when confronted with a difficult question or plan your approach. *"Think about this for a moment"* but don't take too long.

The questions that you'll be asked are not designed to be difficult but are checking a breadth of your experience to check that you are fit to take the responsibilities. So, don't panic when you don't immediately know the answer. Pause, think, organise your thoughts and give a structured response. If you don't know the answer, it will come to you as your present your argument. If the question is about your views on a topic, give both sides of the argument and sum up with your views. Remember that your interviewer may have opposite views and may challenge you to prod you further. Try not to change your views unless you have made a very obvious error (e.g. Euthanasia is legal).

In case of something you have never heard of (unlikely to happen with good preparation), tell the interviewer what you do know, offer some ideas, talk about ways you've worked through a similar problem that might apply here. If you've never heard anything like the question asked before, say that to the interviewer, *"I've never seen anything like this before"* but don't use that as an excuse to quit. This is **your chance to show that you are eager to engage with new ideas**, so finish with *"But I'm keen to try something new!"*. There are many times in life as a consultant when you may come at the cross roads in many ways and you need to show that you can persevere in the face of difficulty (and stay positive and pleasant to work with while doing so).

Understanding Questions

In an interview you will never be asked 'Tell me about revalidation' or a question such as 'Ok – so tell me about a difficult colleague you have had'. Usually the type of question you will be asked is situational, judgement kind of questions. You will be asked a question where you need to put yourself in that situation and give a solution. The best way to deal with these questions would be:

➤ Think: See if you can identify what issues the question is addressing?
➤ Plan: Try to see what component you can fit into that answer
➤ Execute: Try to remember the CAMP (Clinical Academic Managerial and Personal)

Ideally, when you are preparing for your interview you should have thought about these questions. There is a list of questions in the book which you should practice and come up with some similar kind of situations. The most important thing is that you understand the question; for example, if you are asked a question, think for a few seconds and see what is in it, *what is the question asking? Is this a clinical question?* In which case you should have no problem as you have had your training. But if it is a non-clinical question then you need to try to see what aspects of NHS you can bring in. Giving a straight answer will make it a bad response because you are just answering a question.

What the interviewers are looking for is your maturity, whether you can see issues around it. For example, if you are asked a question about the shortage of junior doctors because someone called in sick and you took the call, it is not just about supporting the junior doctor who has called in sick and assuring him, you also have another task because there is patient care involved; patients need to be seen and there is a cost cover as other colleagues will be working extra.

There is a governance issue here (patient safety as patients are not seen in a timely manner) as well as managerial issue (blocked bed due to delayed decision making/discharges). Family meeting may not happen leading to low ratings in friends and family test. Therefore, you have to be able to think outside the box to bring some of these issues into your answer. When you do this, when you have dealt with that, it will come through as a good answer. It will become clearer when you do the questions later on in the book.

Types of Questions

Interview questions can generally be grouped into common categories (for traditional panel style interviews).

> Curriculum Vitae: You are almost certain that you will be asked questions about your experience. You may be asked to go through the CV that is relevant to the job. Be ready. Do not ramble for long about your research experience if this is for an academic post!
> Questions related to your speciality
> Questions assessing your team working ability
> Questions checking your ability to learn from mistake (clinical governance)
> Ethical questions ("Are humans obligated to…", "What are the implications of…")
> Questions testing re: your knowledge of the NHS issues, topical issues, past and changes being introduced within (and why)
> Questions on your ability to bring out changes/managing changes
> Your motivation for the job
> Efficiency and saving, Involvement in cost improvement programme (CIP)
> Understanding of patient safety
> Your interest and involvement in Quality Improvement (QI)
> How to handle a colleague in difficulty

The Medical Consultant Interviews are all about taking your experience, training and – and building on top of them later with clinical experience. By asking the types of questions that you can't just repeatedly practice ("I want to take this job because…") you are forced to **take a step back, think about what you do know and form a logical argument**. It's not the answer they're looking for, but the way you think it through. That's an excellent indicator of the kind of consultant you'll be.

Of course, interview preparation for the 'standard' questions is absolutely necessary – your reasons for applying for that specific job (should be more that "this is the job near my parent's house") will roll off the tongue soon enough. But additionally, for those questions where you don't have a pre-packaged answer, keeping calm and realising that you actually know a lot more than you think and relaying this to the interviewers in a relaxed and confident way – whether your answer is right or not – is a very desirable skill.

List of questions often asked can be access on our website: www.medicalconsultantinterview.co.uk

> **Top Tip:** Practice makes perfect. Take questions, develop your answers, think of examples from real life and see what governance, NHS issues can be weaved into your answer.

PREPARING FOR YOUR INTERVIEW

The obvious way to prepare for your Medical Consultant Interview is to **read widely and start doing this early**. This is important so that you are aware of the issues facing the NHS and in your area.

Some tips:

➤ Prepare your CV
➤ Go through your CV updating at regular interval
   o Highlight your Unique selling point
   o Try to include something that's an achievement you are proud of: Setting up service, courses, a way you could contribute
➤ Read around changes within NHS
➤ Read about your speciality: What's new, what changes and why? How do they impact patient care?
➤ Commonly asked questions: start preparing, make notes

Consultant Interviews are not always about your work. The Consultant job is very demanding and it is important to have stress buster. You may be asked about this. It makes you look like "one of them" "very human" hence likable and appointable.

The NHS: Structure, issues and reforms

We will go through some important issues. Lot of information can be gleaned from resources and links at the end of the book. Google is also a good start.

The NHS: Structure

The secretary of health is responsible for the work of the department of health (DoH) which takes overall responsibility for NHS, mental health, social services and public health. The NHS can be broadly split into primary and secondary care. Primary care consists of General Practice surgeries and other community-based services; secondary care is hospital-based and involves specialist doctors.

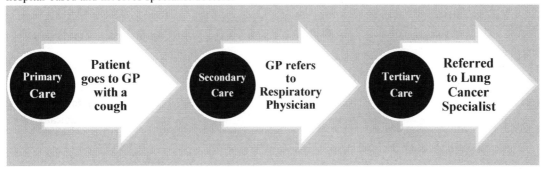

Figure 4: NHS organisations

Patients are generally referred to secondary care by their GP or via A&E. Rarely, secondary care specialists may also refer patients onto tertiary care centres in complex cases. As GPs can resolve 90% of patient's problems, this reduces the pressures on secondary care centres. Therefore, it avoids specialist doctors spending time with patients that less specialised doctors could manage with.

NHS Trust

Each NHS organisation has its own structure and it varies with trusts. Chief executive has the overall responsibility for the organisation. Within the organisation tiers structure exists i.e. division, departments, directors. An example of an organisational flow chart is given below. Depending on the organisation, it may vary and have multiple tiers and other arms. This flow chart is usually given in the job description. Ensure you are aware of the organisational structure of the trust so that you know the roles and responsibilities and your line manager. Most organisations have clinical director (divisional director if the departments within a service are large) responsible for managing consultants within their department.

NHS Regulatory bodies

The GMC

The General Medical Council (GMC) is the regulating body for doctors in the UK. All doctors must be registered with the GMC in order to practice as a doctor. If a doctor is found to be in breach of the GMC's code of conduct, their licence to practice may be revoked – preventing them from practising medicine in the UK.

NICE

The National Institute of Health and Care Excellence (NICE) provides national guidance and advice on how to improve healthcare. NICE's role is to improve outcomes for people using NHS and public health and social services. This is done by -
➤ Producing evidence-based guidance and advice for health and social care.
➤ Developing quality standards and performance metrics for health commissioners
➤ Commissioning and providing access to a range of information services to health and social care practitioners e.g. NICE Evidence, BNF and BNFc.

Clinical Commissioning Group

Clinical Commissioning Groups (CCGs) are clinically-led statutory NHS bodies responsible for planning and commissioning health care services for their local area. They can choose to commission NHS-based services or, in some cases, private ones e.g. Virgin. CCGs basically buy services from hospitals, hospices and other community services. Sometimes an NHS trust provides services to more than one CCG and there may be variation in the service provided depending on the demands of an individual CCG. In preparation for the consultant interview it is useful to find out which CCG's commission services from the trust.

Revalidation and Appraisal

Revalidation for doctors was introduced by the General Medical Council (GMC) in December 2012. One of the main reasons for this was to restore public faith in doctors following a Maori poll that showed public loss of trust in NHS (see NHS scandals). Revalidation is the process by which licensed doctors have to demonstrate that they are up to date and remain fit to practice.

Doctors must undergo revalidation every five years and this requires a recommendation from their Responsible Officer (RO). In most NHS Trusts the RO is the Trust's medical director, who will make a recommendation for revalidation if the doctor has engaged with the appraisal process and demonstrated that they are up to date and fit to practice and if there are no outstanding investigations into their performance.

The system of annual appraisal is used as a vehicle towards revalidation. The process supports doctors in regular "reality check" on their performance across the breadth of their work (clinical competence, team work, regular participation of activities that the clinicians are expected (teaching, audit/QIP). This gives doctors as well as employers that the team remains up-to-date, follows principals of clinical governance and remain fit to practice. Doctors that remain/are fit to practice are issued a "licences to practice" which is valid for five years.

Each doctor has yearly appraisal and the appraisal document is submitted to the GMC at five years interval by the designated responsible officer (RO). The RO is the trust appointed senior clinician (usually the medical director) within the organisation where the doctor performs all or most of their activity. RO can decide if there is sufficient evidence for the doctor to be revalidated or defer the revalidation. The RO makes a recommendation to the GMC and the GMC then uses this to decide a revalidation outcome. There are 3 possible recommendations -

➢ Recommendation for revalidation if there is adequate information to confirm fitness to practice.
➢ A recommendation for deferral if more information is needed or there is an ongoing fitness to practice procedure. This does not affect license to practice.
➢ Recommendation of non-engagement for any doctor not engaging with the appraisal process. This can impact the license to practice.

Doctors with no designated body (locums, career break, gap year) still have to be appraised on a yearly basis. The GMC has created a "Connection tool" to help them identify the person/organisation they need to contact for their appraisal.

Remember, revalidation is not about raising concerns about doctors. There are separate processes for that.

Complaints and Complaints Procedure in the NHS

Any one has the right to make a complaint about any aspect of NHS care, treatment or service, and this is firmly written into the NHS Constitution.

The NHS encourages feedback because feedback is used to improve services. Many service providers have feedback forms available on their premises or websites. Different options are used in various NHS institutions but one of the recognised methods is the "Friends and Family test".

It is recommended that anyone who is unhappy with any NHS service, should discuss their concerns early on with the provider of the service, as they may be able to sort the issue out quickly. Most problems can be dealt with in this manner, however the complainant is not comfortable speaking to the persons directly involved in their care or feel that this approach has not worked are advised to contact Patient Advice and Liaison Service (PALS) which is present in most hospitals.

The PALS team will always try to help resolve issues informally with the hospital if possible. They can be particularly helpful for urgent issues is urgent requiring immediate action, such as a problem with the treatment or care. PALS can also help in logging a formal complaint and direct it to the right people. This is usually via a dedicated complaints team in most NHS hospitals.

The complaint can either be made directly to the NHS service provider or to the commissioner of the services (CCG) but not to both. In the event of a complaint about more than one organization e.g. a complaint that includes issues about GP and local hospital a single complaint needs to be made. The organisation that receives the complaint has to co-operate with the others to provide a co-ordinated response.

Complaints should normally be made within 12 months of an incident; however, the time limit can be extended if there are good reasons for not making the complaint sooner and it's possible to complete a fair investigation.

A complaint can be made verbally, in writing, or by email. A written record of verbal complaints is made and provided to the complainant. An acknowledgement and the offer of a discussion about the handling of complaint is normally made within three working days of receiving the complaint. Different hospitals have varying times within which they complete the investigation and provide a formal response to the complaint. This is usually about 6 working weeks. If no decision has been reached for more than 6 months the NHS organization is expected to communicate the reasons for delay to the complainant.

Once the complaint has been investigated, a written response is provided. The response should set out the findings and, where appropriate, provide apologies and information about what's being done as a result of the complaint. It should also include information about how the complaint has been handled and details of the complainants right to take the complaint to the relevant ombudsman, which for health care is the Parliamentary and Health Service Ombudsman.

Commissioning for Quality and Innovation (CQUIN)

Money flows patients within NHS. Provider bill the CCGs for the care the patients receive. A proportion of the provider's income is linked (since 2009) to quality of care. This ensures that the patients are given care they deserve and the organisations take responsibility to achieve quality over quantity and better outcomes. Aim of this to incentivise the trusts to drive transformational changes to develop innovative pathways leading to reduced costs whilst keeping patients safe without a compromise on the quality. This is updated now to align with the *Five year Forward View: Next Steps,* to have two steps as follows:

➢ Clinical quality and transformational indicators: identified 13 indicators
➢ Local support: develop sustainability and transformation partnerships (STPs) and integrated care systems (ICSs)
See links to read more on CQUIN.

CQC – Care Quality Commission

CQC are the independent NHS regulators incorporating both health and adult social care in England. The aim is to provide health and social care services to people with safe, effective, compassionate, high quality care with a view to improve patient experiences. They act as monitors that inspect and provide guidance on services to regulate with a view to ensure that the services meet the fundamental standards on safety and quality that the patients expect.

When CQC visit an organisation, they are looking at five key questions which include:

➢ Are they safe?
➢ Are the effective?
➢ Are they caring?
➢ Are they responsive?
➢ Are they well led?

This is achieved by the CQC visiting different areas within the organisation, discussing with members of staff, observing and looking at different data provided to them. Most of the NHS Trusts are encouraged to register for the CQC process; this is legally binding and provides an incentive to the organisation to invest in improvement in care if any deficiencies are found.

Most organisations are given a set date or a set period during which the CQC function will take place. The Trust will spend time in preparing and planning for the CQC visit; this would be advertised and, as a result of the outcome following the CQC visit a report is sent and the Trust is marked in different areas as *Outstanding, Good, Requires Improvement* or *Inadequate.* This would provide an impetus to the Trust to initiate projects or look at pathways or care models within to improve care so that at the time of the next CQC they have demonstrated good leadership and bring about changes which will enhance patient care and experiences.

Dr Foster

Dr Foster is an independent organisation which helps Health care organisation to make better and faster decisions with data and insight. It is one of the external organisations which provides an independent scrutiny for the NHS trusts and also compares them against other health care organisations. It is one of the many drivers to assess the trust/department performance and can be instrumental in improving standards, quality of care or need of specific resources. It monitors the performance of National health Service and provides information to the public. It was launched in 2006 and is currently owned by Telstra. It broadly covers 3 aspects as listed below:

1. Population and Health Management: This focuses on identifying patient or patient groups for targeted care, prevention and gaps in care across the health care system to improve patient outcomes and save costs.
2. Cost and Efficiency: Tracks and trends performance, identify areas for efficiency savings to understand and influence demands and patient flow throughout the health care system.

3. Quality and Outcomes Measurement: this aspect investigates risk adjusted quality, patient safety and clinical outcomes data including mortality, benchmarks against other healthcare organizations and identify areas for improvement.

Clinical Governance

The concept of CG was the idea of the Scally and Donaldson in 1998 (G Scally and L J Donaldson 'Clinical governance and the drive for quality improvement in the new NHS in England' BMJ (4 July 1998): 61-65). Liam Donaldson was appointed the Chief Medical Officer of NHS (1998). The original definition put forward was *"A framework through which NHS organisations are accountable for continually improving the quality of their services and safeguarding high standards of care by creating an environment in which excellence in clinical care will flourish."*

Clinical Governance (CG) is about quality and accountability. Here the quality is in terms of clinical care, processes, even booking tests/appointment etc. All aspects of patient/related care need to be robust for clinical excellence. In essence, it is about ensuring that the swiss cheese holes do not line up!

There is no need to memorise this, but understanding is important. Essentially, it is a system through which **NHS hospitals and CCGs** (vs. Doctors and other healthcare professionals) are responsible for:

➢ Maintaining good standards of care
➢ Learning from mistakes
➢ Improving the quality of services that patients are provided
➢ Ensure that the clinicians remain updated
➢ Ensure that research and audit pursued actively

Key principals of Clinical governance

The seven key pillars of the CG are:

➢ Risk management
➢ Audit
➢ Clinical effectiveness
➢ Education and training
➢ Patient and Public Involvement
➢ Using information and IT
➢ Staffing and staff management
The first four are more relevant to clinicians in their day to day work and can be remembered by the Mnemonic **RACE.**

Do not expect that in the interview, you will be asked a question *"So tell me about CG"*. It is up to you to incorporate CG or its building blocks in your answer. An example is when you are asked a question *"tell me what audit experience you have" "Tell us about a Quality Improvement project that you have been involved in" "a mistake that you have learned from"* (more later).

Risk Management

Risk management is the process to understand concerns, identify errors/mistakes, monitor and minimise risk to patients and staff. This is a robust system that's aims to prevent similar occurrence. It is about identifying risk, investigating events and implementing changes to avoid recurrence. Patient care is not just about excellence in clinical care, it is also about the manner in which it is delivered. Risk management is an ongoing process in all areas (patient, clinicians, nurses, ancillary staff, environment, finances and commercial). Patient safety can be put at risk in many ways. Things can go wrong in pateints' care in many ways other than having ignorant employees. When this happens, they should be identified and steps taken to improve safety for better patient's experience.

So, whilst the clinicians may do an excellent job but if this is delivered in an unsafe environment (e.g. bare below elbow, hand washing) or failure to follow acceptable guidelines (e.g. weak audit/research/evidence base care). Errors in booking a patient may lead to wrong patient, procedure, site (left or right) or no booking at all.

Process of risk management include incident reporting, establishing the contexts in which error(s) occurred, identify the risk, analysis of the risk (consequence, impact on patient, future recurrence), developing specific recommendations/plans to avoid in future, communicating results/outcome and monitor to ensure that the robust processes remain in place. Risk Management is not about blaming an individual but about minimising risk by steps taken to avoid recurrence by learning from mistakes in no-blame environment.

In nutshell, risk management is about protocol and guideline, implementing, identifying gaps and filling these gaps to learn from mistakes, near misses and promote a blame free culture where incidences are reported without biases.

Incident reporting: Records/mean to communicate errors. Incidence recording is the reporting tool to ensure learning from mistakes takes place. Within the NHS, National Reporting and Learning System (NRLS) is used for patient safety incident reporting. Local healthcare organisation reports to the national system using the local risk management system (Datix in many places).

Patient Safety Alert: All reported incidents are investigated and if of sufficient severity or if a pattern is identified, Patient Safety Alert are issues across the NHS organisations. This way a specific problem (wrongly sited NG tube) can be identified, lessons learned from mistakes, best practice examples shared. This leads to development of appropriate guidelines/recommendations to avoid a repeat.

Central Alerting System (CAS): Is the web-based system to cascade relevant patient safety alerts. CAS is also used to circulate important public health notices and other critical information/guidance to organisations within NHS and other organisation (Ambulance service, independent organisation, social services etc.

Root Cause analysis (RCA): It is a method of structured risk identification and management in the aftermath of an reported adverse event. It includes a range of tools and approaches (acquired from the fields of human factors and safety science) to determine how and why the incident happened with the aim of identifying how a repeat can be avoided in the future. For the process to work well it has to be undertaken by a skilled multidisciplinary investigation team which includes medical and nursing team members along with representation from the risk management team. The output should be detailed clearly identifying Root Cause Causative Factors (RCCF) along with specific actions with the aim of sustained system improvement. Once the cause of the problem is identified, cause and effect relationships need to be explored to come up to potential solutions. These need to be communicated to the grass root level so that everyone is aware of the issues and mistakes are avoided.

_A_udit

An audit is a systematic process to review a system to assess its performance when compared to acceptable national/regional/local guidelines. It allows us to identify any potential problems that might be preventing good medical practice. Once these problems are identified, changes are made to try to resolve them. After a period of time, the audit is repeated again – completing the audit cycle. Hopefully, the changes result in an improvement in healthcare.

Quality and Improvement project is increasingly used these days instead of Audit cycle. Essentially, this is audit, implementing change and re-audit (completing the audit cycle or QIP).

Doctors are encouraged to do audits/QIP as they can lead to valuable improvements in clinical care. Audits can occur at many levels:

➤ Nationally, e.g. National Stroke Audit
➤ Hospital-Based, e.g. ensuring that all patients are reviewed by a consultant daily
➤ On a ward, e.g. ensuring that all thermometers are correctly calibrated

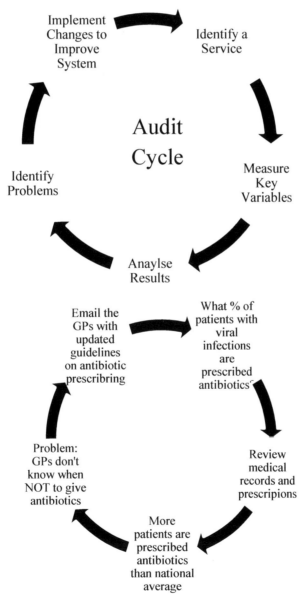

Figure 5: The Audit cycle

Clinical effectiveness

This term encompasses the proposed "right thing at the right time by the right person at the right place". This implies that the organisations follow, develop and implement strategies to provide evidence base care (see later) to the patients in a consistent manner. It incorporates that the organisations follow latest guidelines/recommendations.

Education and training

It is the individual and organisational responsibility that the employee is up-to-date in the area of their work. The individual should be supported in the work to make use of the opportunities to keep themselves updated by attending relevant courses/exams. Training doctors achieve this as part of their regular assessments, with a training record that cover different areas of their trainings. For consultants' appraisal and revalidation is the tool that ensure that the doctors remain up-to-date and fit to practice.

Never Events

Never Events are defined as Serious Incidents that are wholly preventable because guidance and safety recommendations that provide strong systemic protective barriers are available at a national level and should have been implemented by all health care providers.

A comprehensive Never Events list, 2018 as provided by NHS Improvement is listed below:

Surgical
➢ Wrong site surgery
➢ Wrong implant/prosthesis
➢ Retained foreign object post procedure

Medication
➢ Mis-selection of a strong potassium solution
➢ Administration of medication by the wrong route
➢ Overdose of insulin due to abbreviations or incorrect device
➢ Overdose of methotrexate for non-cancer treatment
➢ Mis-selection of high strength midazolam during conscious sedation

Mental health
➢ Failure to install functional collapsible shower or curtain rails

General
➢ Falls from poorly restricted windows
➢ Chest or neck entrapment in bed rails
➢ Transfusion or transplantation of ABO-incompatible blood components or organs
➢ Misplaced naso- or oro-gastric tubes
➢ Scalding of patients
➢ Unintentional connection of a patient requiring oxygen to an air flowmeter
➢ Undetected esophageal intubation (**Temporarily suspended as a Never Event)**

Top tip: Learning from mistakes to prevent future harm. "Financial sanctions" associated with "never events" have been removed to maintain "No blame cultures"

NHS five year forward view

NHS is free at the point of entry. Currently, NHS is not able to meet a number of targets (e.g. 4-hour review in ED) and there is need to improve it. Number of initiatives have been in place and with government agreeing to increase the NHS funding, plan need be in place to improve care. The increased funding will be available over next five years in the year beginning 2019/20. The vision of the new NHS is to develop a plan to use this funding and improvise care and provide:

➢ Measurable changes (patient related outcomes): e.g. cancer survival rates, drug errors
➢ Minimize health inequalities
➢ Disease prevention and chronic disease management
➢ Better and enhances social care
➢ Develop further on work already underway

   ○ Development of new care models
   ○ Sustainability and transformational partnerships (STPs)
   ○ Integrated care systems

➢ Complex need care groups: Older person, frail people, children
➢ Better communication and means to improvise
➢ Motivate staff
➢ Enhanced social care funding

Secretary of state for health and social care has the responsibility for the NHS. The diagram below explains the structure of the NHS. Individual sections later on provide details as relevant.

The EWTD

The European Working Time Directive (EWTD) is an EU law that ensures employees are protected from working excessively long hours as it would compromise their health and safety. For doctors, this means:

➢ Doctors should work a maximum of 48 hours per week on average
➢ Doctors should get at least 11 hours rest per day (i.e. no shifts longer than 13 hours/day)
➢ Doctors are entitled to a rest break if they work more than six consecutive hours
➢ A minimum of 5.6 weeks of paid annual leave

The EWTD helps doctors by ensuring that they are rested and have a good work-life balance. However, it does mean that they get less clinical experience. Furthermore, since doctors get more days off to compensate for periods of long calls (to ensure average hours are <48 per week), it means that there is reduced patient continuity – with different doctors seeing patients on different days. EWTD has been in force for consultants and career grade staff since 1998 and since 2004 for junior doctors.

Working time

Any time spent "working" is counted as "worktime". This includes:
   ➢ Any period where the worker is working (training, at employment related activity)
   ➢ Time spent on work related travel
   ➢ Even if doctors sleep, but on call and onsite, it is classed as working time (SiMAP and Jaeger ruling)

Doctors can opt-out of the EWTD if they wish to but it must be done without any undue pressure. Also, an opt out should not be a necessity for any post and it should never be part of any contract. It remains unclear what the implications of Brexit on the EWTD will be.

Implications of EWTD

➤ Shorter time spent on training
➤ Loss of continuity of care
➤ Missed opportunity for procedural task
➤ Lack of flexibility

Figure 6: European Working Time Directive: Pros and cons

Compensatory rest

Compensatory rest is the time counted towards recovery following a period of work. It is not always possible to take breaks (as stipulated in EWTD). To avoid impact on patient care, or disrupted service, local flexibility was introduced and rotas were created to include time off. This allows time in lieu of the period worked where the weekly worked hours may exceed 48 hours. The provision to take rest at a convenient time ensure patient safety without disruption of the local service. This must be taken as soon as possible after the work period, immediately (as per Jaeger ruling).

Local practices have been developed to calculate working hours. This usually is to follow a pattern or rota cycle (varies between 4 to 26 weeks). Compensatory rest is not the same as annual leave.

Exception reporting

Exception reporting should be undertaken by junior doctors when variations in day to day work exists leading to:
➤ Variable working hours
➤ Changing work pattern (working if areas outside of allocated place of work e.g. a colorectal surgical trainee assigned to cardiothoracic surgery due to shortage in cardiothoracic team)
➤ Overwork: working longer r more frequently than allocated hours
➤ Missing educational: not able to attend grand rounds, speciality training, mandatory training
➤ Missing learning opportunities: unable to attend clinics/procedures
➤ Short staff so no enough support

The exception reporting is sent to the clinical/educational supervisor who should review and discuss with the junior doctors to come up with an action plan, this should be sent to the junior doctor and the director of medical education within the trust. Increasingly, the trusts are using "guardian of safe working" to address these issues.

Do not attempt CPR

The current DNA CPR guidelines were updated in 2016. These guidelines give advice on initiating discussion, engaging people in having that conversation – more so when it is less likely to be successful hence futile - as well as discussing the benefits of CPR based on benefits and burdens. The Trust should develop their own strategies, pathways and regularly audit and review the processes on DNA CPR. The decision about DNA CPR should be carefully recorded in the appropriate forms.

In a situation where DNA CPR is refused, the people need to have capacity assessment - or the Clinician needs to discuss with the next of kin if the capacity is lacking - to involve them in the process. When a DNA CPR decision is made it should be communicated effectively to other healthcare providers and it should be clearly planned whether this is an indefinite decision or whether it should be reviewed at periodic intervals.

End of Life Care (EOL)

EOL is the support that the people are provided in last few months/year of their life. Care plan was introduced to support people to live as comfortable as possible and die with dignity and respect. It is a very emotional topic and subject of litigation sometimes, when handled badly. So, an understanding of EOL care plan is essential for today's clinicians.

The key points are:

➢ Usually for people dying in 72 hours to 12 months (though difficult to predict)
➢ Consider patients' wishes
➢ For people with
    o Incurable illness (cancer)
    o Advanced disease (dementia)
    o Frail patients and have co morbid conditions
    o Life threatening acute conditions massive stroke)
➢ Involve patient or family/carer: right to express on the preferred place to die (home, hospice or hospital)
➢ Expert team involvement: Palliative team
NICE has guidance on care of dying adults in last days on life (https://www.nice.org.uk/guidance/ng31)

NHS Scandals

Failings within the NHS can be at several levels; several scandals have rocked the NHS. Whilst Harold Shipman is an example of an individual failing their patients, Bristol Heart and Alder Hey are examples of large institutions failing to recognise a problem. The Mid-Staffs scandal was also a failure by the regulatory bodies in addition to the institutions and individuals. Lessons have been learned and changes implemented to make NHS better managed and regulated.

Bawa-Garba Case

The Bawa-Garba's case has raised a number of issues for the medical profession. This was a case of the tragic death of a child in 2011 and the consequent criminal conviction of a doctor. Dr Bawa-Garba was involved in the child's care at time of the incident. As the doctor held responsible for the outcome, Dr Bawa-Garba was subsequently convicted of manslaughter and suspended from the GMC register by the Medical Practitioners Tribunal Service (MPTS) in 2015 for a year. The GMC appealed the MPTS decision arguing for Dr Bawa-Garba to be erased from the medical register, and in January 2018, the High Court ruled in favour of the GMC. The relevant Trust where Dr Bawa-Garba worked has acknowledged systemic failures which contributed to the events that day. Subsequently Dr Bawa-Garba appealed against the high court ruling and won her appeal to practice medicine in August 2018.

This entire episode has caused widespread disquiet and concern amongst doctors. It has raised wider issues about the GMC's approach to such cases – this includes its decision to appeal a judgement reached by the MPTS, the lack of adequate consideration of systemic failings, concerns regarding gross negligence manslaughter law as it affects doctors and the impact of using personal reflective learning material which could be used as evidence against doctors.

This ruling has also brought into sharp focus the difficult and pressurised environment in which doctors now work. A climate in which many doctors feel fearful and vulnerable, as they are forced to work without the support, colleagues or resources to provide safe, let alone high, quality care.

Alder Hay Investigation

The Alder Hey organs scandal involved the removal and retention of children's organs without family consent from 1988 to 1995. An enquiry was initiated after a baby died undergoing open-heart surgery at Bristol Royal Infirmary (see Bristol Hearts Investigation). Her mother discovered years later that her heart had been stored by the hospital and generated significant media attention. Hospitals had to pay millions of pounds in compensation to affected families.

An investigation showed that organs were being retained 'routinely' by hospitals across the UK. This resulted in *The Human Tissue Act* that ensured that the removal, storage, use and disposal of human bodies, organs, and tissue was properly regulated and done with appropriate consent. To this day, anonymous organ donation is acceptable but selling organs is illegal.

Harold Shipman

Dr Shipman trained as a practising GP. The death rate amongst his elderly patients was unusually high. Further police investigation revealed that he had:

➤ Falsified medical records on his computer
➤ Overprescribed morphine-like drugs to people that needed them
➤ Falsely prescribed morphine-like drugs to those that did not need them
➤ Collected medicine from the homes of recently deceased 'to collect unused medicines for disposal'
➤ Made false calls to 999 in the presence of family but then cancelled the call, stating that the patient had passed away
➤ Forged wills of his patients that then passed away - benefitting him financially

He was investigated and proven guilty of murdering his patients. Further investigations revealed that he may have murdered at least 218 patients. He was sent to prison where he committed suicide. This eventually led to massive changes in the regulation of the medical profession and introduction of several reforms, e.g. revalidation to restore public's faith in the profession.

Bristol Hearts Investigation

At Bristol Royal Infirmary, a newly appointed consultant anaesthetist noticed that cardiac surgery was taking longer and babies were dying at a higher rate than elsewhere. He did an audit which resulted in a formal investigation.

The investigation found that 29 children died and more were left with disabilities as a result of poor standards. Two cardiothoracic surgeons were permanently banned from practising as doctors again. The enquiry found that the poor performance was due to:

➤ Poor management and lack of leadership within the organisation
➤ Poor quality checks on surgical performance
➤ A lack of monitoring led to a delay in identifying the problem
➤ Raising concerns was difficult as senior managers weren't approachable

The enquiry concluded that the key problem was that there weren't enough hospital quality checks to identify failings early on. The enquiry resulted in several big changes:

➤ Hospitals were monitored more closely by regulating bodies
➤ There was a change in mentality to a 'No Blame Culture'
➤ National League tables for hospitals were introduced
➤ A framework for National standards of care was established

MMR Vaccine Controversy

The Measles, Mumps and Rubella (MMR) vaccine controversy started in 1998 after Andrew Wakefield, a medical researcher, published a fraudulent paper in *The Lancet* that showed an apparent link between the MMR vaccine and autism. The Sunday Times investigated the paper and found that Wakefield had multiple undeclared conflicts of interests, had manipulated data and broken several ethical codes. The GMC found Wakefield guilty of serious professional misconduct and removed him from the medical register. *The Lancet* also fully retracted his paper. Multiple large studies were conducted to investigate the issue – none of them found any link between MMR and autism.

As a result of the paper, vaccination rates in the UK dropped dramatically which resulted in significant increases in measles and mumps resulting in several avoidable children dying. A similar pattern was also observed internationally. There has been a concerted effort to re-immunise children that didn't have the MMR vaccine in recent years to improve healthcare.

Mid-Staffs Investigation

In 2008, Stafford Hospital was reported to have abnormally high mortality rates and poor care. This led to an external enquiry which concluded that there were over 1,000 avoidable patient deaths. It also said that patients had received very poor care with many not being cleaned for prolonged periods of time. It said that these were caused by short staffing, poorly trained staff, poor management, and falsification of data to 'balance the books'.

This resulted in:
➢ Introduction of a duty of candour (being open and honest with patients when mistakes occur)
➢ Financial Compensation for affected patients and families
➢ Resignation of several senior managers
➢ Publication of mortality rates for each hospital online

Duty of Candour

Francis Enquiry led to Duty of Candour legislation. The key recommendations for this include:

➢ Candour including statutory duty
➢ Openness
➢ Transparency

The Duty of Candour legislation was introduced in England in 2014 and is applicable to all health and social care organisations. The basis of this is that all individuals want to be kept informed when things have gone wrong so that organisations must acknowledge the mistakes, apologise and inform them of the facts as well as the necessary steps taken to avoid recurrence.

Any apology or any step taken in accordance with the Duty of Candour **does not** equate to an admission of negligence or breach of a statutory duty. Duty of Candour is applicable in situations where - in the reasonable opinion of a registered health professional - an incident has occurred which has resulted in unintended or unexpected harm to an individual receiving a health or a care service.

How is harm defined?

Harm is defined within the statutory Duty of Candour as the following:

➢ A permanent loss of bodily, sensory, motor, physiological or intellectual functions
➢ An increase in the person's treatment
➢ Changes to the structure of the person's body
➢ Shortening of the life expectancy of the person
➢ Impairment of the sensory, motor, intellectual functions of the person which has lasted or is likely to last for a continuous period of at least 28 days
➢ The person experiencing pain or psychological harm
➢ Death of a person

Key stages of the procedure are:

➢ To notify the affected person and
➢ Provide an apology.
➢ Review the circumstances leading to the incident.
➢ Offer / arrange a meeting with the affected person.
➢ Provide the affected person with an account of the event.
➢ Provide information about further steps taken.
➢ To make available or provide information about support to persons affected by the incident.
➢ To publish an annual report on the Duty of Candour.

The trust's annual report includes the number and nature of incidents and actions taken. It should also include any information about policies and procedures and any changes in the policy as a result of incidents.

Possible outcomes following: Following duty of Candour investigations following are likely outcome:

➢ Development of e-learning modules.
➢ Web based fashions and webinars.
➢ Road shows, pop up clinics.
➢ Face to face training, information and awareness.
➢ Raising material including fact sheets and training of staff.

New Junior doctor contract

In September 2015, Jeremy Hunt, the minister for health, proposed a new contract for junior doctors (FY1 to senior registrar). He justified this by saying the NHS needed to be a '7 Day Service' (even though all inpatients were already looked after 24/7). This was based on the apparent observation that patients admitted on weekends had a greater mortality than those admitted on a weekday. This finding was highly disputed with many prominent academics and clinicians accusing the health secretary of misrepresenting data. The major contract changes were:

➢ Removal of overtime rates for work between 07:00 – 22:00 on every day except Sunday
➢ Small increase in Basic Pay of approximately 10%
➢ Reduction of the number of maximum hours per week from 91 to 72

This meant that doctors would be paid the same rate for working Tuesday morning as Saturday evening. This also meant potentially working many more weekends than previously. The British Medical Association (BMA), the doctor's union, declared several days of strikes. These resulted in the cancellation of thousands of operations and clinics. Despite significant opposition, Jeremy Hunt declared in July 2016 that he would unilaterally impose the contract on all junior doctors with it being implemented from October 2016 onwards.

This has been a very politically charged issue (though it seems to be settling) – it's important you try to remain impartial and apolitical if you're asked questions like, *"Should doctors ever strike?"* or *"Would you strike as a doctor?"*.

Medical Training

At the time of writing this book, medical students after graduating from medical school (5-6 years), must do 2 years of 'foundation training'. At the end of the first foundation year (FY1), doctors will get full registration with the GMC to practice medicine. After the second year (FY2), they have several choices. They can apply for:

➢ Core Medical Training if they wish to pursue a medical speciality, e.g. cardiology, respiratory, endocrine, gastroenterology, rheumatology, nephrology etc. [2 Years]
➢ Core Surgical Training if they wish to pursue a surgical speciality, e.g. colorectal surgery, upper gastrointestinal surgery, vascular surgery etc. [2 Years]
➢ Other Speciality training if they wish to pursue other specialities like paediatrics, psychiatry, obstetrics/gynaecology, radiology etc. [5 – 9 Years depending on the speciality]
GP training if they wish to become a GP. [3 Years]

It can take in excess of 10 years to become a consultant in many specialities – more if you include the time that doctors may take to do additional degrees like PhDs and MDs. It may also take longer if the doctor isn't able to pass all their postgraduate examinations in a timely manner, e.g. MRCP and MRCS.

The speciality training programme is changing from 2019. In 2019, Internal Medicine Stage 1 (IM) replaces Core Medical Training. IM) is the foundation for a career in any medical specialty. Progression to Specialist Registrar training within any these broad medical specialties is dependent on successful completion of IM.

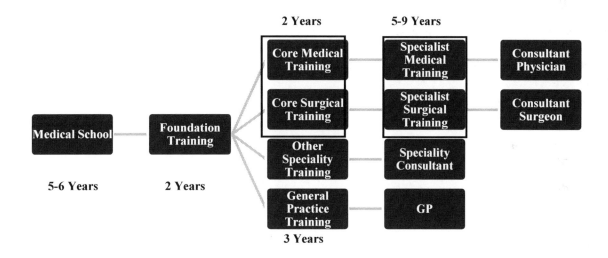

Figure 7: Typical career progression

Doctors entering the 2019 intake will be the first to commence IM training. Internal Medicine Stage 1 will see several mandatory placements throughout the programme designed to address core goals of the Shape of Training reforms. These 'rules' are new compared to CMT, and include:
➢ a minimum of 4 months spent in Geriatric Medicine,
➢ a spell spent in Intensive Care (minimum duration spent in ICU being 10 weeks, but the aim is for all trainees to spend 3 months in ICU)
➢ specific Outpatient training (aiming for weekly or twice-weekly clinics at least throughout IM2).
The two training programmes remain mostly similar in their delivery of experience of the acute medical on call rota, completion of portfolio requirements, and progression in the MRCP(UK) qualification.

Medical Ethics

It is not uncommon for consultant interviews to include a question dealing with an ethical dilemma. While one does not need to be an expert on medical ethics it does help to have a basic understanding of the core principles of medical ethics. We recommend reading *Medical Ethics: A Very Short Introduction* by Tony Hope, which gives a brief and accessible overview. When presented with a question on medical ethics, it can be useful to think about how the main principles of medical ethics apply.

You may be asked questions that appear difficult or one which appears to have no right answers. You need to demonstrate that you understand the ethical issue and apply your knowledge to come up with a plausible reply. Sometimes, the answer may not be immediately obvious to you. Do not panic and think it through. Most importantly do not let your personal or religious views cloud your judgement when answering such questions. Apply the principles of medical ethics and the answer will be clear. The main principles of medical ethics are often said to be:

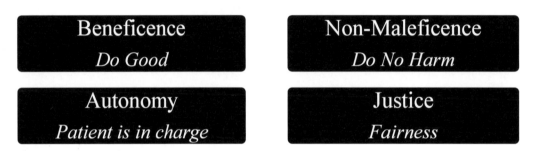

Figure 8: Principles of Medical ethics

Beneficence: The wellbeing of the patient should be the doctor's first priority. In medicine, this means that one must act in the patient's best interests to ensure the best outcome is achieved for them, i.e. 'Do Good'.

Non-Maleficence: This is the principle of avoiding harm to the patient, keeping with the Hippocratic Oath "First do no harm". There can be a danger that in a willingness to treat, doctors can sometimes cause more harm to the patient than good. This can especially be the case with major interventions, such as chemotherapy or surgery. Where a course of action has both potential harms and potential benefits, non-maleficence must be balanced against beneficence.

Autonomy: The patient has the right to determine their own health care. This requires us to consult patients and obtain their agreement before undertaking any medical treatment – essentially an obligation to obtain informed consent. A doctor must respect a patient's refusal for treatment even if they think it is not the correct choice. Note that patients cannot demand treatment – only refuse it, e.g. an alcoholic patient can refuse rehabilitation but cannot demand a liver transplant. Another implication of respecting patient's autonomy is medical confidentiality. Within any health care encounter it is implicit that the doctor will keep confidential any information provided to them. This promise of confidentiality allows patients to divulge sensitive information which assists in the delivery of their care.

There are many situations where the application of autonomy can be quite complex, for example:

➢ **Treating children:** Consent is required from the parents, although the autonomy of the child is considered increasingly as they get older.
➢ **Treating adults without the <u>capacity</u>** to make important decisions. The first challenge with this is in assessing whether or not a patient has the capacity to make the decisions. Just because a patient has a mental illness does not necessarily mean that they lack the capacity to make decisions about their health care. Where patients do lack capacity, the power to make decisions is transferred to the next of kin (or Legal Power of Attorney, if one has been set up).
➢ **Justice:** This is the moral obligation to act on the basis of fair adjudication between competing claims. This includes ensuring fair distribution of scarce resources, respect for people's rights and respect for morally acceptable laws.

Consent: This is an extension of Autonomy- patients must agree to a procedure, treatment or intervention. For consent to be valid, it must be **a voluntary informed consent.** This means that the patient must have sufficient mental capacity to make the decision and must be presented with all the relevant information (benefits, side effects, and the likely complications) in a way they can understand.

Confidentiality: Patients expect that the information they reveal to doctors will be kept private- this is a key component in maintaining the trust between patients and doctors. You must ensure that patient details are kept confidential. Confidentiality can be broken if you suspect that a patient is a risk to themselves or to others, e.g. terrorism, child abuse, informing the DVLA if a patient is at risk of seizures, road accidents, etc.

When answering a question on medical ethics, you need to ensure that you show an appreciation for the fact that there are often two sides of the argument. Where appropriate, you should outline both points of view and how they pertain to the main principles of medical ethics and then come to a reasoned judgement.

It is important to know that sometimes the beneficence and autonomy may be in conflict. For example, a patient is denying treatment that could be lifesaving. It is possible that sometimes the patients make decisions that are not correct or in conflict with beneficence duties of a doctor. When faced with such scenarios, try to understand the reasoning of the patient. Is it because of fear, ignorance or something different, e.g. religious beliefs. If the decisions of the patients are fully informed and the patient has the capacity to make well-informed decisions (patient is not confused due to illness/drugs or mental illness), clinicians should respect the autonomy of the patient.

Caldecott Guardian

Caldecott Guardian is a senior person within the NHS trust, to ensure that the personal information about those who use the service is used and shared legally, ethically and appropriately and that confidentiality is maintained. A Caldecott Guardian should be able to provide leadership and inform the guidance on complex matters involving confidentiality and information sharing. The Caldecott principles are used to determine when confidential information might be used and when it should not. These are as follows:

➢ Justify the purpose for using confidential data
➢ Do not use it unless it is absolutely necessary
➢ Use the minimum necessary for the purpose
➢ Access on a strict need to know basis
➢ Ensure those with access are aware of their responsibilities
➢ Comply with the law
➢ The duty to share information can be as important as the duty to protect patient confidentiality

The Caldecott Guardian hold the key to ensure that organisations satisfy the highest practical standards for handling personal identifiable information. The Caldecott Guardian role should be given to a person who is senior enough, has sufficient experience and champions confidentiality issues at different levels within the organisation including the Governance and Information management and technology. They must be able to instil confidence in their colleagues and make justifiable and practical decision about uses of confidential information.

General Data Protection Regulation (GDPR)

In May 2018 the new General Data Protection Regulation (GDPR) came into effect, replacing the Data Protection Act 1998 (DPA). The DPA gave the GMC power to control how data is collected, recorded and used. Personal data under the act is defined as identifiable information. It's important that data is:

➢ Processed fairly and lawfully
➢ Gathered for specific purposes.
➢ The data is adequate, relevant, accurate, and kept up to date

This governs how doctors collect patient information and who they can share this information with. Practical examples are doctors being allowed to break confidentiality for acts of suspected terrorism and road traffic accidents. The introduction of GDPR has led to updating of GMC guidance on confidentiality.

Medical Law

Understanding the principles of medical law is essential. Here is a brief overview of some key legal cases and principles that you should familiarise yourself with:

Mental Health Act

This act basically governs how heath care professionals interact with people with mental disorders and their rights to force treatment. The original act was passed in 1983, but there has been a significant amendment in 2007. The most significant components for health professionals are the definition of holding powers which allow doctors to detain and treat a patient with a mental illness against their will. Most notably, these are the section 5(2) and 5(4) defining doctors' and nurses' duties respectively. Other orders to be aware off are Section 135 (magistrate order) and section 136 (police order).

Gillick Competence

Competence is an essential requirement for valid consent to medical treatment. In UK law adults are presumed competent to consent, and their competence only comes into question if their decisions appear irrational. However, the age at which children under the age of 18 can legally consent to or refuse a treatment is much more complex and children are often presumed to lack competence. As per UK law a child's ability to consent or refuse treatment depends on their capacity to understand the nature, purpose and consequences of what is proposed. In England for a 16-year-old to be deemed competent they should meet the criteria set out in the Gillick judgement as scribed in italics below –

"Provided the patient-whether boy or a girl-is capable of understanding what is proposed, and expresses their own views, I see no good reason for holding that he or she lacks the capacity to express them validly and effectively and (for them) to authorise the medical man to make the examination or give the treatment which he advises." (Per Lord Fraser – Gillick v Wisbech and W Norfolk AHA, 1985).

The above principle has been further formalised in the Scottish"Age of Legal Capacity Act 1991" , which states that – A person under the age of 16 years shall have the legal capacity to consent on his own behalf to any surgical, medical or dental procedure or treatment when in the opinion of a qualified medical practitioner attending him, he is capable of understanding the nature and consequences of the treatment.

Bolam Test and other tests for medical negligence (Done AG)

The Bolam test is a legal rule that assesses the appropriateness of reasonable care in negligence cases involving a skilled professional. The Bolam test states *"If a doctor reaches the standard of a responsible body of medical opinion, he is not negligent"*. Essentially the practice of the doctor in question should be in line with the practice of his peers. In order for someone to be shown to be negligent, it must be established that:

➢ There was a duty of care
➢ The duty of care was breached
➢ The breach directly led to the patient being harmed

More recently the courts have become more critical about how they review and assess medical practice and the Bolam test is no longer accepted as the sole basis for decisions about medical negligence. In what is described as "Bolitho gloss on Bolam", a judge can overrule the Bolam principle if he can be satisfied that the body of expert opinion cannot be logically supported at all. Likewise, as the test for breach in consent cases Bolam has been replaced by the Montgomery test. As per the Montgomery test the adequacy of information given to patients in order to seek consent is judged from the perspective of a reasonable person in the patient's position.

Mental Capacity Act (2005)

The Mental Capacity Act (MCA) has been developed to protect and empower individuals who may the lack the mental capacity to make decisions about their care and treatment. The MCA only applies to individuals who are 16 years or older. The kind of conditions which can be associated with lack of mental capacity include, learning difficulties, dementia, brain injury and stroke. However just because an individual has any of these conditions does not mean that they lack mental capacity to make a specific decision.

The National Safeguarding Steering Group (NSSG) has set up a sub-group to support delivery of MCA in the UK. This is known as the National Mental Capacity Act and Deprivation of Liberty Safeguards Subgroup.

The MCA sets out the following key principles:

➢ A person must be assumed to have capacity unless proven otherwise.
➢ A person is not to be treated as unable to decide unless all practicable steps to help them to do so have been taken without success.
➢ A person is not to be treated as unable to decide merely because they make an unwise decision. Everyone has a right to make life style choices where they have capacity to do so.
➢ When someone is judged not to have mental capacity a
➢ Treatment provided to an individual who lacks capacity should be least restrictive with regards to their basic rights and freedoms.

Top Tip: Capacity exists if someone cane hear/understand, retain, decide and communicate back. Any missing step can lead to lack of capacity. It is point and subject specific.

Medical Capacity

Medical capacity arose from the Mental Capacity Act. It's the patient's ability to decide that they can make specific decisions about their care. The capacity is time and 'point' specific, meaning that they may not have the capacity to make complex financial decisions but can take decisions if they would like to have/decline specific treatment. This can change in time so there may be a time when they have capacity but other times when they don't (even within days or hours, depending on their clinical condition). For example, a patient admitted with a severe infection may not have capacity on their first day in hospital but this may change as they improve with treatment.

When assessing capacity, it is important to know that the individual does not have an underlying mental illness or a reason to compromise their decision-making abilities.

Important things to consider are:

➤ Can the patient understand the relevant information?
➤ Can the patient retain the information for sufficient time to make the decision?
➤ Can they analyse the information correctly?
➤ Can they communicate their choices clearly?

Euthanasia and Assisted Suicide

Euthanasia is a deliberate intervention undertaken with the express intention of ending a life to alleviate pain and suffering. Assisted suicide is the act of deliberately assisting or encouraging another person to kill themselves. The two main types of euthanasia are:

➤ Active Euthanasia: Doctor causes the patient to die, e.g. by injecting poison
➤ Passive Euthanasia: Doctor lets the patient die, e.g. withdrawing life-sustaining treatment, switch off life-supporting machines

Currently euthanasia is legal only in the Netherlands, Belgium, Colombia, Luxembourg and Canada. Assisted suicide is legal in Switzerland, Germany, Netherlands and some US states. **Active Euthanasia is classed as murder in the UK and is illegal. Passive euthanasia is legal.** You should know the main arguments for and against active euthanasia (covered in '*Why is euthanasia such a controversial topic?*')

TYPES OF INTERVIEW QUESTIONS

Whilst the list of questions provided is not exhaustive, it does cover the vast majority of styles of questions that you are likely to be asked. However, there are no guarantees and you could potentially be asked things that you've never heard of anybody else being asked in interviews. Nevertheless, don't be afraid of the unknown. Keep in mind the qualities that interviewers are looking for and go for it! Remember, what's more important is your ability to deliver genuine answers that are tailored to you – **don't try to rote learn and recite the example answers given in this book**.

Once you have gone through the book and recognised style, patters and how the question is dealt with, you should have sufficient skills to meet any eventuality. Practice with people. Some commonly asked themes are grouped as below:

Attributes	Reason and Method
Clinical	Your experience: usually tested from your application, CV
Motivation	Your reasoning to apply for the specific job, trust and continue as clinician
Team working	Your skills in working with different people, understanding making and breaking of team, value and significance of a team player
Governance	Your ability to understand components of clinical governance and its implications in day to day life
Teaching/Academic	Teaching experience, keenness, publication posters abstracts
Management	NHS and changes
Personality	To know what you are, how you react and are you "like them"

Table 1: Different types of questions and assessment methods

MOTIVATION

1. Why this job? Or why you have applied for this job/this trust?

You are almost guaranteed to be asked this question in your consultant interview. Hence it is essential that you have prepared a flawless answer for it. The best way to approach this question is by being very honest and very detailed in your answer. It can be difficult to know where to start when answering this question. You could look at your CV/application form and bullet point the reasons you stated there. This is an often asked and discriminating question and make a difference to the outcome. We have given few examples to understand and develop your own for real interview.

Bad Response A:

"I have always been a caring person and I always wanted to work in a big city. This job gives me the opportunity to realise my dream. I have always admired doctors at this organisation and looked up to them as role models in my life. This is close to my parents so a great place to work with nice social life."

Bad Response B:

"I want to be a consultant in a district/teaching university hospital as I like the pace of working in this setting."

Bad Response B:

"This is the first job that I could apply to as I am not keen to do another set of nights as SpR."

Bad Response Analysis:

This answer shows very poor insight into the intricacies and the unglamorous reality of being the medical consultant. The candidate's example of their caring nature is distanced from the reality of using specialised medical skills and knowledge to treat patients. This answer is very focused on the "city life dream" does not mention how the candidate currently feels about the job or organisation. He has failed to grab the opportunity to cite the strengths the organisation has and how his attributes compliment the organisation. The candidate does not explain him/herself in enough depth, nor their skills/experience that matches what the organisation requires (e.g. the job description/pre-interview visit may have shown a need for setting up a neonatal unit or develop colposcopy service in which the candidate has experience; they need to reflect more (how their experience matches the job advertised, how the organisation will help them realise their own dream. The opportunity to show your qualities, i.e. hard work, keenness to learn, your empathic nature, is missed in the above response.

Each point has been poorly expanded on and leaves a lot to be desired. The answer is idealistic and does not demonstrate an understanding into what life is actually like as a consultant. Work life balance is critical and whilst it is not a bad idea to bring in the dream of living in countryside or city life, it should be at the end rather than "main reason" to apply for specific job. It is never a good idea to even allude that the district hospitals are less busy or work at low intensity. In fact, the opposite may be true (shortage of staff, need for referral to tertiary unit, more of the service component and less training posts).

Good Response A:

"I love working as part of a team and forming personal and professional relationships with others. I find it exceptionally rewarding to learn about how other people view the world. This job provides me the opportunity to work with world class team with excellent links with the university where I feel I could fit in with ease. My clinical experience matches what is required by the department e.g. writing guidelines on OPD colposcopy as well as my teaching experience at different levels (Junior doctor, membership exam such as FRCA, and regular teaching at the University. I feel I am going to be a good fit. In addition, the organisation has good reputation with quality work emerging in research. This means I will also have the opportunity to contribute and develop personally. In summary, this job offers what I have trained for, in an organisation that takes pride in values of kind, caring respectful and responsible at the its core. Last but not the least, who can deny the charms of living in a larger city/country life."

Good Response B:

"The advertised job offers the skills and interests that have been my strong points during my training. My work in setting up the non-invasive ventilation has been appreciated and I feel there is need for setting up the NIV service in this organisation which I would be able to do. I also feel that I have all the essential and desired criteria. The organisation is well established and offer unique (transplant/complex cardiac surgery) services and I would like to be part of such a great organisation with excellent leadership (various national audits have shown fantastic results showing strong

leadership and team working). The CQC ratings are great in most areas except some improvement required in patient flow in ED. There is an excellent research set up and I would like to continue in this part. I believe this marriage is going to be perfect as I can offer what the organisation needs and the trust can make me develop professionally whilst keeping my passion for teaching and research alive."

Good Response C:

"There are many different reasons for why I think being a consultant at this trust is the right career path and lifestyle choice for me. The Dr Foster data suggests that the hospital has a longer LoS for diabetic people when admitted to surgical wards. This can be minimised by innovative use of the nerve centre (which you use) and communicate effectively between ward teams and diabetes team to make early referrals. I can use my IT skills to develop and launch the in-patient virtual ward to reduce LOS, facilitate early discharges which would improve patient' flow, reduce 4 and 12-hour breaches (another big issue faced by the trust). This would improve patient's experience and keep the Cl Difficle rate as low as the trust is proud of!

My other area of interest is working in intermediate care. My excellent interpersonal skills mean I can develop close liaisons with the community team and reduce referrals to the speciality services avoiding delays in patients being seen in clinics (keep 18 weeks target). Lastly, given the opportunity, I would like this job in this organisation as it offers me the opportunity to use my training as well as work in a great unit!"

Good Response Analysis:

There is no one right answer; there should be lots of reasons for why you want to take this job or in this organisation! The above answer incorporates lots of different reasons to do so – think about the qualities/attributes you think are important to being a consultant, and which ones reflect you personally. Match them to what the trust is looking for, there needs and what their weaknesses are. Fill that gap and the job is yours.

Some of these mentioned above include: academia and hard work, practical skills, adaptability, communication and teamwork. It may sound cheesy/over-used to say you want to work in a great organisation but it is true (most people want to be part of the best team). So, find a unique way of expressing this. Despite this answer being relatively short, all of these features are incorporated into it and demonstrate an insight into what is expected of the consultant and touches on different responsibilities (teaching, research, academia, service development). Moreover, I think it is also important to demonstrate an understanding that being a consultant is a lifestyle, and not just a job!

These answers are robust and complete. They show that the candidate understands that a wide range of skills are necessary to be a good consultant, that they have made a well-considered application to this job, and that they are passionate about a range of aspects of their job. References to a candidate's training and past experience is especially creditable as it shows an active interest in and a realistic perspective of new services and patient care.

Overall

You must avoid a generic answer by making your response personal and including fine detail. Your answer to this question should be relatively long, highlighting your passion for your subject using reflective language. Give examples to show that you can as you have. You should have sussed out what the trust needs (job description, pre-interview visit) and then match what you have that they need. Make some leading comments, if needed, knowing that the interview can ask you follow up questions on; this can allow you to take control of the direction of the interview and show off your strengths. Your research should have been thorough on the organisation (google trust/leaders, check CQC/Dr foster ratings, googles leading people, know any new clipping etc). This way you are aware of the non clinical but equally important attributes e.g. yearly STAR awards. Be warned that your answer may be dissected by follow-up questions. For the above example, a potential follow-up question and a good potential answer are outlined below.

A good candidate uses the follow-up questions to give more details about their motivations and demonstrate even more of the qualities that the interviewers are looking for. Equally, if you give an interest in research, be prepared to explain why you would not rather go straight into a career in research. You may be asked about what challenges you faced when you tried set up a new service? How did you evaluate it to demonstrate effectiveness? You can use what you have included in your CV/application to build your answer. For example, you could say "my project on the genetics of diabetes drew my attention to the rising epidemic of obesity and diabetes". Be prepared to have some discussion about your project, diabetes or obesity or something completely different, e.g. public health issues and clinicians playing a role in disease prevention! It is important to be aware of what you have stated and read around relevant topics.

2. Why should we offer you this job?

This is a very commonly asked question. This is your opportunity to sell yourself by matching your skills to the essential and desired criteria in the JD and more if you can.

Bad response:

"I have applied for this role showing that I am keen for the post. I have done good Registrar training and I have the CCT in orthopaedics. I have performed a number of activities as a Registrar and I was well liked. My 360 assessment has shown that I am a very good and likeable person; most people like to be with me. Therefore, if offered this role I would be someone who is a good person, a good team worker as well as a trained orthopaedic doctor."

Response analysis:

Not a bad response, it discusses the training and that the person is a good doctor with team working activity; it does lack a structure, it does not link the key factors required for a consultant i.e. the clinical skills as well as other attributes such as the ability to work as a manager or teacher. It does not give any examples of previous work and does not add any value by bringing in the Trust requirements and linking it with their experience. This response can be improved by giving it a better structure as shown below.

Good response:

"I should get this role because I have had structured training in orthopaedics rotating through various districts & teaching university hospitals, giving me a well-rounded experience of good feel of the needs of different people as well as different ways of handling similar kinds of situations based on the resources available to oneself. I also feel that besides the clinical skills, I have acquired a good research background by participating in research trials, particularly dealing with fracture neck femur as well as spinal surgery for complex cases. This experience gave me the research skills, awareness of the research governance e.g. Helsinki declaration etc and made me aware of the research methodology; I would be able to bring in to the Trust my research experience. By participating in a research trial, I would be able to be aware of the new changes, bring in the new skills and technology so that we can improve the services for the patient that we provide. In the past I have worked in different capacities and led the teaching activities within the organisation. I contributed to the MRCS examination and I was one of the examiners and I intend to continue to do this. I am also trained to provide SIM training and written module for Sim learning.

I believe I match the essential and desirable criteria given in the job description. I would be able to bring in my expertise from the teaching which I carry out at the local university. This will not only improve junior doctors' training but improve the patient's outcome, as the better trained doctors provide good care to their patients. All of this would add to the Trust's values and improve patients experience. I believe I should get this job because I am clinically competent, have had structured training, I am a good team worker, hardworking goal orientated person and I can assure you that I will give 100% of myself to ensure that the care that I give to the patient is of highest standard and matches the Trust expectations of me."

Response analysis:

This is a very good response; it not only covers the different roles that a consultant plays (clinical, teaching, management) but also alludes to how the candidate can develop the existing services to the next level by bringing in the skills. There is a brief mention of the candidates experience with the fracture neck femur or surgery (this could have been extended slightly, to make it even better and open up more probing questions later on). The candidate has also read the job description and matched his skill.

Finally, the candidate sums up his experience, matches up his needs and ends up by saying how he would add value to the Trust. This is an all-round response which would make interviewers like the candidate.

Overall:

The panel is basically asking you why you should specifically get this job considering that everybody who has applied for the role has had similar training, has worked in a similar capacity, has rotated through as a trainee; this is an opportunity for you to bring up your experiences and what you have learned. Your research about the trust should have given you an idea on what the trust is looking for – their needs, the gaps in the services and match it with what you have (your experience) and see whether you have the capabilities with the existing resources. You need to demonstrate this in an enthusiastic manner, you need to show commitment to the service by demonstrating the previously completed project so that you can show that you have what it takes to start or build a new service or take the service to a new level. This is an example where there is an opportunity for you to shine and highlight your experience to finally nail the job.

3. Why should we *not* give you this job?

The question often surprises the candidate. Understanding this question is the key. Without understanding the logic in the question, its very easy to fall into the trap and candidate may start to give a list of why they should not get the job they have prepared so hard! This could be something that they are worried about: move to a big teaching hospital, working with well-established people, travel or simply something that they feel is an integral part of the work but they don't have enough experience to take on that responsibility. This is a dangerous approach. A good candidate will give a positive spin, appear thoughtful and come up with "I can't think of a reason for that" or something along the lines. Some candidate may start giving list of work required in the job but that they do not have experience to do so.

Bad response

"I can't tell you why you should not give me this job. I am a hardworking person and I have everything that you need in a good consultant."

Response analysis

This is a very bad response. Not only it is short, it shows that the candidate does not have an idea on the selection process. The opportunity to sell oneself is totally missed here. The candidate has not connected the job description, training and his/her own strengths. The question appears to be a negative but it can easily be answered with a positive spin as shown below in the good response.

Good response

"I don't think that there is any reason why I should not get this job. I have had a structured training and am fully competent to work independently. I have also been involved in research and participated in research trials with thorough understanding of the research and clinical governance. I have kept myself updated with the current guidelines and contributed to the local hospital guidelines. I am an avid reader and enthusiastic teacher with regular teaching for junior doctors at various levels (FY/CMT/PACES). I have all the essential and desirable criteria in the job description. In addition, I feel that my experience of work in the liver unit where I was the coordinator for the Fatty liver/diabetes would be very handy in this trust (considering the high prevalence of diabetes in the area as obvious from the HES data. Lastly, I should get this job as I will bring my teaching experience from the University and could contribute to the teaching activity and make the organisation an education hub. All of this would ensure that I would contribute to the organisation's ethos/values and improve patients' journey/experiences."

Response analysis

This is a good response. It links the job description, the organisational needs as well as the experience from past. The candidate is well read and has done the research to a greater depth (knowing HES data). He is selling himself well and is bring up different skills (clinical as well as other areas where he is useful) and add value to the trust. He has thought about his role in the organisation and feels that he can fit in and able to contribute in a variety of role.

Overall

Do not be put off by the negative in the question. It is very easy to get drawn into giving reason "I have not done this in my training or that I don't have this experience which is essential for the job. On the other hand, second candidate seems to have done well as he has focused more on why he should rather than why not! Whichever form the question is asked (why should or why should you not) you are being asked your attributes to match the needs. If you do that, it is an easy sail.

4. Do you have what it takes to be a Consultant?

A Bad Response:

Of course; I am a fully trained doctor. I have worked as a Locum Consultant for a few months now; prior to that I was a Registrar and I was actually making decisions which would be made by a consultant. In fact, there would be some time where I would come in before even my consultant started and I would be post-taking patients or doing the ward round and just report to the consultant. I have had good training and am a confident person. I can make correct decisions. I have had no complaints and people feel happy with me. I therefore think that I am a strong clinically sound person who can be appointed as a consultant.

A Response Analysis:

This response is inadequate at it does not allude to the pressure in which a consultant works. There is always a tug on their time. There would be pressure for them to make the target, develop the service and handle the different personality traits that they work with. In addition, they need to be on top of their administration work and the clinical tasks cannot be left behind as they all pile up.

The candidate has actually completely ignored the pressure that a consultant goes through and has not touched on it; in addition he has missed an opportunity to bring in some examples from previous experiences as a Locum Consultant or at Registrar level and has not given examples of where he has demonstrated what it takes to be a consultant.

A Good Response:

I have had good training during my time as a Registrar and my time as a Locum feel it has prepared me to take on the responsibility at consultant level. When I was a senior registrar I used to work with my consultant who trusted me to take more responsibility. As a trainee representative on the SpR training committee I have had some management experience. I have attended management meetings during my final year of registrar training and understood that the consultant role extends far beyond simple clinical service delivery. Consultants often work under pressure and there is a constant need for them to be on their toes to ensure that only the clinical work is completed timely but the training of junior doctors continued unhindered and service development is achieved at the same time. This requires a great commitment, good time management, interpersonal skills and a team working spirit.

In my Locum post I was able to develop a service in short space of time because I was able to work well with the team. I was able to use my time efficiently and I was able to contribute effectively to the Trust. I believe my experience, training and personal attributes of a good team player working in a team and remaining calm under all types of circumstances combined with my zest to continue and contribute gives me the strength to become a consultant.

Response Analysis:

This is a good response – although it could be further improved. This exam touches on the previous experience where the candidate has set up a service (it would have been slightly more useful to give an example of this service). It talks about the pressure the consultant lives by; it gives an example of how it can cause defragmentation of the service and put the whole service at risk. This is a good example.

The candidate finally sums up by giving his view that he is fit for the purpose and ready for this responsible position. Therefore, the response goes through the various aspects of the consultant role and then gives an example of "yes, I can do" followed by the summary of why and how he can deal with it. This is a good response overall.

A question that is asking you whether you are able to meet the challenges is clearly not just going to be yes and no answer. You will need to give examples from past experience in order to stipulate that you have what it takes to take on such a responsible job as a consultant in an NHS organisation. As alluded above, being a consultant has lots of commitment at different levels which not only includes the clinical role but also the educational and supervisor roles. They have to be able to teach not only to contribute to junior doctors training but to stay updated themselves because teaching requires learning for the teachers as well as their students. In addition, the consultants have to participate in managerial meetings, listen to other people's views and embrace them into their way of working and the wider departmental practice. All this requires good leadership and time management skills without which the team loses its productivity. It is important therefore that an answer to such a question touches on these numerous issues and is able to convey that the candidate has the maturity to take on what it takes to be a consultant.

5. Why this trust?

This is another way to ask the question "Why do you want this job" which is different than "Why should we give you this job". The answering phrases will vary (see later) but it is about using knowledge gained from the job description, pre-interview visit etc. This is testing you on your knowledge of the trust (what you know, what is missing, how can you fit in). This question is about your enthusiasm and about your background work on the job advertised. You should have gleaned a lot of information from your research about the trust/organisation/people working at the trust/your future colleagues.

In your consultant interview, you need to sell yourself to the interviewers and part of that is explaining why you have chosen to apply at that trust? How much you know about the organisation? It is important to know these because you are going to be doing this job for long time. You need to know how this organisation works, the weaknesses and strengths of the organisation. Try to research about the trust/people/department before your interview and think about what attracted you to apply. Was it something that you liked or something that you could change? Try to highlight what you will bring to them. You may have discovered a specific problem e.g. the long wait list for Paediatric ECHO (which you can provide) or your teaching award so that you can set up extra teaching,
All trusts are different, so it is important to have researched what they have to offer that would benefit you and why/how you would fit in there. It is essential that the candidate knows what they are signing up for and must show that they are the kind of person that would thrive in the sort of environment at that particular trust. Thus, the answer to this question should make clear that you understand about the trust and are the right sort of person for the challenge. Remember, the aim of the game is to portray how well you would fit into the organisation, and to demonstrate how you would contribute to the trust. Sell yourself!

Having had your pre-interview visit and met some of the staff and managers, you should have a good idea about the organisational working. Obviously, the interviewers will assume you've applied to other trusts, but for this question a little ego massaging can go a long way!

Bad Response A:
"I've always wanted to be at your trust because it has such great facilities for both medicine and for other aspects of consultants' life. These facilities combined with the excellent research you have makes me think that working here as a consultant would work well for me. I looked into the colleagues and I am impressed at the number of publications they have and would like to join the club!"

Bad Response B:
"I want to be at this trust as I was a junior doctor here and I liked the friendly nature of everyone. This trust is the largest NHS trust in the country and I would enjoy being part of the big organisation. It would also be good for private practice, which I am keen to pursue."

Bad Response Analysis:
This response sounds far too generic and does not give the interviewers the impression that you've visited the trust or spoken to any current members. Try to explain why that specific trust is good for you and also why you would be good for them. This response goes some way to doing that by saying that you are aware of the research work but does not go deep into that. However, lots of places have research and similar facilities so your answer should be tailored to the "haves and have nots" of the organisation and how you can fit the "haves" and bridge the gap to "have nots" of them. This makes you look more attractive as you not only are complimenting them but helping them bridge the gap on what they are missing (a skill or service that you can provide or develop: PACES exam or a new technique to do lung biopsy that reduces the hospital length of stay post procedure. Make sure your answer is specific to that organisation. A poor candidate will often give an answer that does not properly answer the question, is not very specific to the issues faced by the trust and shows no/little consideration of the working environment.

This answer completely misses the point of selling the skills that the candidate has. Remember this is your opportunity to sell yourself. Tell them what you can offer, how can you improve what is wrong and continue to excel what is good in that organisation.

Good Response A:

"I understand that this trust is extremely demanding and challenging, but this sort of pressurised environment is one in which I would thrive. I work well under pressure and am also sure that the strong support networks that are established here will help me to function to the best of my ability. I am very enthusiastic teacher and am always keen to be involved in teaching opportunities and set up new courses e.g. MRCP teaching. (I have organised a number of PACES courses that have received great feedbacks). Whilst the CQC rating have been great for the trust, the trust requires "some improvement" in staff and patient experiences in people with diabetes as shown by the National Diabetes In-Patient audit. This could be due to the lack of dedicated in-patient diabetes team. I will bring my experience from my last trust where I set up this service. In addition, this organisation has shown strong leadership, it is close to my aging parents and the country life with nice golf clubs are a big magnet to me personally!"

Good Response Analysis:

This response demonstrates that the candidate is aware of the sort of working environment that they would be working and seems determined that they would do well under that sort of pressure. They also show knowledge and the challenges faced by the trust and how they can contribute to the growth of the trust. Additionally, the candidate seems to have done a good background search of the area (talks about golf clubs) and shows a compassionate nature as he moving close to "aging" parents. The candidate offers a "complete package".

A good reply as it is specific and will highlight the trust's achievements, matching them to the applicant's own interest, linking what is said elsewhere to compliment this, e.g. personal statement, information in the job description and information gained during pre-interview visit. Candidate has also done a good background check (aware of CQC ratings and actions by the trust, diabetes issues and offers solutions).

Overall:

Overall, to answer this question well, it is essential to show knowledge of the trust and how your own attributes would make you suit that environment. It is important to show that you actually want to come to this trust for reasons other than its prestige. The candidate must demonstrate that they have thoroughly researched the trust and really do want to be part of the organisation, for well thought through reasons.

You need to give **specific** reasons for the trust for which you are being interviewed. Answers like "this is the best trust", or "my parents wanted me to be close to them in their old age time" may please the interviewer but you need to say something of substance. The trust's website will usually detail success stories but the real success of you is to read between the line (what projects are undergoing and read the rational (the trust may have performed poorly in those hence the drive to achieves better outcomes.

Show that the leadership style is similar to yours. You have the experience of what is missing (at the trust) and hence you can sell to this trust. So, the question asking you "Why this trust" is checking if you have what they are looking for? Tell them what they need and what you have is a perfect marriage!

Sell your organisation abilities and how the excellent education centre there is a magnet to you. During your pre-interview visit, you may have discovered that the trust has had a problem in some aspect (long clinic waiting time, breach of 18 weeks target).

You could start your answer by adding something that you found interesting that matches with your style/personality, and if possible, link it with something in your CV/application/experience. Following this, you can highlight the other equally important aspects of consultant's life (life after work, family) e.g. local library, roving club, golf course etc. Showing that you have put well-rounded consideration into your choice of place of work. Thus, if the trust has a good sports team or runs a drama club/ cricket tournament, you could link your sport/drama skills.

Top Tip: A good candidate will demonstrate specific knowledge about the trust, be positive about it, and have a matching personality/portfolio for choosing it. They would also be aware of what they can bring to the trust.

---

6. What do you expect to get out of this job?

Every one need a job. They are asking you what is your expectations from **"this"** job? What are you hoping to gain out of this job, other than salary? This is a variant of "why do you want this job or why you have applied for this job?" Give it a little thought. What is it that you want from your consultant job? Is it just the stability of a job, reputation and personal gain by working in xxx trust, professional satisfaction as the trust has resources that match with your future plan/ambitions (transplant facilities, research facilities) or links to the university etc. It is important to show in this response that you are passionate and enthusiastic about both, your job as well as the organisation. It is also important to recognise that this means more than just the clinical/academic/anything else that attracted you to apply for this job? There is much more to than just being a consultant. This question is indirectly asking you on what you have, how can you use it and develop in future.

Bad Response:

"I expect to get this job as I am nearing the end of my training/locum post. I would like to continue to excel as a consultant to make my patients feel better. I expect to contribute as a good doctor, and also to develop myself as a person. I expect to make some good friends who will hopefully stay friends for life. I also hope to make some good contacts in the medical profession and find something to give back to the society."

Response Analysis:

Although none of this response is technically incorrect, it only shows the bare minimum that you could get out of this job for yourself. It is possible to get so much more out of the consultant post than just providing the basic clinical stuff (looking after the patient, attend meeting, audit etc). This candidate has not demonstrated that they are aware of this, or perhaps they are just not enthusiastic enough to put in the extra effort. This suggests that the candidate may not be as much of an asset to the organisation as others may be, as they are not willing to reap the many other benefits that the organisation has to offer.

Good Response:

"Of course, the main thing that I want to get out of this job is to be an excellent clinician, teacher, colleague and a person. However, I am aware that this incorporates many more aspects than just the academia/patient care. I am eager to go above and beyond the duty of call for patient care component of a clinician. I am keen to pursue my research interest and the award winning newly opened research wing with state of art islet cell harvest facilities would complement my work that I started at the Joslin Diabetes Centre.

Therefore, I will be able to extend my knowledge and understanding of medicine beyond what is required as a consultant. As well as academia and personal satisfaction, I expect to develop myself as a teacher and contribute to the training of the next generation of doctors. This will include both clinical skills and other important life skills which all form part of the job. This job would give me a good mix of personal, clinical satisfaction."

Response Analysis:

This response is thorough and shows that the candidate is genuinely passionate about the job and will gain a lot out of it. Candidates are able to get through the consultant post by putting in minimal effort (although this is still quite a lot), but the interviewer will be impressed when you can demonstrate that you want to get out a lot more than just the bare minimum. It is true, as in most things, that the more effort you put in, the more you will get out of it. This response demonstrates that the candidate is keen to make the most out of all of the fantastic opportunities that are available at the organisation and will fully benefit from the job in the organisation. Happy employee is most productive and hence this will be a perfect marriage!

Overall:

Overall, a good response to this question will demonstrate that the candidate is passionate about the job so will gain a lot more out of it than someone much less enthusiastic. Candidates should recognise that there are many other aspects to be gained other than knowledge, such as life skills and lifelong friendships. It is a good idea to link any past experiences or skills that you have and link them to what the organisation has to offer. This way not only you are showing that you have researched the organisation well, you are also demonstrating that you have thought about different activities as consultant and that you would contribute and gain personally as well as professionally (see reference to Joslin diabetes centre).

7. Being a Consultant is very demanding and intense; how will you manage your time to deal with all of your work?

Part of the interview is not only to judge your suitability as a doctor but also as a person. In this kind of question, you need to demonstrate a mature approach to the possible challenges that you will face in your job as consultant as well as some of the possible ways that you will overcome them.

Bad Response:

"I understand that being a consultant can be challenging but I can assure you that I am a very competent clinician. I have always managed to meet my targets and move on to new ones. I passed my exit exam (and all my previous exams) in first attempt, despite doing a busy work schedule. I feel that I am ready to take on the challenges of being the consultant and I look forward to it. Furthermore, during my training period, I participated in many extracurricular activities which took up a lot of my time, If needed, I can plan to give up on these to make even more time."

Response Analysis:

This response is at one end of the spectrum; the applicant completely fails to acknowledge any of the challenges that the life as a consultant mean and says that they are more than competent enough to time-manage. The applicant may be very competent but consultant jobs are very demanding and challenging for everyone (in a multitude of the ways) and the interviewers are looking at a realistic understanding of these challenges. The applicant says that they finish their work quickly and leave, almost showing disinterest in their work. Furthermore, the applicant at the end says that they will give up all of their hobbies to make more time for job - this will make the interviewer wonder if the applicant really cares about any of the activities that they do.

Good Response:

"I completely understand that being a consultant will be a very challenging experience but I believe I will be able to deal with these challenges. For me personally, I find that a schedule really helps me focus my time. I wasn't too organised initially but then I use the calendar and use the diary function, set aside time every day for each task. This allows me to meet my deadlines in time and it also ensured that I meet my targets in plenty of time with time to spare to learn Spanish! I realise that the transition from registrar to consultant (or from locum consultant to substantive) will be even bigger but by setting a schedule for myself, I will be able to manage my time effectively. Finally, I have a number of hobbies but I realise that, regretfully, I may have to give some of them up. I am very passionate about them so it would be hard to decide what to give and what to pursue but if I must, then I will choose and keep some to pursue and leave some. This way, I still have some relaxing time for myself whilst doing a demanding job and when time permits, revisit what I left behind"

Response Analysis:

This response is significantly better than the previous response as the applicant has a mature approach to the challenges that they could face as a consultant. They outline a previous time they faced time issues and then showed how they learned from that. Self-reflection is key to the realistic approach that interviewers are looking for. Also, notice the difference in approach to hobbies. Both applicants say that they might give up some activities but there is a genuine sense of regret in the second applicant. This also shows that the applicant has thought ahead about how they might manage time in their life as a consultant.

Overall:

A balance is needed to answer this question; the applicant should be confident that they will be able to overcome the challenges of time management. They should not be too overconfident like the first response but at the same time, they should not be scared or panicking in any sense. The applicant must show that they have thought about this previously and give a measured response.

8. What can you add to the trust? Or What would you bring to the trust?

This is to see if you understand what are the expectations from your future employer and weather you understand them. A quick google search should have revealed trust's plan for next few years, trust's reports and what is missing and/or require improvement. You should try to find out if there is any area of service that the trust lacks and you can provide.

You pre-interview visit, job description should have given you the requisite information. Identify where the gaps exist and try to bridge them with "what you can do that the trust does not have". This will add brownie points to your application.

Bad response:

"I am a very good motivated doctor. I like to work with my team and provide great care. I have glowing references and I will bring a very committed person to the job. I have skills that could be useful to the organisation"

Response analysis:

The response is short, lacks structure, no depth in the answer and completely ignore the question. The question is about you, your experience and how you would be useful to the trust. This is about your experience and how you can improve performance of an organisation. An opportunity to expand on previous experience and linking with missing services at the local trust is missed.

Good response:

"I have had good all rounded training in Urology. I have worked in different set ups like district general, teaching university and academic centres. This has given me different skill sets including research and teaching. I also learned robotic surgery in my last post and performed a significantly higher number of procedures. I know when we met during my visit that you are aiming to set up the robotic Prostrate surgery and I can definitely positively contribute to that.. This way we can reduce our income gap by performing surgery locally and not refereeing to the tertiary centre. In addition, I would also use my research training and teaching skills to contribute to the ongoing activities. I have organised MRCS exams and I am in the question writing group for the Royal College of Surgeons. Thus, I would be an extremely useful addition to the teaching group within the institution. I would make the organisation proud by bring my teaching clinical research skills to the trust."

Response analysis:

This is a better response. This response directly references the information gleaned during the hospital visit. The candidate has done the thorough search. The candidate is well read and seems to have read the trust board meeting minutes (they are public and available on the trust website). He is also aware of the future service plan/directions and has linked his previous work in the robotic surgery unit and how his experience can be of use. He also covers others areas where he can contribute to the organisation's finances. He has used this opportunity to include his clinical skills/experience, academia and appear as an all-round person.

Overall

These questions are looking at your understanding of the job you will be doing. This question is very similar to an earlier one and you need to bring in your experience. A good read of the job description and understanding of the criteria for selection (essential and desirable) is important. One must try to match what is essential to the job. Anyone being interviewed will have training and experience. You need to shine by adding that extra which could be anything but must have some value to the trust. If the GMC survey was bad for the trust, they may value someone with teaching experience whilst lots of publication may be a magnet for a tertiary reference centre.

Top Tip: you are so lucky if you are asked this question. Sell yourself well. Tell them what you can do, what you are good in, what they are missing and job is yours.

9. What is the worst/most difficult aspects of being a consultant?

This might seem like a surprising question; you have just spent lot of time with passion for this amazing job and forming a perfect answer as to why this job interests you; now they suddenly ask you to give some negative aspects of the job. This, in fact, is a very serious question designed to see if you really have the maturity to become a consultant. Being a consultant, just like any other job will have its advantages and disadvantages; you must show that you have thought about both of these aspects. This could be a follow-on question to something like "why this job or why should you get this job"

Like other professions, doctors face many challenges that have the potential to permeate through to their personal lives. However, the nature of these challenges is quite unique. The aim of this question is to get you to identify these difficulties and discuss how they may impact on your life as a consultant.

Bad Response:
"By far one of the most difficult things about being a consultant is about dealing with sick patients and screaming family/relatives as the buck stops with myself. I myself have a very short temper and feel at a loss sometimes when confronted with such behaviour. However, I have thought about this and developed the skills to delegate my work greatly. I choose and delegate some of my work so as to minimise direct family contact. Being consultant is demanding and involves long hours and too much of the paperwork; Despite this the pay is good and brings in a lifestyle that most dream of. It is a prestigious job so despite the stress and responsibilities, I am keen to leap into my life as a consultant."

Response Analysis:
This is an exaggerated response but each of the drawbacks highlights a key issue (stressed family/patient, long hours). The response on the first issue shows that the candidate seems to lack any kind of empathy and patience; they view "screaming family" as something to be avoided and they suggest that the best method to do this would be to delegate to someone else. There will always be difficult patients but it is your job as a consultant to be understanding and provide the best possible care. Whilst the delegation is required in the job and some task have/should be delegated, it should have done on the merits of the job, as part of the training of the others, that you would be supervising as consultant and not because you don't like it hence shying away from it. The second point on pay, is factually correct but suggests that the candidate is only after the money. Finally, there is lot of paperwork to do as a Consultant but it is not specific to being a consultant and does not display the maturity required.

Good Response
"I think there are a lot of difficult aspects of being a consultant, however, the most difficult part would be the personal sacrifices they have to make on a daily basis. Most people do not realise that being a consultant isn't just a job but a lifestyle. It requires a lot of dedication and time, often to the detriment of their own personal and family lives. It can be a toll that is often hard to bear and its impact should never be underestimated as the daily stressors one faces as a consultant are unique. Doctors face complicated choices in patient care which can involve life and death decisions. This can have a heavy psychological impact. Although they face many difficulties, I believe the upsides of patient' satisfaction go a long way to helping doctors overcome some of the inherent challenges that come with the profession. Moreover, I think it is vital to focus on maintaining a healthy work-life balance and taking care of yourself as much as you can within the demands of the profession. There are, of course, many wonderful things about being a consultant, but it is important to be realistic about the challenges."

Response Analysis:
This response aptly identifies some difficult circumstances a consultant finds themselves in and the impact it can have on the health care professionals. Because it is not such a generic answer that any member of the public would be able to come up with, it shows that the candidate has done their research and understands the reality and the challenges of being a consultant.

Overall:
While considering your answer, make sure you expand on the points you make by explaining the reasons behind your beliefs and provide examples when you can. Examples show that you have thought thoroughly about not only the benefits of becoming a Consultant but also the hardships that comes with it. You need to show that you are prepared for the challenges you are likely to face as a consultant and that you are prepared for the task. Be ready for a follow-on question, asking you give an example where you made a choice?

10. Why do doctors leave the NHS? Would you?

This question tests your understanding of your future employer, being well read you can show your dedication and motivation to pursue your consultant career within the NHS (other options are private sector, pharmaceuticals, academic jobs, research, overseas). There are many reasons for doctors to leave the NHS and your answer could speak generally about them or focus in on one specific reason. Either way, you need to acknowledge the complexity of the situation. The best people to find this sort of information from are doctors themselves who have or know people who have left the NHS. Thinking broadly about the destinations of people who leave is a good starting point – generally, people leave to continue medicine elsewhere (abroad or private practice) or to pursue a different career (in pretty much anything!).

Bad Response:

"One reason some doctors choose to leave the NHS is to work for private practices. This throws up some ethical questions over private practice and whether those that can afford it should be able to jump waiting lists and see specialists that would not be available to the general public. To me, it doesn't seem right that the government and NHS help to fund the training of doctors who then leave the organisation to work in direct competition but for a select group of the population."

Response Analysis:

This response does well in considering doctors that leave the NHS to work in private practice, but more elaboration is needed about other areas that the NHS loses its doctors to. It's worth mentioning the breadth of the issue and reasons people leave, even if only to frame your answer to focus on one aspect as that will show your appreciation of the bigger picture. The candidate does not answer the second part at all and maybe perceived by your interviewers that you are being discreet or deceptive.

Good Response:

"There are number of reasons for why doctors leave the NHS – to continue medicine elsewhere, to have a different career, to take time out to do research, or even to have a family. I have come across doctors that have left the NHS to work in management consultancy in London, migrate to in the Australia or that took up a research post with a big pharmaceutical industry. These are some good examples of the quality of doctor and training that medics receive with the NHS – that these persons had the transferable skills to be able to enter a completely different work environment. However, I feel uneasy about the idea that the NHS and government subsidises medical education if people then leave the NHS so early.

Another reason that the NHS may lose doctors is to work abroad due to the issues surrounding the junior doctors' contracts. We have yet to see whether the high numbers (I read 7 out of 10!) quoted in the media that suggest they may leave to work elsewhere actually do. However, this would start a very new era for the NHS and medicine more internationally if doctors were less compelled to stay to work in the country they train in. As far as I am concerned, I have not given much thought about leaving the NHS. I feel I would like to maintain my patient contact, stay in clinical areas though, I may consider getting into some research/teaching element to my NHS job after some years."

Response Analysis:

Starting your response by showing your knowledge of varied reasons that doctors may have for leaving the NHS will show the interviewers your understanding of this complicated situation. Doctors themselves are probably the best people to comment so having an example from your discussions with fellow doctors is likely to be a good idea. Also, notice how much you can respond before you have to justify any of your own opinions about the topics. Topical news stories relating to the issue would definitely be a good thing to bring up (assuming you know enough about them in case they ask you follow-on questions) as it shows you are interested and aware. The candidate has answered the second part and shown his commitment whilst admitting that he may consider changes in practices/role with time.

Overall:

This is a tricky question so try to highlight what you know about the NHS. Where possible, including topical issues is a good idea but make sure you know enough about the issue so that if the interviewers probe you further, you offer intelligent answers. Any experience/opinions of doctors you know/have met would also be good to include. Reading topical news, BMJ, royal college publications would all give you ideas on recent changes being discussed. Be careful in responding to a follow-on question asking if you would consider a career outside NHS or abroad. Whilst you need to be honest this question is tricky and actually testing your motivation towards NHS, your commitment to the organisation and hence should be answered with utmost care (more so if you are even contemplating). A hint of you being unsure, may lead to the trust thinking that you are not committed to this job and are taking it as a stop gap post. Remember, being honest is the key but revealing *every future plan of yours is not necessary*. In addition, plans change!

11. Would you choose a party over a patient? What if they weren't your patient? What if you weren't on call?

This kind of question is very common in interviews - it is a hard question to answer as you want to show commitment to your patients, but at the same time, your answer needs to be realistic- there are going to be times in your professional life where you will have to decide between a professional and personal commitment.

Bad Response:

"I would always choose the patient first. My first commitment is always to my patient; the Hippocratic Oath states that as doctors we must all look after our patients. I myself do not go to any parties and spend most of my spare time reading medical journals. It doesn't matter if the patient is my patient or someone else's patient; When I chose to be a doctor, I made a lifelong commitment to the betterment of everyone in the human race."

Response Analysis:

This person might at first seem like the perfect doctor; they spend all of their time reading medical journals and would drop everything to treat a patient. The first problem with this is that the response is not realistic. No person would actually spend all of their time reading medical journals and if they did, they would quickly burn out. Even if you do not go to many parties, you should always try to answer the essence of the question; would you stop a leisure activity to go to help a patient?

Remember that medicine is a stressful career and it's important that you have some time off so that you can de-stress. Spending all your free time on reading medical textbooks/journals or sacrificing your personal time to look after patients is likely to lead to burn-out which is not a good idea!

Good Response:

"This all very much depends if I am on call and if I have something else planned at the time. I understand that it is very irresponsible to plan on going to a party when I am on call and I would never do this. Even if the patient was not my patient but I was on call, I would choose the patient. My duty as a doctor does not just extend to my patients but anyone who requires my help. However, if I was not on call, I would be less likely to go because doctors must balance their social life and work life. Some downtime is required for doctors to recuperate and this will allow a better performance on the job. Obviously, if there is an emergency and the on-call doctor was suddenly unreachable I would feel compelled to go out of basic human compassion."

Response Analysis:

This response is significantly better as it demonstrates the responsibilities that a doctor must have; being a doctor does not just end at the hospital, it is a profession that you must carry with you wherever you go. The answer clearly delineates some circumstances in which they would/wouldn't go to work and provides justification for these.

Overall:

For this question, you must not be afraid to say that there are some circumstances in which you would choose your social life. If you do end up saying that you would always drop anything you are doing to go to see any patient, then a particularly cynical doctor might ask if you believe doctors should have any free time at all!

12. What are your long-term plans in life?

This question is somewhat complex as it does not really have a set answer. It really depends on what exactly you see yourself doing in the future. There are however a few things that can come across as a little one-dimensional and should be avoided.

Bad Response:

"In the future, I see myself working in a large university hospital making life-saving decisions, whilst also having a good personal life where I am able to travel the world and devote to leisure activities like golf. I am hoping to own a house in London and send my children to private schools for them to receive the best possible education money can buy."

Response Analysis:

This is a rather poor answer as it is solely focused on money. It does not give any indication of other goals and completely ignores some of the key roles that the consultants have to play such as training, service development, research and providing good care. Whilst financial safety and gain are a valid goal, it reflects rather poorly to fully ignore aspects such as patient care in this type of answer. Also, the days where medicine was essentially a money printing profession are long over.

Good Response:

"For the future, I am hoping to achieve a variety of goals both on a professional and private level. On a professional level, I am hoping to reach excellence in my chosen field of practice enabling me to deliver the best care I can to my patients. I am hoping to positively influence their lives by caring for them. On a personal level, my goals include caring for my family and providing for them. I also hope to be able to spend time with them to see my children grow up and become responsible adults. In my free time, I would like to pursue my other interests, e.g. music and photography. I also hope to progress further in my career and be either a clinical director/medical director in the trust."

Response Analysis:

This answer is better than the previous one because it draws a clear distinction between professional and private goals. Your professional goal should always be to provide the best care for your patients that you are capable of and some thoughts on how you see your career progressing over the years. On a private level, you can pretty much have any goals you want. Just make sure that they are reasonable and don't conflict with what people generally see as good moral conduct.

Overall:

This question is tricky as you have a lot of freedom in answering it. The best way to deal with this question is to answer honestly about what you want to get out of life. Spending a few minutes thinking about this question prior to the interview will make answering it a lot easier. It is also acceptable to say that you haven't really planned that far ahead, but then make sure you can argue why.

13. Where do you see yourself in 5/10/20 years' time?

This question can be asked for a number of reasons – simply to get to know you a little better and stimulate further questions, to assess your ambitions/aspirations or to assess your understanding of the NHS organisational structure. You don't need to know what you may pursue but you may have an idea about the options you may have considered. If you do have some idea, then don't be afraid to suggest it provided you have done the research and know a bit about that aspect of progression.

Bad Response:

"In twenty years, I hope to have moved to New York and be the chief paediatric heart surgeon at Mount Sinai hospital. I also hope to be a tenured professor at New York medical school after developing a technique that allows us to engineer heart tissue from pluripotent stem cells- earning a large amount of money as a result. By this time, I will have found a husband and will have settled down with three children. Finally, having established myself at the top of my field, I will begin looking at the political office- I eventually hope to join the US senate."

Response Analysis:

This is obviously an exaggerated response but there are a few key lessons. Never say in an interview that you are planning to move abroad and leave the NHS, even if this is your intention. The NHS provides significant funding to your medical course and they see this as an investment; they need you to stay with them in the future. By committing to the trust, you are making a commitment to the NHS (even if this is something you intend to go back on at a later date). The second big mistake with this answer is that everything is too definite. You have no idea what you will be doing in a few years' time let alone the next 5/10/20 years. Whilst such a detailed answer can show that you're ambitious, it also shows a lack of realism. Finally, never mention money in a medical interview (if this is the primary reason you have chosen this career- think again!).

Good Response A:

"In 10 years' time, I hope to have established myself in my speciality as a paediatrics endoscopist. It's an area I've had a lot of experience, although I'm very open to having my mind changed as the situation change! I would also be an examiner for the royal College of Paediatrics or might pursue a role in education (take up RCP tutor post at the trust or be the director of education. If I do focus my career in paediatrics, then in 20 years' time I would hope to be a senior consultant/clinical director /medical director or a professor in a university."

Good Response B:

"Hopefully I'll get this job so then in 10 years' time I would be settled well into my post as Consultant Radiologist. I would have pursued my research dream and taken up more interest in research and established my research service with participation in research trials. On a professional front, I would have taken my MRI training further and developed neuroradiology service. I hope to have become well known in the research circle with number of publications. On a personal note, I would like to pursue my roving training which I had to put on hold as I was training to be a consultant."

Good Response Analysis:

This response demonstrates your knowledge about the career options available to consultant (beyond patient care). They can choose/develop as researcher/academician or pursue managerial skills. The comment about broad-based training also shows dedication and ambition as you are clued up and seriously considering the shape of your future career. The candidate does not talk about personal progress (family, hobbies etc) and it is OK. One does not need to go through everything/all aspects of life in an interview. If challenged, admit that the plans can change, though you are very committed and would like to stick to plan but for reasons beyond control, you have the flexibility and maturity to recognise this and have the maturity to handle such life changing situations or when dreams change!"

Overall:

Use this question to demonstrate your understanding of the life you are committing to. Be open and flexible for things like research/academia/starting a family etc showing that you have a realistic grasp of the future and the demands of a career as a consultant. It may seem daunting, but it is not that difficult to predict where one might be as the path after taking up consultancy is very well defined. One may not be able to predict if they see themselves as a researcher/professor or president of the royal colleges, so it is fine to accept that you do not know exactly what direction your career may take but you are very keen to develop research or a role in education. It shows maturity to appreciate that what interests you and the priorities you are looking for in your job may change somewhat along the line. You can use a question like this to demonstrate your knowledge of how NHS organisation works. one cannot always expect to stick to a rigid career plan.

14. We have much better applicants than you – why should we take you?

The aim from the interviewers is to play 'bad cop' and try and stir you up a little. Do not be fazed by this- it is their job and they do not mean to make you feel bad! They are simply assessing your ability to deal with criticism, which you will be inevitably faced with at some point in your career. The simple answer is that you are actually the correct person for this job - don't be afraid to say so! This, of course, needs to be backed up by evidence of what specifically sets you apart from other applicants.

Bad Response A:

"I guess you probably do have much better applicants than me. I just wanted to try to get to an impressive trust like this. I guess, like you have highlighted, I am probably not good enough for such a high-profile trust (or a trust in a district hospital setting). There are perhaps a lot of applicants better suited than me, but I have wanted to be part of this trust and contribute. I have the right experience and I think that is a good enough reason for you to choose me."

Bad Response B:

"I'm confident that I'm the best candidate for this job. I have the right skills, experience and training. I have prepared for this job as it is my dream to be in a trust like this. I would be crushed if I didn't get the job. I can do all things that you need doing. So, you have no reason not to choose me."

Response Analysis:

The first candidate shows a concerning lack of confidence in themselves. A confident answer accompanied by confident body language (good eye contact, sit up straight) will go a long way. Contrastingly, the second candidate is on the opposite extreme and comes across as arrogant. A lack of personal insight and willingness to take feedback on board is equally as bad in an interview setting.

Do not accept that there are other applicants that are better than you - you will find things that differentiate you from others. Make sure to highlight your positive attributes during your interview.

Good Response:

"I should get this job as I am the right person. I have all the essential and desirable criteria, as in the job description. I have the necessary skills and experience to take on this job like a fish to the water! I have had a structured training and experiences that match your needs. I am well versed with the audit/research process and will bring that experience to contribute to the trust. I also bring with me great academic skills- I have shown that I have a great scientific aptitude by my publications and presentation awards in various national and international meetings. I am also a hard-working goal-oriented person with great team work spirits. I like to meet my targets, set my bars high and work diligently. In addition, I can assure you that I will contribute 110% to provide great patient care and actively contribute to the trust projects/values."

NB: be prepared to be quizzed on "what are the trust' values?" as a follow up question.

Response Analysis:

This answer demonstrates confidence and enthusiasm. The candidate is able to utilise his/her achievements as a selling point and shows the interviewer what he/she can bring to the organisation. Remember that you are an investment for them and they love to hear what you aim to bring to them during your time with them. The candidate does mention "I will bring to…" it could be further tightened up by using the information gleaned during pre-interview visit: any challenges the trust is facing? Any service they are missing and bring up your experience in those areas to be a perfect match"

Overall:

The aim of the interviewer is to try to shake you up a little. If you know that and are expecting that from the beginning, it won't be a big shock and you will be prepared for tough questions like these. Remember to highlight your achievements to date and try to sell yourself to the interviewer by showing them how much you plan to contribute to their organisation. You can impress them using the trust's CQC rating, data from Dr Foster or any information gleaned during your pre-interview visit (any areas that they need improving? Anything that's a big hurdle for them?) and align your experience to offer solution to these. A guaranteed way to get them to like you!

15. What would you do if you didn't get this job?

The reason interviewers may ask you this question is to assess how determined and motivated you are towards this job/trust. The most important thing to remember in your response to this question is to demonstrate **self-improvement.** It is crucial to accept that the reason you may not be successful could be due to the quality of your application but demonstrate that you are willing to improve to try again.

Bad Response:
"I am very hopeful to get this job and all my plan revolves around me getting this job. I would be very disappointed and gutted if I did not get this job. So, I would try again if the job was advertised again or a new one appeared."

Response Analysis:
This response is very passive and bland. Remember that the question demands a response that demonstrates that you actually want to improve your application and not just apply again! A good response would express that you have a clear plan if your first job option does not materialise. You should be demonstrating organisation and foresight. The answer is also very vague and gives no specific description as to why you would be disappointed (an opportunity to impress with nitty gritty of the trust: the positives as well as negatives that you could work on to improve). Although you are showing determination by stating that you would re-apply, it's unrealistic to apply again and again if you have been unsuccessful on two occasions. You would need to have insight into your own shortcomings. It is also unlikely that a job in similar capacity would appear in the time scale that you are looking. You are already looking the job and can't wait too long to get the stability (unless you choose to do locum in between). So, when you say, you would wait for advertisement, you need to add in what you would od in the interim and how would add value to your CV to correct mistakes from this round of selection. Many people apply for few jobs so if you are dead committed to this specific organisation, you should be showing it in your answer (and that might get you the job).

Good Response:
"In all likelihood, with my experience and training I should get this job. If I didn't get one, I would be very disappointed. However, I would receive as much feedback as possible regarding my application, interview skill and how can get better so that I could improve before reapplying again, when opportunity came. If it means taking some interview course or do some audit/research or get some publications. I would make the most of the situation and try and take part in as many enriching experiences as possible – I could enrol in a teaching diploma. As I am very keen to have this job, I would opt to take on some locum posts here or nearby to work on improving applications (based on the feedback).

If I didn't get the job after my second application, I would need to have a realistic expectation of my abilities. I would need to realise that I possibly need to reconsider my application and apply where my experience is better matched with the job."

Response Analysis:
This response is far better. Not getting this job would leave you disappointed and stating this shows that you definitely *don't* want to be in this situation. 'Receive as much feedback as possible' demonstrates that you are not only going to improve your job application but are willing to listen to criticism and critiquing before self-improvement, an important attribute to have as a doctor (regardless of the grade). Show a clear plan, publication, teaching diploma. Demonstrate how would you use the time between this job and new application. A teaching diploma would improve your chances of securing an academic job. This way, the time while waiting is not wasted as well. This answer, unlike the last, shows that you understand your personal limitations and that other options are also available although not ideal. It's preferable to state an alternative (teaching/research).

Overall:
This question will usually be asked at the end of the interview just to see whether you have a backup plan. Stating that you have planned an alternative option, reapply does not mean that you don't want to get in the first time. It makes you look better as you understand the challenges of the job application process, realise how competitive the process is and are willing to improve.

MEDICAL ETHICS

Questions testing ethical dilemmas may get asked directly in the consultant interview in formats shows or could be a follow up question in a situational question. We have decided to keep the format of direct questions related to ethical issues so that you are aware of the framework. Some questions may actually be speciality specific e.g. Sports injury for Orthopaedic consultant interview or IVF question for an Obstetric interview. You may think of these questions not relevant to you but get yourself familiarised as you may be asked something similar.

16. What are the main principles of medical ethics? Which is most important?

There are a few principles which are generally accepted as the core of medical ethics. You should be fully versed with them in your position. It can be useful to read a little about them to make sure you have a good grasp on what they mean. See the Medical Ethics section for more details.

You are less likely to get asked a direct question in this form but it could be a follow-on question when you are discussing ethics related questions. So a grasp of these would be handy. In answering this question, good answers will not just state what the main principles of medical ethics are, but why they are so important. You don't need to go into too much detail, just show that you know what the principles mean. In choosing which principle is most important, it is good to show balanced reasoning in your answer, i.e. that you recognise that any single one of the principles could be argued to be the most important but for specific reasons you have picked this one.

Bad Response:

"It is really important for doctors to empathise with their patients, so empathy is probably the main principle. If doctors empathise with their patients, this means they will do what is in the patients' best interests, so it is the most important principle in medical ethics."

Response Analysis:

Empathy is obviously an important component of the doctor-patient relationship and the ability to empathise is crucial for all medical professionals, but it is in itself not a principle of medical ethics. The candidate seems to be getting at the idea of beneficence but does not really explain what they mean or why it is so important. If you are asked to make a judgement on which medical principle is most important, it is a good idea to have mentioned other medical principles earlier in your answer to compare it to. Thus, the main way in which this answer falls down is in having shown no real appreciation for other medical principles and not coming up with the whys of the chosen one.

Good Response:

"The main principles of medical ethics are beneficence, non-maleficence, autonomy and justice. It is very difficult to say which is most important as, by definition, they are each crucial in medicine and they are all very linked with each other. For example, if a patient wants a treatment that a resource-limited health system, like the NHS, can't offer without compromising the healthcare to someone else then this is a conflict between autonomy and justice. If I had to pick, I would say that beneficence is probably the most important principle as if it is applied to all our patients then it should imply justice and if a patient is properly respected, then it should also consider the importance of autonomy."

Response Analysis:

This candidate knowledges the main principles and understanding of what they mean and how they could be applied practically. Notice how this candidate showed their understanding without actually defining each principle, though there wouldn't necessarily have been anything wrong with doing so. This candidate recognised the difficulty in picking a 'most important' principle, in so doing showing balance and humility. Their insight into the conflict between different principles further shows a good understanding and suggests they have given medical ethics a good degree of thought. Do not be afraid to admit it as such.

Overall:

This question is really easy one. In your role you are familiar with the main principles of medical ethics so that you know you can define them and recognise how they might apply in a clinical setting. The question of which is 'most important' has no single right answer – it can be good to say this and then make sure you have a reasonable justification for whichever principle you pick.

Be prepared for a follow-on question like "give an example where justice is most important." Do not be put off by these, they are trying to stretch yourself to ensure that your replies are from the understanding of the principles rather than prepared answers.

17.Should pharmaceutical companies advertise on merchandise?

This question is asking whether it is right for drug companies to advertise their drugs for the treatment of various diseases directly to patients and doctors. This is an interesting question that could allow good candidates to shine if they can present a well-thought-through argument. The major considerations here are whether it is fair for advertisers.

Bad Response:
"Yes, they should be able to advertise because patients will then be aware of the additional drugs available to them to treat their disease. In addition, doctors will be more informed about drugs and know what drugs to use in specific conditions."

Response Analysis:
Though the candidate touches on the important point of making sure patients are fully informed of all treatment options, he fails to address the significant other issues associated with this problem. For instance, what if the evidence base for the use of this drug is poor? Will the drug company ensure that the merchandise they advertise on is widely disseminated around the country to people of every social demographic (ensuring equality of healthcare opportunity)? The candidate has taken a rather simplistic and blinkered approach to this complex question that requires far greater thought and balance in the answer. It also does not look at the biased prescribing that may pop in from gifts to prescribers.

Good Response:
"On one hand, it seems fair that patients should be made aware of all the potential drugs that may help their disease even if they are not currently licensed by NICE. This allows patients to make a fully informed decision and not providing all available options encroaches upon their autonomy. On the other hand, suggesting to patients that a potentially very expensive new drug that is the key to their survival will put patients' families under pressure to potentially self-finance the drugs and/or put their doctor under massive pressure to prescribe the drug. In the circumstance that the cost-benefit of the drug is not deemed acceptable by NICE, then this raises the issue of having patients who can afford these new drugs receiving different treatment from those who cannot. This directly contravenes the principles of this country's national healthcare system. Furthermore, advertising to doctors raises the issue of influencing them to prescribe the drug. It can be argued that the product being advertised will lead to a bias in the prescribing habits regardless of the proven efficacy or cost benefits."

Response Analysis:
This answer provides several different dimensions that demonstrate careful consideration by the candidate. Impressively, the candidate manages to slip in references to NICE, ethical principles, and topical issues such as healthcare being stratified based on patients' wealth and finally, alludes to the post code lottery. This shows a deep appreciation for topical healthcare issues as well as providing a balanced view. To improve, the candidate could have presented their own opinion and conclusion. Be prepared for follow on questions.

Overall:
This is an opportunity to shine as the question provides a wide scope for dropping in lots of your "extra" reading (see the "good" answer). Other points may be that legislation should be in place to ensure that the drug companies follow firm evidence when advertising these drugs (e.g. regarding drug superiority over another). Candidates should be aware that this sort of starting question might then lead onto a wider discussion regarding the application of the free market to healthcare and all that entails. Therefore, in preparing for these sorts of questions, candidates should read more widely than just that directly relevant to these questions. There's no point being polished and efficient for a precise sort of question given that it's likely a variant of the question that will be asked come interview time anyhow!

You may have follow-up questions on post code lottery (variations in prescribing and drugs available to patients depending on where they live), NHS philosophy (free at the point of entry), conflict of interest (drug company's interest Vs patients' interest etc.

18. You are returning home after a busy day, at the car park, you find someone who has collapsed and requires CPR. What would you do?

This is a potentially tricky question and some background reading into the laws that govern the application of healthcare in the UK would, of course, be desirable. You should be familiar with the intricacies of the law to simplify good reasoning ability. You should approach this question systematically. An example of such a systematic approach is the following: Firstly, do you have a duty of care to this member of the public? Secondly, what standard of care is expected of you? Thirdly, can you be held accountable for increasing the harm to the member of the public?

Bad Response:
"I am not ALS trained and if something goes wrong then the person's family may sue me. I won't be able to give any drug as none is available in the carpark. I don't think that I have a duty of care to this patient anyway."

Response Analysis:
Several issues arise with this answer. Firstly, the law states that you are only liable for damages if their action leaves the recipient in a worse position than if no action at all had been taken. Given that the person would have almost certainly died without CPR, it seems that you would be justified in administering CPR without fear of liability. Secondly, the candidate states that they have no duty of care because the person is not their patient. This may be true; however, the interviewers would begin to severely question this individual's morality if they were to not apply their potentially lifesaving skills in this situation simply because they did not have a formal duty of care. Remember that even as a member of public, it is crucial to raise an alarm, seek assistance to ensure that the patient gets the treatment. Least that could be done here by the doctor in question is to at least call for help and offer basic life support.

Good Response:
"I'm not entirely sure of the finer points of the law, however, I believe that a we as a doctor should give CPR in this scenario. This is mainly from a moral point of view due to myself having the knowledge to save this person's life. Doctors can administer treatments without consent if the individual is unable to give consent and it is in the patient's best interests. Both these conditions seem to apply here. I have my basic life support training and I can provide basic life support so I feel I would call for help and provide basic life support/CPR. Even if I am not able to provide CPR, I would raise alarm to get help by calling 999. On the other hand, if I were to encounter this situation on my out from a pub, when I may have had a pint or two, I would rather raise an alarm by calling 999."

Response Analysis:
The candidate does well to present a good, logical argument with a nice conclusion at the end. Importantly, they admit to the interviewer that they are not an expert on the law but show how the small bits they do know (when treatment without explicit consent is appropriate) may be applied to this situation. The candidate even touches upon counter-arguments, e.g. what if the doctor is incapacitated for some reason (the candidate suggests a situation whereby the off-duty doctor may be drunk on a night out). This response is good as it leads the interviewer and invites them to ask follow up questions. They touch on capacity and negligence. Both important in patients' care. So, an opportunity well used.

Overall:
This is a typical question where the interviewer is likely to expect you to know what the law is, however, wants to see how you think your way through tricky problems. This is also an example where they are subjecting you to challenging situation to see if you would "just choose to see the other way" or work in the best interest of the patient. Plenty of practice in thinking about these sorts of dilemmas will make you more comfortable with these questions. An extended question to think about relating to this would be: Has the patient clearly denoted a Do Not Resuscitate wish? Again, you should be aware of the latest resus council recommendation. YOU may get stretched far into power of attorney, living will etc.

Being a consultant is a job that often leave you holding the bucket! You should have a detailed knowledge of the law, not the sections and subsections and in greater depth, but know what you need to know and what is relevant. As a doctor, you are often needed in unlikely situations (in an airplane up in the sky: you may have had a pint or two). You need to decide your responsibility in this situation. If the risk outweighs benefits, that is the side you should follow.

19. Do you think people with extreme sports injury should be treated by the NHS?

The crux of this question comes from the implication that those who do extreme sports, such as skydiving, are people who voluntarily take risks with their health and should not expect taxpayers to pay for their medical care if they are injured. This is reflected in a private healthcare where people who take risks would have to pay a higher fee. Patients often argue that they have the right to healthcare since they themselves are taxpayers and by paying to support others they also have the right to seek treatment.

We can analyse this question with the principle of justice because healthcare systems, such as the NHS, have limited resources so we must place restrictions on how funds are spent. It would release funds that could be spent on others who have not purposefully put themselves in harm's way. However, the principle of autonomy also plays a role; a person's autonomy has to be respected. They have a right to decide how to live their life and participate in extreme sports if they wish. Looking at a third principle, beneficence, it is important to be non-judgemental and act in the best interests of the patient, which means treating injuries. Most medical professionals will prioritise the principles of autonomy and beneficence over justice.

We can draw a parallel between the situation proposed and denying treatment to those who are ill due to lifestyle choices. These conditions are often seen as "self-inflicted" and include smoking- or obesity-related diseases. If we begin excluding those who participate in extreme sports, it is a slippery slope before we exclude lifestyle diseases from public funded treatment.

Bad Response:
"People who do extreme sports put themselves at risk; their injuries can be avoided by simply following a different lifestyle. This is not fair to others who are leading normal lives. However, people who do extreme sports also pay taxes which contributes to the running of the NHS so they are entitled to use it."

Response Analysis:
The response is good because it shows a balanced view. However, it misses the opportunity to get into detail. For example, they did not discuss patient autonomy and the patient's right to lead their life as they see fit. Doctors can give advice but should not penalise them for not following it. Another ethical principle that was not fully discussed is justice. The NHS has limited resources so should we redistribute our funds to only people who cannot avoid their injuries? Another fault with this answer is that it misses the key connection between the question and the treatment of alcoholics and smokers with a self-inflicted disease.

Good Response:
"The NHS is a publicly funded institution and free at the point of entry for the general public. We should not limit anyone's access to it. This goes against the principle of non-maleficence. Others may argue that people doing extreme sports are causing themselves avoidable harm and their injuries are self-inflicted so the NHS funds could be better spent elsewhere – thus following the principle of justice. However, this is analogous to the treatment of alcoholics and smokers. We treat such people within the NHS because the service is for the promotion of better health (beneficence) so it is not ethical to withhold treatment."

Response Analysis:
This answer starts with a strong opinion and gets straight to the point – this will catch the interviewer's attention. This is then followed by a balanced argument showing the candidate is able to consider opposing opinions. Drawing a parallel between the question and the treatment of other lifestyle diseases is essential in an excellent answer. Being able to refer to current topics or issues in the NHS is the sign of an excellent candidate. This answer also discusses all the ethical principles apart from autonomy – the answer would be improved if autonomy was also used.

Overall:
When answering an ethical question, use the ethical principles (**autonomy, beneficence, non-maleficence and justice**) to structure your answer. Giving a balanced view also shows you understand both sides of the argument and makes you stand out as a strong candidate.

20. Should the NHS fund IVF? What about injuries that arise from extreme sports such as mountain climbing?

This question essentially addresses two different subjects, both relating to a similar basic issue: shortness of funds. Since we're in the UK and are arguing on the background of the tax-funded NHS, the basic question is how far society can be held responsible for covering the costs of treatment resulting from the actions of individuals.

Bad Response:

"The NHS should fund neither IVF nor health care for extreme sports injuries. IVF is a service that is hugely expensive and has a fairly low success rate. Funding cycle after cycle of IVF is just not sustainable and at some point, the patient has to accept that they just cannot get pregnant – especially if the difficulties are simply due to the mother putting her career first and now being too old to conceive. There are plenty of children looking to be adopted. The same applies for injuries resulting from extreme sports. It is unacceptable for society to pay the bill for when somebody's hobby goes wrong. If individuals believe that they need to go mountain climbing and get hurt in the process, it is up to them to cover the bill, not society. The NHS just does not have the funds for this."

Response Analysis:

The candidate has very strong views. This response is very judgemental and shows very little understanding of what the NHS is about and, more importantly, what it means to be a clinician. The idea of the NHS is to provide healthcare for everybody – indiscriminate of their income and social class and that includes support with conception. In addition, there are tight regulations in place when it comes to cyclic treatments such as IVF, where 2 cycles are covered by the NHS and all further cycles have to be covered by the patient. In regards to the extreme sports, this answer shows great ignorance with regards to a doctor's duty of care (and GMC's Good medical practice). Whilst it can be argued that extreme sports-associated injuries are the individual's fault, what about diseases associated with smoking and alcohol, poor diet or even simple activities such as driving? These can just as easily be attributed to individuals and cost the NHS much more money than extreme sports.

Good Response:

"This is a very complex question. It addresses the question of what treatments are affordable and logical in times of shortening funds. Instead of focussing on these two very specific examples, this question should be approached on a more general level. In principle, the NHS is based on the idea that everybody living in the UK should have access to healthcare. This includes treatments for infertility as well as for injuries associated with extreme sports. The most fundamental idea of the NHS is to not differentiate between diseases themselves but to ensure that everybody gets treatment. Unfortunately, during times of shortening funds, there need to be limits to this as some modern treatments are very expensive. It is for that reason that in IVF, for example, only a limited number of cycles is NHS-funded. On a more doctor-centred level, being non-judgmental is of central importance. It is our duty to treat everybody, irrespective of race, creed, gender or the cause of their injury or disease."

Response Analysis:

This is a good response as it acknowledges the complexity of the issue whilst relating it back to the specific question. It is non-judgemental in that it does not assign blame and tries to address the root cause of the problem. For a good response, it is important to provide a differentiated and logical answer that does not fall victim to personal opinions or rash impulses. Notice how cleverly, the candidate has avoided committing himself to either side but has given views on why an approach is desirable and the pros and cons of both.

Overall:

Medical Ethics is rarely ever black or white, there are always grey areas. The main challenge of this question is to avoid rash and sweeping statements and to answer in an undifferentiated manner. The IVF part of the question is a particularly difficult subject, mostly because it is very difficult to assign responsibility for the inability to conceive. The mountain climbing part is somewhat less challenging as blame is assigned more easily. Be careful, though, as it is very easy to fall into the blame trap.

21. Why is euthanasia such a controversial topic?

Euthanasia is a topic that comes up a lot in many forms during clinical work. It can be a straight question of a follow up to a question in some specialities (oncology, anaesthesia, medicine, surgery). It is a very controversial topic as the definition of euthanasia itself is a complicated one and it also stands in fundamental conflict with what it means to be a doctor: to preserve life. There are countries like Switzerland, where euthanasia is legal. Be careful and differentiate euthanasia and physician assisted suicide (see next question).

Bad Response:

"Euthanasia describes the medical killing of people. It can be seen as controversial as the bottom line is that it is murder to end a life. In euthanasia, a doctor kills his patient because the patient's life is considered not worth living and he (the patient) would be better off being dead. In that sense, it represents the most merciful step to take."

Response Analysis:

This is a bad response as it is too undifferentiated for an issue as complex as euthanasia. The question asks about the controversy surrounding it and this is in part due to the very nature of euthanasia. Whilst the above answer superficially touches on these issues, it does not explore the issue sufficiently to be an appropriate answer. Be aware of how complex the matter is and do not trivialise it.

Good Response:

"Euthanasia is a controversial topic for a multitude of reasons that come from a variety of different backgrounds. One of the reasons for controversy lies in the very definition of euthanasia. Euthanasia is defined as the ending of life to alleviate suffering. This almost makes it sound like a form of treatment. The controversy arises when one considers the very meaning of being a doctor. It is the doctor's duty to safeguard and protect life, not to end it. On the other hand, the idea of duty of care and patient well-being is the very thing that may justify the ending of life to alleviate suffering. In essence, the controversy on an ethical level arises in part from the conflict between safeguarding life and ending it to reduce suffering.

Other causes for controversy lie in issues such as communication where the question is asked how, for example, a comatose or paralysed patient cannot communicate their wish to live or die. A further point to take into consideration is the idea of life not worth living. Once we accept that there is a life that can be declared as not worth living, where does that lead us? Some fear that it will lead to a slippery slope where definitions of unworthy life become increasingly arbitrary. The GMC code of good medical practice and UK law currently don't permit euthanasia."

Response Analysis:

This is a good answer as it directly addresses the complexity of the issue and then attempts to provide explanations and examples for the different issues. The answer also attempts to demonstrate the controversy in that it provides the point of view of the two main camps involved in the discussion. This is important as only with opposing opinions can there be controversy.

Overall:

This question is a challenging one as it is easy to get lost in one's own opinion. It is important to have a correct definition of euthanasia as it is very easy to answer this type of question wrong if the definition is incorrect. Whilst one has to be careful with one's own opinion, it provides a good starting point as it will allow for examples and arguments of both sides. Remember, "worth living" is very subjective. What means unworthy living may not be the view held by the individual or their near ones. A person may be perfectly happy being bedbound and being dependent on others for everything but gets the joy from watching children/grandchildren.

22. What is the difference between euthanasia and physician-assisted suicide?

Euthanasia is the act of deliberately ending a person's life to relieve suffering. Assisted suicide is the act of deliberately assisting or encouraging another person to kill themselves. In a practical example, a doctor administering a patient with a lethal injection to stop their suffering would be euthanasia. If the doctor handed the lethal injection to the patient so they injected it themselves, this would be physician-assisted suicide. The best answers to this question will go beyond knowing the different definitions to being able to interpret what implications these definitions have on the differences between euthanasia and physician-assisted suicide legally and ethically.

Bad Response:

"Aren't they basically the same thing? It means when a doctor helps someone who is seriously ill to die so that they are not in any more pain. I know it is illegal and I think maybe that when it is counted as murder, then it is euthanasia and when it's counted as manslaughter then it is called physician-assisted suicide."

Response Analysis:

This is clearly wrong. In an answer like this, it is better to simply admit it if you don't know what the definitions of these terms are, instead of trying to guess them.

Good Response:

"The difference between euthanasia and physician-assisted dying is that in the former, the doctor is actually doing the act that kills the patient, whereas, in the latter, the doctor is merely assisting the patient to kill themselves. There are several important differences between the two. For example, in physician-assisted suicide, the patient's desire to die is, by definition, a requirement. This is not necessarily the case for euthanasia, which can be voluntary, non-voluntary or involuntary. It is because of this that some people argue that physician-assisted suicide is more morally acceptable because it is in accordance with patient autonomy whereas euthanasia is not necessarily. However, it is sometimes argued that this discriminates against those who are too disabled to commit suicide, even with physician-assistance, and that in these cases, active voluntary euthanasia should be allowed as ultimately the intention is the same. Legally, there is also a big difference – active euthanasia is regarded as murder or manslaughter whereas physician-assisted dying is not, though it is still illegal."

Response Analysis:

This answer shows good knowledge of the definitions of euthanasia and physician-assisted suicide, as well as the different types of euthanasia. It shows an appreciation for the ethical distinction between the two and some of the controversy that surrounds the issue. It is always a good idea to include ethical principles like autonomy/beneficence in your answer. The candidate could perhaps do more to explain whether they think there is an ethical difference between physician-assisted suicide and active voluntary euthanasia.

Overall:

These distinctions are of huge importance in medicine and are the source of much debate and controversy, so it is worth familiarising yourself with them now. The best answers will demonstrate not only knowledge of these concepts but also an understanding of what they mean and how ethical arguments tie into them.

Your answer may have a follow-on question on legal issues/implications of both processes for the survivors. In Euthanasia (mercy killing as in the case of Sara Stakes who took her husband to Switzerland), the law of the country may consider this a crime but if the husband went to the Switzerland on his own, she is not to be held responsible.

23. Do you think it's ethical that drugs are trialled in third world countries but once they're developed, they can't be used by most of the country's population because of their cost?

It is important in answering this question to address both sides of the argument and reflect on the benefits and disadvantages of both. Here, the interviewer wants to see that you are able to consider different perspectives other than your own. That you are able to argue your point clearly and logically and that you have a valid and credible understanding of medical ethics. It is essential that you develop a good awareness of medical ethical issues in preparation for the interview. It is very important that you are able to make a good ethical assessment of a given situation and make ethically-informed arguments.

Bad Response:
"I think it I s very unfair that drugs should not be given to the people of the countries in which they were trialled. These people are so close to drugs that have the potential to cure them or their family. These people suffer disproportionally to those in other countries because third world countries lack the functional resources. We need to help third world countries and not withhold resources from them to disadvantage them further."

Response Analysis:
The candidate is focused on a very narrow-minded view of the situation. This impairs the candidates' ethical analysis of the situation, preventing a balanced viewpoint being expressed as well as a lack of logical reasoning given to support the viewpoint expressed.

Good Response:
"People in many third world countries are not able to afford drugs independently from other sources of financial support. Consequently, the third world country is being exploited for financial gain by other countries and organisations; its resources are being used but the country receives very little - if any - benefit. As a result, third world countries are likely to fall further into poverty, increase inequalities within the global community, and inequalities within the population of that third world country. However, many research studies can only be afforded if they are undertaken in third world countries. Therefore, we need to ask ourselves if we would rather not run the drug trials and not have these lifesaving drugs available for anyone or run the drug trials in countries that will not benefit from them in the foreseeable future. It could be argued, from a utilitarian perspective, that developing the drugs is always worthwhile as the drug will ultimately be able to save lives somewhere in the world. It would be ethically correct if one could use some of the profits from the production of the drug to support the third world country."

Response Analysis:
This response goes through a step-by-step logical approach to addressing all the different factual and ethical issues involved. It tries to explain why both sides of the argument are justified as a result of the contextual limitations of the situation. It identifies the key ethical question at the centre of the discussion and ends on that. The responses go further as to suggest a solution, demonstrating a good grasp of the ethics involved. The response is detailed. It does not reach a fixed conclusion which suggests that the candidate has explored each side of the argument and has found both arguments similarly convincing.

Overall:
Answering ethical questions requires a different technique to answering most other interview questions. The basis of answering these questions relies on a good understanding the basic theories of medical ethics and requires practise. You should listen to and engage in ethical discussions with peers, consultant to give you practice interview or anyone who is interested and try to gain a balanced view of medical ethical situations.

24. Parents who withhold vaccines from their children commit a form of child abuse. Do you agree?

Parents have to make decisions in the child's best interests, making sure they are safe; thus acting as the child's advocate. Previously, the law viewed children as property that parents could control as they saw fit; we now recognise that parental authority arises from parental responsibility. Parents need to intervene when children's immaturity could lead them into danger. They also need the power to make medical choices because most children do not have the capacity to do so. This could be a direct question or a follow-on question when you are/have been quizzed on MMR scandal.

However, it is essential to consider the large scale of harm posed by infectious diseases. The primary risk of this parental decision is borne by the child. The danger is very real; a parental choice not to vaccinate can directly harm other children and increase the risk of outbreaks. If vaccination rates are high enough, the concept of herd immunity offers additional protection to everyone – both vaccinated and unvaccinated.

On the other hand, vaccination is not risk-free. They can carry side effects of fever, joint and muscle pain, and swelling. However, in comparison to the much greater risks of not receiving vaccination – many of these diseases kill – vaccination remains the best option.

Bad Response:

I believe these parents are guilty of child abuse. A vaccination is highly important to prevent disease in a child. By knowingly preventing a child from receiving a vaccination, they are allowing the child to be susceptible to a host of dangerous diseases. Thus, putting the child at risk."

Response Analysis:

This response conveys a very strong opinion. In interviews, it is always best to give a measured response that shows both sides before concluding. This opinion is also contrary to current law – parents can refuse vaccinations and the law does not prosecute for child abuse – so this answer seems poorly researched. However, the answer does contain correct information, it has just not been presented well.

Good Response:

"I think it is important to explore the reasons that parents may refuse a vaccination for their children. Some refuse based on religious grounds and it is important to respect that. However, some may be refusing due to misinformation; we are still recovering from the Andrew Wakefield scandal that linked autism to the MMR vaccine. In these cases, it is important to give information and educate parents.

Parents have a duty of care to their children and often want the best for them; they could believe that the best is refusing a vaccine which is where education comes in. A vaccination also provides a protective effect to the community to herd immunity so it is not just their child at risk, and it is important to explain this as well. There are also risks and side effects associated with vaccines so parents could believe they are protecting their child based on this. I believe it would be misguided to label all parents who refuse vaccinations for their children as child abusers. It is important we address the underlying issues."

Response Analysis:

This is a very comprehensive answer. It provides ideas for both sides of the answer and gives a balanced response. Always avoid condemning patients/people and instead promote education/disease prevention – doctors need to educate the public as well as treat them. All the information provided is correct and used as evidence to their argument. The candidate also demonstrates empathy by placing themselves in the parents' position. Worth noting is the ending. It almost feel like as the candidate is waiting for a follow on question (MMR scandal) and a good strategies and indicates well prepared candidate.

Overall:

A good answer will demonstrate knowledge of current procedures and will try and view the issue from the patient's perspective. Avoid condemning patients or their actions but instead give a more neutral opinion.

25. Should doctors be banned from smoking?

This question revolves around the idea of how far doctors not only act to improve patient's health but are also responsible to provide an example of healthy living. The question is if it is legitimate to demand of doctors to live a healthy lifestyle since they will be advising their patients to improve their lifestyle by, for example, quitting smoking. Doctors are human and have the right to choose but have an image to portray.

Bad Response:

"Doctors should not be banned from smoking because they have a right to do what they want to their bodies, as long as it does not harm anyone else. Doctors have an important position in the public eyes as they act to improve public health and demand of their patients to do their best to improve their health as well. It is common knowledge that a healthy lifestyle is central to maintaining good health, which includes smoking cessation. Having your doctor tell you that you are supposed to stop smoking as it is bad for you, but then he is smoking himself will make the patients lose trust in the healthcare system. It is the health professional's duty to provide a good example to his/her patients by living a healthy lifestyle. This includes smoking. Therefore, I believe that doctors should be banned from smoking."

Response Analysis:

The response is very superficial and doesn't explore any of the key ethical issues. It lacks insight into the complexity of the question. It fully ignores the ethical component of the question. Whilst it can be argued that medical professional should lead by example and not smoke, the same principle of autonomy and self-determination that applies to the patient also applies to the doctor. One's choice of career does not limit these freedoms. This is important to recognise.

Good Response A:

"This is a challenging question as doctors hold a special place in society. On one hand, they are mere individuals like everybody else with the same rights and responsibilities as every other citizen, which includes everyday choices such as smoking. On the other hand, they hold a special position in the public eye by providing an instance of moral direction giving. This is where the question of the smoking ban for doctors comes into play. Doctors will advise their patients to improve their lifestyle in order to improve their health and in many instances, this includes smoking cessation. If now the advising doctor himself is a smoker, this advice can be seen as losing a significant degree of strength as he does not act on his own advice. It is, however, important to realise that besides the professional side of the doctor, he or she also has a private side to which they are entitled to make whatever decision they want, provided it is legal, and this includes smoking. Therefore, whilst it would be preferable for doctors not to smoke simply because it would be preferable for anybody not to smoke, it is wrong to ban doctors from smoking merely because they are doctors."

Good Response B:

"The main arguments for a ban on doctors smoking are that it may indirectly have a negative effect on the health of patients. By setting a bad example, it could be said that doctors who smoke are failing to discourage their patients from doing the same. If a patient knows that their doctor smokes, they are perhaps less likely to take the advice from that doctor to quit smoking as seriously, as they know it is hypocritical. On the other hand, it could be said that banning doctors from smoking is interfering in doctors' private lives: why not ban them from drinking alcohol and give them target BMIs as well? These clearly start to impede on the doctor's autonomy. In balance, I think that doctors have a right to smoke if they want to, as long as they ensure it is not having a negative impact on their patients. This could mean banning doctors from smoking on hospital premises, for example."

Response Analysis:

This answer is better as it acknowledges the complexity of the issue and also tries to explain the background to why such a question arises in the first place. It attempts to describe the role doctors play in society and how this is related to the judgement of their choices and decisions when it comes to their private life. This is important as it considers the ethical idea of autonomy and self-determination that is a central part of this question.

Overall:

This question ties in with the idea of leading by example. Similar questions include obesity or alcoholism in doctors. When answering any of these questions, it is essential to realise that doctors, just like everybody else, also have a private life in which they are separated from their profession and are just as entitled to making decisions out of their own free will as anybody else, especially when it comes to their own bodies and health. They are doctors and humans. Sometimes the role and responsibility may be at conflict and one must find a way. Doctors, as humans, have the autonomy but also have a responsibility in preventing disease. Passive smoking can be dangerous and a doctor that smokes may not be a good role model for his patients. Candidates should be exploring this in their reply when putting up arguments for both and summarise with what they think would be a better option.

26. What are the ethical implications of an obese doctor?

Obesity is an escalating global epidemic in many parts of the world. Obesity affects virtually all age and socioeconomic groups. It is no longer limited to developed countries but has spread to developing countries as well. The UK has the highest level of obesity in Western Europe. Obesity levels in the UK have more than trebled in the last 30 years and, on current estimates, more than half the population could be obese by 2050.

The media has created the perception that obese patients are "lazy, noncompliant, undisciplined, and lacking in willpower". Such negative attitudes place the patient–physician relationship at risk if patients agree with this belief; it can damage the trust and confidence patients must place into their doctors to receive optimum care. Obesity in doctors can be another barrier to good patient care as they may be reluctant to discuss weight loss strategies with their patients. Physicians should work to avoid bias in health advice regardless of their own BMI status.

Obesity poses a major risk for serious diet-related non-communicable diseases, including diabetes mellitus, cardiovascular disease, hypertension and stroke, and certain forms of cancer. Its health consequences range from increased risk of premature death to serious chronic conditions that reduce the overall quality of life. Care of obese people will require the doctor to expend more time and medical resources. Thus, obese patients often place an increased burden on the healthcare system and have regular interaction with the healthcare system to receive advice from doctors. It important that doctors can act as health advocates. Obese doctors may be seen as hypocrites as they try and advise patients on weight loss. It is also important that doctors remain fit – they often have to stand for long periods of time and will have to at times, run in medical emergencies. An obese doctor may have difficulties with this task which will impair their ability to fulfil their role.

Bad Response:

"Obese doctors pose an ethical dilemma. They are supposed to offer health advice and patients who see doctors who are overweight, they are unlikely to follow their advice. This can impact patient care."

Response Analysis:

This answer merely touches on a few of the issues and does not use key phrases, such as "trust" or "patient-doctor relationship". The positive aspects of this answer include acknowledgement of the ethical dilemma associated with the situation and its possible impact on patient care. A better answer would discuss the health conditions associated with obesity and why it is important for doctors to counsel patients on this, as well as the possible consequences of an obese doctor giving this advice.

Good Response:

"The concept of an obese doctor may appear as paradoxical to many patients. Many patients are aware of the health implications in obesity so they can start to question the doctor's ability to act as a health advocate. These doubts can adversely affect the patient-doctor relationship. However, doctors face great stresses at work and whilst it's a good idea in principle to have thin doctors, it is difficult in practice, e.g. comfort eating. Finally, being obese could help some doctors empathise with their patients to get them more engaged in discussions about lifestyle advice."

Response Analysis:

This answer provides specific buzzwords, e.g. 'patient safety', 'empathy', and 'health advocate'. These words always add "brownies" to an answer and present the candidate as a knowledgeable and competitive applicant. It also highlights the potential consequences related to the patient-doctor relationship and offers a realistic viewpoint on the current paradigm.

Overall:

A good answer will employ topical phrases, such as exemplified above. It is important to always discuss any concept brought up in more detail and develop further. This gives a more interesting answer and shows interviewers that you are a reflective thinker.

27. Are disabled lives worth saving?

When asked ethical questions, there are rarely right and wrong answers. However, with this question, the answer is clearly yes. As a doctor, it is not your position to decide that someone with a disability is living with a quality of life that is not worth sustaining. It is worth discussing cases in which patients decide their lives are no longer worth living but it is not a doctor's decision to make.

Bad Response:

"If an individual with a disability requires lifesaving treatment or an individual requires treatment that may leave them with a disability then I do not think that the treatment should be given. Individuals with disabilities have a much lower quality of life and it is not fair to subject someone to this kind of life."

Response Analysis:

A response like this would raise a lot of concerns about the candidate giving the answer. The first issue to address is that individuals with disabilities are often able to live with good quality of life, there are lots of ways that individuals can learn to cope with their disabilities. The second is that doctors cannot make decisions about treatment based on quality of life judgements. Doctors must make decisions based on their medical knowledge and the likelihood of success of the treatment. It is not a doctor's place to suggest that life is not worth living if you have a disability.

Good Response:

"The answer to this question is definitely yes. Whilst disabled people might face difficulties in life that others are fortunate enough not to face, this does not mean that disabled people do not have a good quality of life. However, quality of life is a subjective thing. The idea that disabled lives might not be worth saving suggests that disabled people would be better off dead than living with a disability. There are a lot of disabled people who be offended by this judgement and would tell you that their lives may be sometimes difficult but that they find ways to cope with their struggles in order that they can enjoy life.

There are some cases in which individuals with a disability may make a decision that they do not want their life saved. For example, an individual with locked-in syndrome whose only remaining form of communication was his ability to blink, said that once he was no longer able to blink, he wanted doctors to turn off his life support. The doctors respected this patient's wishes but it would have been wrong for doctors to make this judgement on behalf of the patient. Disabled lives should be saved if the individual with the disability wants to have their life saved."

Response Analysis:

This is a good answer which makes a clear distinction between a doctor's decision that a life isn't worth saving and a patient's decision that their life isn't worth living. Importantly, the answer is very positive about the lives of disabled people and understands that individuals can still enjoy a good quality of life. As a doctor, it is important to support patients with disabilities and to ensure they can have as high a quality of life as possible.

Overall:

Being especially abled should not influence the decision to treat or treat an individual in any way. As a consultant, you will come across this situation often. These individuals often have remarkable stories of their resilience and fight and they will tell you that their struggles are worth it to be able to still enjoy life.

28. What would you do if your patient with Huntingdon's disease does not want anyone else in the family to know.

Huntington's disease is a devastating neurodegenerative disease with no cure; it affects the coordination of movement and leads to mental decline. The diagnosis is usually confirmed by genetic testing and affected individuals show disease progression in a predictable way. The genetic testing can even predict when symptoms will begin to affect the individual. In the latter stages of the disease, sufferers require full-time care which often affects life for the surrounding family. The disease is inherited in an autosomal dominant fashion which means offspring have a 50% chance of developing the disease, however, it should be noted that individuals suffering from the disease often choose not to have children because of this risk. There is a wide range of ethical issues which arise from the diagnosis of Huntington's disease and they will be explored in more detail in the answers below. When approaching ethical questions like this, the key thing is to explain your reasoning for your thought and to discuss both sides of the argument. Ensure you answer the question too, explain why this is a 'dilemma'.

Bad Response:

"Huntington's disease is a devastating neurodegenerative disease which develops predictably and sufferers require full-time care in the latter stages of the disease. This is likely to put significant pressure on close family and friends. Importantly, the disease is inherited in an autosomal dominant pattern which means that any offspring have a 50% chance of suffering from the disease. For both of these reasons, it would be wrong for a sufferer of the disease to keep it a secret from their family and partner. Family deserve to know that their relative is certain to require care later in life and details about the potential effect on offspring should not be kept from a partner. It is, therefore, GP's duty to inform the family and partner in a situation where the individual with the disease does not wish to share their diagnosis."

Response Analysis:

This answer raises two of the important ethical dilemmas surrounding a diagnosis of Huntington's. The progress of the disease is devastating and sufferers will come to require full-time care. This is something that families understandably would like to prepare for however many sufferers do not want this sense of impending doom hanging over their family's heads and would rather break the news later. Similarly, when it comes to reproduction some couples would like to undertake IVF and use pre-implantation genetic testing to ensure an embryo with HD will not be used for reproduction but there are individuals who feel this is morally wrong and so may prefer to keep their diagnosis a secret from their partner. Whilst the answer raises these two points, it doesn't discuss why an individual may not want to share their diagnosis. The question asks about the ethical dilemma so both sides of the argument should be offered. The answer also incorrectly states that it is the GP's duty to inform the family and partner. This would be a breach of confidentiality; the GP can only encourage the patient to share this information with their family.

Good Response:

"Huntington's disease is a devastating neurodegenerative disease which develops predictably and sufferers require full-time care in the latter stages of the disease. Genetic testing can predict when symptoms will begin to appear which can be very stressful for sufferers. An individual diagnosed with HD may not wish to share this information with their family for a number of reasons. The disease is inherited in an autosomal dominant pattern which means each of the sufferer's siblings has a 50% chance of being a sufferer and also that at least one of the sufferer's parents will also suffer. Since this disease does not have a cure, some say it is unethical to inform people that they will develop this disease long before they ever develop symptoms.

However, others argue that knowledge that the disease will progress allows patients to plan their lives. Other important factors to consider are the ages of family members, some members may be too young to be tested because they may not be deemed mature enough to deal with news of a diagnosis. Individuals may also hide this information from family for financial reasons. If family members are aware of the diagnosis and get tested themselves to discover they too have HD, they will be required to pay much higher costs for medical insurance.

Whilst you may argue that individuals can access free healthcare on the NHS, often the provision of care for individuals with debilitating chronic conditions is not good enough and health insurance is an important safety net. Despite these concerns, if I was the GP for a patient in this situation I would encourage them to tell their family members. Obviously, I would be unable to inform the family myself due to confidentiality but I would stress that it is important that everyone in the family should have the opportunity to think about their long-term plans should they have HD or if they will end up caring for someone with HD."

Response Analysis:

This is an excellent response which really explains why this is a dilemma for a patient. It gives both insightful reasons why a patient may want to keep the diagnosis a secret but also offers the conflicting thoughts that a patient may have in weighing up a decision to tell someone. Finishing the answer by stating what the candidate would do as the patient's GP helps this answer to really stand out and shows that the candidate is thinking about these issues from a perspective of a potential doctor.

Overall:

In any ethical question, ensure you provide a balanced argument but try to conclude if you can. You will get extra credit if you can understand how doctors fit into these situations and can demonstrate knowledge of legal issues limiting doctors' actions e.g. confidentiality.

29. You witness a doctor fill in a DNA-CPR with the patient, but without consulting with the patient's family. What issues do you see with this?

There are two main issues. Firstly, how do DNA-CPRs work, and secondly, to what extent should a patient's family be involved in a decision that is primarily the concern of the doctor and patient.

Bad Response:

"This doctor is clearly breaching his professional obligations. End of life questions such as resuscitation orders always have to be discussed with the patient's family in order to make sure they adequately represent their wishes. Ignoring the family's wishes would be both unlawful as well as unethical. Every patient is entitled to all necessary treatments to maintain their life. This includes resuscitation at all cost."

Response Analysis:

Whilst this answer is in part right, it also has significant flaws. It is always preferable to consult with the family of a patient, especially when dealing with questions such as resuscitation, but ultimately the decision lies with the doctor as resuscitation is a treatment like every other. The decision to withhold or deliver treatment should be discussed with the patient, but once again, the ultimate decision lies with the doctor. In general, the doctor must always keep in mind the patient's best interest and this might include the decision to withhold resuscitation.

Good Response:

"If the patient wishes to discuss their end of life plans without involving their family, then the doctor has to accept this. Ideally, we would like to involve the patient's family, it is ultimately the patient's decision and ignoring this would represent a breach of confidentiality."

Response Analysis:

This is a good response as it delivers a short & succinct answer whilst acknowledging the finer points surrounding DNA-CPR. Remember that like with many ethical questions, there is no clear-cut correct answer.

Overall:

This is a challenging question with many both ethical and legal components. It's important to acknowledge the ethical challenges. It's important not to get carried away by your own opinions about end of life care. Not only will this impair the quality of the answer, it might also be misunderstood and reflect badly on you. Remember, medicine is not just about curing the ill – it is also about palliating those we cannot cure.

30. What is a DNA-CPR? Why is it so important?

A Do Not Attempt Cardio Pulmonary Resuscitation order (DNA-CPR) refers to a decision, usually made between doctors and a patient approaching the end of life, not to attempt cardiopulmonary resuscitation on that patient in the event of cardiac or respiratory arrest. This question, therefore, includes the end of life issues and you will stand out if you can answer it sensitively and with empathy for those patients reaching the end of life. The most impressive interviewees are those who show awareness of what real life issues in discussing this with patients/family and understand why patients might not want to undergo CPR.

Bad Response:

"DNA-CPR is a decision made by doctors not to attempt CPR on a patient in the event of cardiac or respiratory arrest. It means that doctors do not spend time and resources trying to resuscitate a patient for whom CPR is unlikely to be successful."

Response Analysis:

This answer shows a lack of understanding that these decisions are usually made by doctors in conjunction with their patients and, therefore, also misses the reasons why it is important for doctors to discuss the DNA CPR with their patient. However, it is important to acknowledge that doctors do have the power to decide upon a DNA-CPR without patient involvement and patients cannot demand doctors to carry out treatment against their clinical judgement.

A good point is made that DNA CPRs are often made for patients for whom CPR is unlikely to be successful but it shows a lack of sensitivity with its reasoning. These decisions are not made to save time and resources for doctors but instead are made with a patient's best interests in mind, i.e. it is not advisable to perform CPR on a patient if it is not likely to be successful. CPR is often traumatic and invasive.

Good Response:

"DNA-CPR refers to a decision, usually made between doctors and a patient approaching the end of life, not to attempt cardiopulmonary resuscitation on that patient in the event of cardiac or respiratory arrest. The decision is usually made because the chances of successful resuscitation are very low and, even if successful, many patients will suffer broken bones and brain injuries. A large number of patients with DNA-CPRs are those with terminal illnesses or with chronic progressive debilitating conditions e.g. end stage COPD or advance cancer. In this case, it is important to discuss a DNA-CPR early so that patients can think about their decision and discuss with their family. This is also important in patients with dementia who will gradually lose the capacity to make their own decisions.

In reality, CPR is a traumatic and invasive procedure with only 5-20% success rates and explaining this to patients will assist them in making decisions regarding the end of life. For many people, the most important factor in death is dying with dignity and not performing CPR allows patients to die peacefully and with dignity. This also allows patients to choose a preferred place to spend their final days/hours by avoiding emergency admission to hospital. It is important that patients know that having a DNA-CPR does not mean they will be denied other treatment and pain relief as they approach the end of life."

Response Analysis:

This is an excellent answer which addresses medical reasons why CPR may be inappropriate at times and also personal issues surrounding the end of life. It clearly demonstrates an understanding of the implications of attempting CPR and also the reality that CPR is most often unsuccessful in patients who have reached the end of their natural life. Mention of a DNA-CPR in patients with dementia shows a wider awareness of issues surrounding capacity and decision-making.

Overall:

The best answers to this question address the needs and concerns of both the patient and the doctor. In medicine, your patients will often have a different agenda to you as the doctor and, therefore, to be an effective doctor, you must show an ability to understand your patients' concerns and find a way to reach an optimal outcome for both of you. The key point with DNA-CPRs is to remember that although it is a clinical decision, it is good practice to involve the patient and their family (especially if the patient's capacity is an issue).

Now that you understand more about the reasons behind a DNA-CPR, think how you might respond to a follow-up question asking, "How would you react to an angry relative of the patient who disagrees with your DNA-CPR decision?"

31. You are treating a dictator who is responsible for the murder of thousands of people in his country. You are alone with him and realise killing him could save millions of lives. Assuming that you wouldn't get caught, would you do it?

As with any ethics question, the first thing to do is to recognise that there are **two sides to the argument** and to think about what these are. Ultimately, it matters less which side you choose than it does your ability to ethically justify your decision and the personal values you show in your argument. This is an opportunity to demonstrate a good understanding of relevant ethical principles and your ability to apply them practically. If there are potential flaws in your argument, it is much better to recognise them overtly than to try and gloss over them. Arguments of both sides should be given and then a reasoned decision on which is more powerful should be made.

Bad Response:
"I would never kill someone, so I would definitely not kill the dictator. But maybe I just wouldn't treat him as well as I could and so hope that the disease kills him."

Response Analysis:
This candidate has failed to demonstrate the ability to use ethical reasoning to justify their decision or to show an understanding of any of the main tenants of medical ethics. He also has not recognised that there could be another perspective on this problem and that arguments exist for killing the dictator. Finally, the suggestion of compromising care to the dictator certainly requires more justification. While it is true that there is an ethical difference between acts (killing the dictator) and omissions (failing to treat the dictator properly, in the hope he will die), this candidate does not really explain what they mean by this. This is also not aligned well with the good medical practice.

Good Response:
"The arguments for killing the dictator seem reasonably clear – if doing so will save millions of lives then a utilitarian argument could state that this would achieve the best for the most people and so is the right decision, though there are a few problems with this. Firstly, you can't be sure of the assumption that killing the dictator will save lives as an equally bad dictator may come through the ranks to take his place. Secondly, a murder by a medical professional completely breaks the implicit trust in universal beneficence to individuals and political impartiality that medical professionals rely upon to practice, especially with organisations like Médecins Sans Frontiers (MSF) in conflict regions. If regimes stop trusting these organisations and allowing them to practice, it could be that more people are harmed than saved. Murdering the dictator is a clear violation of pillars of medical ethics: respect for the sanctity of human life, non-maleficence and beneficence - the priority of the wellbeing of the patient in front of you, whoever they are. It is also inappropriate when doctors start to judge whether or not the patients in front of them are worth helping. Ultimately, murder is fundamentally wrong in any situation. It is for these reasons and because we cannot even be sure of the utilitarian argument for killing the dictator that, on balance, I would not do so and follow good medical practice."

Response Analysis:
Although this response is quite long, such a difficult moral problem warrants a suitably thorough answer. This candidate clearly outlines ethical arguments for and against killing the dictator and then comes to a reasoned judgement. The candidate also shows a clear understanding of the concept of utilitarianism and knowledge of the principles of beneficence and non-maleficence, giving the interviewer the opportunity to ask more on those if they want.

Overall:
Notice that both the bad answer and the good answer came to the same conclusion: neither would kill the dictator. It was not the ultimate decision that was the difference between them, but rather their ability to reasonably justify their opinions with ethical argument and explain what they meant.

32. A Jehovah's Witness is brought in by an ambulance to A&E after being in a road traffic accident and suffered massive blood loss. They need an urgent blood transfusion but the patient is refusing it. What do you do?

This is a classic ethical dilemma and variants on this frequently get asked. It's very important that you're aware of the law surrounding capacity and consent (see medical law section). The key here is to explore the patient's refusal for transfusion rather than falling into the trap of assuming that they don't want it as they are a Jehovah's Witness.

Bad Response:

"I would give the blood transfusion anyway because the first duty of the doctor is to do what is right for the patient. Therefore, if a blood transfusion is needed to save her life or prevents serious harm, then that would be best. This patient may not know what is best for them right now, but could be thankful after we give her the blood transfusion if it then saves their life"

Response Analysis:

This response fails to consider the finer ethical and legal implications of transfusing someone against their wishes. There is no mention of patient autonomy or capacity. Nor does the response explore the reason for why the patient is refusing the transfusion nor consider the situation where they may have decided earlier to be Jehovah's witness but may have changed their mind.

Good Response:

"Initially, I would try to establish why the patient is refusing a blood transfusion – is it because they lack capacity? Or is it because of a phobia of blood products/needles? Or based on religious beliefs? There is a conflict in this situation between wanting to do what we, the healthcare professionals, perceive is in the patient's best interests, which is giving the blood transfusion and respecting the patient's autonomy. To balance these, I would first make sure that the patient understood the potential consequences of what could happen if they refuse the blood transfusion – including potential death. Also, I would check that they still have the mental capacity to make this decision, including asking about whether they have made a prior declaration about what they would want in this situation, and assessing whether they suffered a head injury in the RTA or could be delirious due to blood loss.

It would also be important to check that the patient is not under undue influence from any friends or family who are with them. If the patient seems to have full mental capacity, understand the consequences of their decision, and not appear to be under the influence of anyone else, then I would respect their wish not to have a blood transfusion while consulting with colleagues so that they can check my assessment of the situation. In addition, I would also explore alternatives to blood transfusion".

Response Analysis:

A fantastic response that gives a structured step-by-step guide as to what the candidate would do. They clearly have a sound grasp of the medico-legal implications and also avoid the trap of assuming the refusal is due to religious purposes.

Overall:

You might get asked follow-on questions of this theme, e.g. *"Another unconscious patient is admitted following a car accident. They are believed to be a Jehovah's Witness. Would you transfuse?"* *In this case, as the patient is unconscious you are able to act in their best interest assuming there is no advance directive or family member preventing you from doing so (in which case, you should seek urgent legal advice).* A Jehovah's Witness with full capacity can refuse blood transfusion but, in this situation, it is possible he may have changed his mind or became a Jehovah's Witness unwillingly.

MANAGEMENT AND NHS ISSUES

33. Do you agree with the privatisation of the NHS?

This is a highly charged question. The interviewee must be able to give a balanced argument whilst still demonstrating a clear point of view. The interviewer wants to ensure your understanding of the healthcare system you are applying to be a part of, and how politics permeates the day-to-day function of the NHS and also weather you could leave to work in privately funded health care. It is also a chance to demonstrate keen debating skills.

Bad Response:

"I don't believe in the privatisation of the NHS. I believe the average UK citizen would end up worse-off both financially and in terms of their health if privatisation were to be taken further. It is financially viable for the NHS to remain free at the point of use. This is simply a way of attempting to turn healthcare into a competitive, profitable market, which I believe to be immoral."

Response Analysis:

Although the content may be true, this answer is too unequivocal and does not provide a balanced view of the topic. This answer is also perhaps too emotional and could be perceived as more of a rant than as part of a lively debate.

Good Response:

"Before we can answer that question, we need to understand what privatisation of the NHS actually entails. The concept of privatisation can be viewed as a spectrum with an entirely publicly funded NHS at one end of the scale, and America's private system with commercial insurance at the other. Commencing privatisation of the NHS involves private companies bidding to provide particular services currently already covered by the NHS, which is already happening. Those who are pro-privatisation believe that this increased competition provides patient choice and may actually stimulate improvements in the standard of care.

However, I believe that in the UK we are incredibly lucky to have access to a unique and world-class health care service, and it can be accessed free at the point of use by all. Privatisation directly erodes these fundamental socialist principals the NHS was founded on and could deepen existing inequalities, thereby worsening the general health of the UK population. Since it's conception, the NHS was never set up to be a profitable franchise and privatisation seems to involve prioritising profit over health – something which I don't feel represents the moral values of the NHS. Having different providers for every service also further breaks up an already fragmented system, resulting in less transparency. Overall I believe that privatisation of the NHS is detrimental to patient care."

Response Analysis:

This comprehensive answer incorporates the pros and cons of the question whilst clearly articulating a strong point of view. It is a good idea at the beginning to demonstrate knowledge about what privatisation of the NHS actually involves in practice. Whatever your personal opinions, it is important to acknowledge that we are very lucky in the UK to access free, world-class care and that privatisation represents a threat to this.

Overall:

Take time to explore the meaning of the question and consider your argument. It is important to be balanced and convey both the advantages and disadvantages before arguing your conclusions. It is also important **not** to be afraid of expressing your opinions, as long as you can back this up – this is not the platform for a political stance.

34. Should doctors ever go on strike?

This question offers the candidate an opportunity to show an awareness of contemporary issues in medical governance and an appreciation of some dilemmas faced by doctors who try and balance a duty of care with a right to strike.

Bad Response:

"Doctors should always feel able to strike. It is their right to demonstrate their disgruntlement at any perceived unfairness in their working conditions. Why should they put up with poor pay just because the government is trying to save money? Doctors have spent years training and have an extremely stressful job and should be remunerated proportionally to this. Cutting pay is outrageous!"

Response Analysis:

The candidate has failed on a number of fronts. Firstly, the candidate focuses purely upon the idea that a strike is due to poor pay. Though this could be the case, it is certainly not the major issue that junior doctors took with Jeremy Hunt's proposed reforms. Indeed, it was more to do with concerns regarding patient safety in relation to new working hours for junior doctors. Secondly, the candidate takes a very uni-dimensional approach and completely ignores the idea that the conditions of doctors striking should perhaps be different from other professions given that their strikes may well have a direct effect on the health of a large number of the population. Thirdly, the candidate has trivialised the aims of the government to the extent that it seems they do not really understand what the government are trying to get out of this situation (or at least have an appreciation for what the government's true position is).

Good Response:

"I think it is important to balance the right of doctors to strike when they perceive unfairness and concern with patient safety. Doctors are in a unique and difficult position in that their striking will undoubtedly have an impact upon the health of those patients that they commit their lives to helping. This is a very difficult situation but we must also remember that doctors deserve to be provided with safe and fair working conditions. This I seven more important in light of Dr Bawa-Graba case. Therefore, as long as an adequate emergency cover is provided, I believe that the right to strike is a key means for doctors to alert the government to issues in the way that some of the country's most vital healthcare staff are being treated."

Response Analysis:

This response shows a deeper appreciation for the difficulty of the question of doctors going on strike. The candidate balances the two sides of the coin well and then comes to their own conclusion. This demonstrates that the candidate has thought about this and they present their opinion clearly and concisely in a way that invites healthy debate between the candidate and the interviewer. Candidate even brings in an example of a recent, highly charged and emotional issue of Dr Bawa-Garba (be prepared to get a follow-on question and bring this up only if you can present both sides of the argument and come up with something).

Overall:

It is important to always present a balanced view, demonstrating consideration for both sides of the argument. It is fine to eventually present your opinion on the matter (indeed this is what's encouraged by the question!), however, it must be educated and balanced. Do not be too much like a bulldozer in your approach and not consider the other side of the argument (even if you do think it's a rubbish one!).

35. What do you understand by "confidentiality"?

It is unlikely that this question will be a direct opening question but a follow-on question where issues related to confidentiality are being discussed e.g. a follow-on question in a scenario where an epilepsy patient continues to drive and the right to confidentiality will need to be breached in the public/patient's safety interest. This is why such questions are included in here.

Confidentiality is a legal and an ethical obligation (required by professional codes of conduct). It means not sharing information about patients without their consent and ensuring that written and electronic information cannot be accessed or read by people not involved in the patient's care. Informed consent and patient capacity are considered essential in maintaining the privacy of the patient. Confidential data is any information that could be used to identify the patient; this includes name, address, etc.

Confidentiality is important for several reasons. One of the most important elements of confidentiality is that it helps to build and develop trust. Patients may not trust a healthcare worker who does not keep information confidential and we know that trust is key to a doctor-patient relationship. A client's safety may be put at risk of discrimination and stigma if details of their health are shared publicly, e.g. a HIV diagnosis.

Discussions about the patient should take place in the workplace and not be overheard to general public. To ensure confidentiality, information should only be disclosed to third parties (such as another government agency or a family member/carer) where a patient has consented to the release of the information. Further all of us need to ensure that any information that is collected is securely stored and disposed of.

There are few exceptions to the general rule of confidentiality and they all have legal bases. These include: if a serious crime has been committed; if the client is a child and is being abused/at risk of abuse; or if you are concerned that the client might harm someone else. When legal obligations override a client's right to confidentiality, there is a responsibility to inform the patient and explain the limits of confidentiality.

Bad Response:

"Confidentiality is what prevents us from sharing patient information with others. It means that we cannot talk about patients in open places in case others overhear or pass information unless absolutely necessary."

Response Analysis:

The response itself is correct and contains all true information but it is lacking in detail. Using the word "cannot" implies that the candidate does not understand the ethical obligation; it would be better to use "should not". This answer does not discuss the importance of confidentiality and how it gives patients the confidence to disclose. It also doesn't address the limitations of confidentiality and scenarios when it can be breached.

Good Response:

"Confidentiality is the legal right of the patient to not have their information disclosed to outside parties. Patients entrust us with sensitive information relating to their health and other matters when they seek treatment so we also have an ethical obligation to keep confidentiality. Patients share information with us in confidence and this help in development of healthy patient-doctor relationship. There are also some circumstances where confidentiality may be breached. These can include notifiable diseases and cooperation with social services or when a crime is involved."

Response Analysis:

This answer has a clear definition of confidentiality and mentions the ethical framework that healthcare workers have to follow to keep confidentiality. This candidate clearly understands the importance of patient trust and how it affects the patient-doctor relationship. They also discuss the conditions in which we can breach confidentiality which shows that the candidate has a great understanding of the issue.

Overall:

A good answer will clearly define confidentiality and discuss its importance with "patient trust" as a buzzword. It will also discuss the conditions in which confidentiality may be broken. Be prepared to be asked "have you ever had a chance to breach patient confidentiality? What ere the grounds?" This question is your opportunity to bring in your knowledge of Caldecott guardian, data protection issues. Remember, you are unlikely to get asked about these. You need to look for opportunity to use these phrases as they show you are keen and well read. If someone is aware of the mistakes, they are less likely to make them. The following question could be combined with the previous one.

36. You're given £1 Million to spend on either an MRI machine or on 50 liver transplants for patients with alcoholic liver disease (cirrhosis). Which one would you choose?

Decisions about resource allocation are hugely important in a system like the NHS where resources are so limited and those making the decisions must be able to justify them to the public. Analysis of the cost-effectiveness of treatments is done by NICE, which assesses how money can be best spent to achieve the best for the most people. This uses measures such as QALYs (Quality Adjusted Life Years). The other ethical decision here is whether patients should be treated for arguably self-inflicted conditions.

Bad Response:

"I would pay for the MRI machine. This is because for the patients with alcoholic cirrhosis, their condition is self-inflicted and so they should be given less priority than patients whose diseases are not self-inflicted, like many of those who would be helped by the new MRI machine."

Response Analysis:

This alludes to a common ethical debate about whether, in a resource-limited public health system like the NHS, those with conditions which could be considered self-inflicted should be given less priority than other patients or perhaps be asked to pay for their healthcare. The arguments put forward for this include the idea that this would discourage people from unhealthy or risky lifestyle choices and so remove some of the burdens that these patients present to the NHS, while also benefitting the patients themselves. In contrast, arguments against this state that in many cases the causes of a disease can be multi-factorial, including lifestyle risk factors but also genetic predisposition for the disease, so it cannot be said with complete surety that a person's lifestyle choices are responsible for the disease. Furthermore, such a move would represent a slippery slope towards doctors making dangerous judgements about which patients are worth treating and which are not. What makes this answer bad is that the candidate has failed to support their decision with an ethical argument or to recognise that their valid counter-arguments to his position. Furthermore, the candidate hasn't shown any awareness about how these resource allocation decisions are really made.

Good Response:

"I suppose my decision would have to depend on a number of factors. To start, I would want to know if there has been any analysis from NICE regarding which of these options has the potential to contribute to the most QALYs. While liver transplants make a relatively quantifiable improvement to the recipients' lives, it is difficult to quantify the amount of benefit from using an MRI machine – use of the machine does not generate QALYs in itself, but the earlier and more accurate diagnosis that it can offer certainly has the potential to do so. Another factor would, of course, have to be the relative need for MRI machines vs. liver transplants. For example, giving a hospital a second MRI machine will be of substantially more benefit than giving it its sixth MRI machine. Ultimately, I think this approach would probably lead me to opt for the MRI machine. This is because, although the liver transplants are of very obvious and substantial benefit to the 50 people who get the transplant, the MRI machine has the potential to last for decades and so help thousands of patients so that its cumulative contribution to wellbeing is perhaps greater."

Response Analysis:

This answer shows that the candidate has an idea about the process behind resource allocation decisions in the NHS and the role of NICE. It is also a thoughtful approach to the problems of working out how to fairly compare very different types of expenses, such as diagnostic tool versus a treatment. It is good that the candidate ultimately picks one of the options as the question explicitly asks for this and their choice is supported by the caveats that it would require deeper analysis and rely on an evidence-base.

Overall:

What matters more is not whether you pick the MRI machine or the liver transplants but your ability to give a balanced and rational ethical argument to support your answer, to demonstrate relevant knowledge and consider the practicalities of applying this in the real world.

37. If you get the job, would you be happy being a 9 to 5 consultant?

Being a doctor is a commitment and a lifestyle. Many a time, patients remain under the care of the consultant though they may be away. It is not always possible to start and finish at exact time and often being very rigid is not practical. On the other hand, work life balance needs to be maintained to avoid burn out. This question is exploring your attitude on work ethics.

Bad Response:

"I would like to be a consultant; I have trained all my life to become a consultant and now it is time for me to enjoy my life. I would like to pursue my other interests e.g. paragliding; I would therefore like to do this early in the morning so as to be able to take some sunrise aerial photography. I would also like to start a family and travel. Therefore, being in a 9 to 5 consultant post would actually fit in with my requirement and make me happy – although during those hours I would like to make sure that I am very useful and productive and most efficient for the Trust so that I get some clinical satisfaction as well."

Response Analysis:

This is not such a bad response because it does discuss the candidate's aspirations to contribute and be useful for the Trust-although the initial focus seems to be on personal development rather than an all-round development. A question like that is usually looking at your aspirations, what you would like to achieve in time to come and how else you can contribute. Therefore, it is not a good response.

Good Response:

"I have trained all my life to become a consultant and this is my opportunity to leave my mark on the speciality. While being a 9 to 5 consultant most of the time is hard work there are opportunities when doctors are needed out of hours – for example, being on-call. Sometimes the demand of the service, e.g. late meetings or early meetings with the CCG's may require that I have an early start or late finish to the day. I possibly would be happy to work around those commitments because this would lead to an improvement in the service and the patients will benefit. As a result, although a 9 to 5 is an ideal job which most of us would prefer, I don't think it is always possible and I would have the flexibility to continue as long as I personally develop myself I maintain a good personal work/life balance as well as knowing I am contributing and doing some service development which will be good for both the patient and the organisation."

Response Analysis:

This is a good response. While this response is also saying that the candidate would like a 9 to 5 job but they recognise the need that doctors also have to be available out of hours and is happy to work flexibly. In addition, there is an insight that sometimes they may have to start early or finish late and, again, there is the flexibility making this a good response.

Overall:

Consultants jobs are for life; although with the new consultant contract, though the changes to the contract are very lucrative and time-binding to the consultant; it also means that the role of the consultant would be extending with a 7-day service looming on the horizon very soon. Hence, the rigid attitude of just being a 9 to 5 consultant would not go down very well with the panel as they are looking for flexibility as well.

38. What is the role of managers in NHS?

Remember, your panel include several managers. Get a realistic balance between managers and doctors. Avoid the catch. You are not here to criticise managers. Managers are trained to look at the processes whilst clinicians provide care. Both must complement each other. Managers integrate and are a go-between between the Clinicians and the service provision/users. They are responsible for ensuring that the service is delivered in a timely manner without any disruption. They are there to take that pressure away where Clinicians and the clinical team can continue to deliver the part they are trained to do.

Bad Response:

"NHS managers ensure delivery of care is happening and people are doing their job. They are also seen everywhere – rushing around with a clip board and pen in their hand chasing people to undertake certain things. I personally feel that sometimes managers could be obstructive in the care that we offer as they could come across as 'annoying' and may not achieve what they are supposed to. I still believe managers do have a place because that way the Clinician can be free to do the clinical part of their role."

Response Analysis:

Underplaying the role of a manager in the NHS is not a good way forward; it is not something that would be appreciated at an interview and will not put you in a better position. Obviously, criticising is never a good idea and one should refrain from it in an interview setting - in fact, one should refrain from in every setting.

This candidate has no idea about the role of the managers. They do not understand the hierarchical system which the NHS has where there are different tasks and roles and team members play different roles based on their skill mix and capabilities. Managers play an important role within the organisation and take away the pressure from the Clinicians enabling them to undertake specific skills for which they have trained. Recognition of this is lacking in the above response and takes away the contribution and showcases managers in a bad light (annoying, irritating, obstructive).

Being unduly critical in the interview poses the risk of you being perceived as a person who has a natural dislike for managers. In fact, the interviewer may feel that because of your dislike for managers you will struggle to get on with them and therefore be detrimental to team working.

Good Response:

"The managers play an important role in the NHS; they are aware of the bigger picture in that particular segment that they work on; they have their skills and they have demonstrated abilities in the past as part of their training or in their role to show that they are able to work in a team and bring about a change. Like clinicians their focus is to improve patient care. Some of the managers are from a medical or nursing background and this allows them to have an even better understanding about how to deliver good clinical care. Non-clinical managers should work closely with clinicians sharing their varied skills to achieve the same goal. Once that understanding is bidirectional, the NHS working will improve as both are working towards a common goal of best patient care, meeting NHS targets and the organisational values."

Response Analysis:

This is a good response; it looks at – the Clinician's as well as the manager' perspectives. It also talks about Clinicians acting as managers and the pressures that the managers have. There is suggestion about managers being able to hold the team together and keeping patients at the centre of the care. This response is not biased and does not demonstrate a dislike for the managers; it is seen as putting them in a better light because it is recognising and giving value to the hard task that they do.

Overall:

A question such as this – asking the role of the manager – is trying to understand what is your understanding of how the NHS works. The NHS is a big organisation and a Trust is a component of it. NHS trusts have a different skill mix of people working at their capabilities. Individual clinical staff may not be aware of the bigger picture, nor of the regulatory and financial constraints whereas the managers are likely to have a better understanding of the organisational priorities and vision. It can therefor appear to a clinician that managers are not listening to them and don't care about an individual patient. Closer working between clinicians and managers is key to avoid such misunderstanding. Clinicians who are in a management role are able to see the picture from both points of view and they are in a better position to fine-tune and paint the picture correctly.

39. Should doctors that are managers, stop doing clinical work?

This is a step up from the previous question and could be a follow up question.

Bad Response:

"Being a manager is a tough task; managers have to scurry around all over the place trying to get things done in an orderly and timely manner. When Clinicians take on the responsibility of a manager obviously they will be doing the same thing but will not have enough time to do the clinical work and I feel that people should either undertake the managerial task or just should continue to be a Clinician."

Response Analysis:

This response lacks an understanding of the manager's role; it does not demonstrate the expectations from clinicians as well as the managers. It fails to recognise that lots of organisations have clinicians taking on the managerial roles with good outcomes. This response does not bring out any governance issues within too.

Good Response:

"Managers have an important task to do. Working alongside clinicians, managers contribute to the service development and ensure smooth delivery and robust logistics. They also ensure that the service provisions are governance safe. It means that when Clinicians take on the responsibility they have sight of the bigger picture because they are continuing to do the clinical work, on the shop floor and they know the day to day problems which clinicians face. I therefore believe that Clinicians taking on managerial responsibilities could be very productive as they will be able to see both sides of the coin. This way they will be able to provide safe evidence-based care and governance because when/if mistakes happen the clinician, acting as manager, would be able to see why the mistake happened as they are in that situation themselves. They will also be mindful of the clinical impact of management decisions about service changes. I believe that this would be productive for the organisation as we can learn from the mistake in a no blame culture."

Response Analysis:

This is a good frame work and the candidate understands the role of the Clinicians as well as the role of the managers. The candidate has given insight into when both roles are played by the one person and actually brings in the patient safety aspects and learnings.

Overall:

This question is checking your understanding of NHS working, whether the partition between clinicians and managers should be a clear divide or whether integration can happen and managerial posts can be taken by clinicians. It is always nice to give both sides of the argument whereas if managers continue to do the clinical job they would not be as efficient as they would not be able to attend all the meetings that the managers have to attend. They will not have enough time to disseminate the knowledge or the results of the meeting because they are going from meeting to meeting or are doing the clinical work. Therefore, clinicians in management roles who continue to do excessive clinical work will struggle to deliver on their management commitments.

The desire and pressure to deliver 100% to both roles can be very stressful and ultimately not very good for the individual or the team. How these roles are balanced is ultimately a personal choice and if someone can continue to do this they should. If a clinician continues to do a managerial role it means that there would be more clinicians and managers with work distribution to enhance efficiency. Instead of few people being inundated with tasks, more people are doing different tasks and all people are working to a common goal; it could therefore produce a better understanding of each other, good team working, excellent communication skills and may result in a harmonious environment where clinical care would be excellent.

40. What is RTT?

This question is looking to see if you are aware that as per the NHS constitution patients have a right to access certain services commissioned by the CCG's within a defined period of time. It is not just exploring whether you understand the abbreviation. RTT. You need to define the term but go further and explain the legal consequences of not delivering on the promise.

Bad Response:

"RTT is an abbreviation for referral to treatment time. It is thus the time taken for a patient to receive treatment from a consultant, from the point of GP referral."

Response Analysis:

The response is factually correct confirming that the candidate had made the effort of familiarising himself with NHS jargon. However, it fails to highlight the logic and legal basis for this constitutional commitment and why it is considered important for patient care.

Good Response:

"RTT or referral to treatment is the time interval from the point of a GP referral to the delivery of treatment by a consultant. The concept is based the patient's right as per NHS constitution to have access to certain services commissioned by CCG's within a defined period of time. As per the NHS constitution patients should not wait for longer than 18 weeks from referral to treatment for any non-urgent referrals. The maximum waiting time for suspected cancer is two weeks from the day the appointment is booked through the NHS e-referral service or when the hospital receives the referral letter. The RTT clock starts at the time the referral is received by the hospital and stops once the treatment is carried out. Interestingly the clock does not stop if the patient cancels their appointment in advance or if the patient cancels their surgery.

NHS Trusts have to provide data to CCG's about RTT and their waiting times. This information should be readily available to the service users and it is considered good practice for Trusts to inform patients about the RTT in their organisation via their appointment letters. Trusts are expected to reach a 92% threshold for this target. In the past missing the target led to financial penalties in the form of fines but this has been discontinued as it was recognised that imposing fines made it even more difficult to deliver services on time.

There are exceptions when the 18 week waiting time is not applicable. This includes patient choice to wait longer, when delaying the start of treatment is thought to be in the patient's best interest e.g. where stopping smoking or losing weight is likely to improve the outcome of the treatment or when the patient fails to attend the appointments that had chosen from a set of reasonable options."

Response Analysis:

This is a much better answer as it demonstrates an in-depth understanding of the concept of RTT. The candidate has clearly communicated the legal basis for RTT, the national expectation and the consequence on failing to deliver.

Overall:

It is a reasonable expectation that someone wishing to become a consultant in the NHS needs to have a good understanding of the operational processes in the NHS, especially those linked to patient care and patient flow. It is not enough just to be familiar with the jargon, rather one needs to demonstrate the logic as well as the limitations of these processes. You can also provide an example of how the system operates in practice.

41. What is your understanding of choose and book?

This question is exploring your understanding of certain operational systems in the NHS, which support patients having a say in the service they receive.

Bad Response:

"The Choose and Book is an online system which allows patients to choose and book an appointment at the hospital of choice on the date and time of their choice. It is very similar to the choice supermarkets provide for delivery of online shopping, with the customer (patient) making all the decisions."

Response Analysis:

The response is very brief and perhaps misleading as it suggests that patients can choose to see a hospital specialist whenever they feel like and at any hospital they like. While choose and book is certainly about giving patients a choice in deciding their hospital appointments, it still requires agreement from their GP and appointment choice is hugely dependent on availability in any given hospital. In practical terms this does not remotely compare to the choice offered by supermarkets for home delivery.

Good Response:

"Choose and book is a system which was introduced to ensure that patients needing specialist treatment have a say in deciding which hospital they get seen and when. While the system definitely provides patients with a choice to choose their secondary provider this choice is limited, only allowing patients to book their first appointment with a specialist in the hospital/clinic of their choice. Once both the Patient and GP agree that the patient needs a specialist appointment this can be booked at the hospital of choice and generally date and time can also be chosen as per patient preference.

The appointment can be booked by the GP while the patient is in the surgery or the patient can be provided with an appointment request letter with a unique reference number, which can be used to book an appointment of their choice from the comfort of their own home. This is done using the NHS e-referral service. This choice is not applicable to follow up appointments which are provided by the hospital. From October 2018 all referrals are expected to be made using the NHS e-referral service, with the paper referral process being switched off. It is important to remember that in actual terms the choice is very dependent on the availability of appointments in any specialist clinics in the hospital."

Response Analysis:

This is a much better response explaining the concept of choose and book. It shows that you have real understanding of how the system operates in practice and its limitations. Choose and book does not apply to follow up appointments which are normally decided by the specialist. The answer also shows that you are aware of the developments in this area.

Overall:

This is again a question related to your understanding of operational procedures in the NHS. Often while candidates are familiar with the jargon they miss out on how the system operates in practice. The second answer clearly demonstrates that you are familiar with the real life operation of choose and book and what it can and cannot do.

42. What is latest NHS drive to improve patient care?

This question is an attempt by the interviewers to find out if you follow the developments in the NHS and patient improvement initiatives planned at the national level. It also tests if you are aware of the government's flagship policies on NHS and if you have bothered to read about the vision of the NHS chief executive for the NHS.

Bad response:

"NHS has always been focused on improving patient care. This is about providing the best available evidence- based treatment to all the patients. Extra money has been pledged by the government which should help with buying more diagnostic equipment and expensive medicines to improve patient care."

Response Analysis:

While factually correct the response is very generic and does not show awareness of what is being planned at the national level.

Good Response:

"There is increasing recognition that with an aging and expanding population the demand on the NHS continues to increase. People are living longer with increasingly complex medical needs and the new more expensive treatments continue to arrive stretching the NHS budget. There is clearly a need to be more effective and efficient and this may be achieved by smart use of technology to make earlier diagnosis and reduce the need for hospital visits. The NHS is looking to use technology to address major health care challenges. As a part of this the UK space agency working collaboratively with NHS England is looking to invest 4 million pounds to facilitate technological advancement geared towards improving the health of the nation. The key areas which are planned to be addressed are –

- *Managing long term conditions including joining up health and care services*
- *Earlier diagnosis of cancer*
- *Transforming GP services and other primary care*
- *Meeting mental health needs"*

Response Analysis:

This is a good response demonstrating that you understand the challenges faced by the NHS and the actions being taken at the national level to improve patient care. You have the option of expanding the answer further explaining how you think technology can be put to good use for improving patient care citing examples such as Skype clinics, Patient monitoring at home for chronic conditions such as diabetes.

Overall:

As a consultant you are expected to have an interest in improving patient care. This is an opportunity to demonstrate that you are committed to improve patient care and are up to date with the developments in this area at a national and international level. It may also be helpful to express an opinion about the initiatives you feel are most valuable and how they are relevant to your speciality.

43. What differentiates the NHS from all other healthcare systems in the world?

This question could be the start or follow up of the previous question (and vice versa). This question is obviously aimed at the funding structure of the NHS as well as the question of eligibility. The founding idea of the NHS is to provide medical care for everybody living in the UK, irrespective of their income or social situation, i.e. 'free for all' at the point of entry. The funding model of the NHS is to assign a certain proportion of the general tax income to healthcare. The exact amount is dictated by a judgement of need of funding. Other healthcare systems use different funding models. For example, privately funded, insurance-based or a mix of both.

Bad Response:

"The NHS is superior in all aspects to other systems of healthcare provision as it is free for everybody and you can get all the treatments without having to pay anything. This ensures that everybody can get all the treatment they want without having to worry about how to pay for it. Having access to the most modern and effective treatments free of charge is essential for the maintenance of good population health, making the NHS the best healthcare system in the world."

Response Analysis:

This is a poor response because it is too one-dimensional. First of all, the question does not ask to make a judgement on which system is better but merely asks for the differences. Secondly, the answers show a principle misunderstanding of the resource allocation within the NHS. The NHS provides only NICE approved treatments and part of the approval process is a cost-efficiency calculation, which is particularly important in the context of modern cancer drugs that are highly effective but also very expensive. Some of these modern drugs do not satisfy the NICE cost-benefit calculation and are not available on the NHS, despite their affectivity.

Good Response:

"The main points differentiating the NHS from other healthcare systems is the funding structure. Some countries like the USA rely on exclusively private funding for healthcare where every individual is responsible for covering the cost of their own treatment. Other countries like, for example, Switzerland rely on an insurance-based reimbursing scheme where medical costs are paid back by the insurance. In comparison to that, the NHS is funded by tax income. This means that a certain proportion of the overall income is allocated to healthcare in order to cover the anticipated needs of the system during the fiscal year."

Response Analysis:

This response is significantly better. It answers the question and provides examples from other countries, demonstrating good knowledge of healthcare overall. It avoids judgement and provides a good clear answer to the question. It also shows insight into the funding structure of the NHS.

Overall:

In this question, it is important to avoid judgement and being too rash with the decision-making. The question does not ask about superiority, but about differences. Other than the obvious difference in the funding structure, other differences include bodies such as NICE that evaluate treatments for cost-effectiveness and also provide guidelines for appropriate care delivery, as well as the organisation of care delivery with GPs almost functioning as triage points responsible for the distribution of patients.

44.If you were in charge of the NHS what would you do?

This is a very broad question, you should narrow down your answer right from the start and say that you will focus your answer on a specific bit. For example, say you focus on a particular problem you have encountered in your locum consultant post or during training in not so recent past. Whilst this seems like a tricky question, your response can demonstrate your understanding of the structure of the NHS and some of the problems currently faced by the organisation. The interviewers may be asking this question to see how much you know already about an organisation you will be spending at least another 20 – 30 years of your life or they may be asking it simply as stimulation for debate and discussion to see how you think through a problem. Being in charge of large national organisations is something you're unlikely to have experience of and that's absolutely fine! But do expect to have your ideas challenged and to defend your opinions.

Bad Response:

"If I were in charge of the NHS, I would want to reduce waiting lists so that patients get quicker access to the right health professionals. The waiting times for some clinics and operations can be very long and this is not conducive to an efficient system or happy patients. In order to achieve this, I would channel funds into employing extra staff in one area at a time until the waiting times in that area are reduced and then hopefully with the backlog cleared, the future waiting times will stay reduced."

Response Analysis:

This response does well in highlighting a specific subject to tackle, however, it comes across as overly confident and unfortunately with an unfeasible idea. The response also lacks an example or explaining where this idea has come from; either of which would help the interviewers to frame what they hear and ask more productive questions in return.

Good Response:

"Right now, I must admit there are multiple aspects that we could focus on. Rather than suggesting draconic changes, I would start with improving patients'' experiences with NHS. So, with that in mind, if I were in charge I would invite employees of all skills and levels to offer their experiences and ideas as to how to make specific systems more efficient and a better experience for both staff and patients. I think it's the staff on the ground that can offer the best ideas as to how their jobs could be improved. I think it would be easier for people to accept changes if they were proposed by colleagues rather than seen as imposed on them by management.

For example, in my current locum post as a vascular surgeon, in my outpatient clinic significantly high number of patients do not attend their appointments. If I were in charge of the NHS, this could be an example of something I would investigate using staff feedback – is it that the no-shows are actually needed to keep the clinic running to time or is time/appointment being wasted?"

Response Analysis:

This response uses your experience about the subject, a gap in the process and spins it into a positive, focusing on the people on the ground doing the work and experiencing the system every day having the most informed opinions about it. The use of an example helps to illustrate the argument and reminds the interviewers that you are observant (DNAs in clinic can easily be taken as free time to relax between patient) but you are suggesting this as a problem and coming up with solutions from the users and the people that are directly affected by DNA (staff in clinic that are waiting, missed opportunity for someone else to be seen and treatment planned).

Overall:

There are infinite things one could do if one were to take over charge of the NHS, so narrowing down your discussion points will really help you here. Current issues seen in the media would also be a reasonable springboard for your response to this question. If the interviewers start to debate with you, then try to explain the rationale behind your ideas but don't feel you have to continue to defend ideas if it quickly becomes apparent they are not feasible! The interviewers are almost certainly interested in seeing how you think through the problem rather than what you actually come up with – no-one is expecting you to have a management degree. Some issues to think about are junior doctor's shortage and staffing crisis, hospitals on edge, NHS dependence on locum doctors, training of doctors, skill mix use within NHS etc.

45. What have you read recently about NHS?

The NHS is constantly in the news and not all of it is good news. There are issues with waiting times, problems in Emergency departments and cancelled operations. It is easy to forget what a great service NHS provides and how it continues to develop and evolve. This question should therefore is best responded by talking about the new developments and not about scandals.

Bad response:

"I like to follow news about developments in the NHS. I have just read about the problems ED's are having with meeting the 4-hour target. Ambulances are having to wait for long periods simply to off load the patients to ED. The system appears to be at breaking point and something needs to be done about it."

Response analysis:

The response is factually correct but rather than focusing on positive developments in the NHS it presents the difficulties NHS is having. Of course, one could choose to highlight the problems in the NHS but then it would be worthwhile providing an informed analysis of the reasons behind the problems and the steps being taken to address them.

Good Response:

"I have read about a number of developments related to the NHS which should have a huge positive impact on the service that NHS delivers. There is some thought being given to prevention of disease rather than just on treating illness once it happens. This is a more progressive way of managing the nation's health. One such development is the NHS Diabetes Prevention Programme which is recruiting people at risk of developing Type 2 diabetes into behavioural change programmes. Another development is the use of innovative digital technologies which are empowering patients to manage their own health at their convenience. Examples include The Big White Wall, one of the first services to be endorsed by the NHS Choices website, and which was backed by NHS England's Regional Innovation Fund. The service, which addresses mental health and wellbeing issues, offers users secure, anonymised access to a novel combination of peer support and professionally-trained therapists. Users' feedback is adding to the growing body of evidence which points to the effectiveness of mental health services delivered online."

Response Analysis:

This is a much better response giving examples of real meaningful and positive developments in the NHS, which have been in the news. The candidate is able to demonstrate that they have an interest in the NHS above and beyond their daily job.

Overall:

It is wise to read widely and have a good knowledge of national and international developments for any interview. For a consultant interview this reading should necessarily include developments about health in general and NHS in particular. It is even better if you are prepared not just with a knowledge about these developments but also are able to express a personal view about what is of value and why.

46. Tell us about NHS plan

This question is looking to see if you are familiar with the NHS plan, the reasons it was developed and its underlying importance. Of course, you need to define it as such but go further and explain the ramifications and implications both to the provider and user.

Bad Response:
"NHS plan was strategic plan developed in the year 2000 to outline working guidance for NHS for next five years."

Response Analysis:
The response is factually correct confirming that the candidate had made the effort of familiarizing himself with the developments in the NHS. However, the reply is brief and limited.

Good Response:
"The NHS Plan was a strategic plan developed in the year 2000 which was presented as the biggest change to healthcare in England since the NHS was formed in 1948. It set out to modernise NHS to make it a health service fit for the 21st century and putting patients' needs at its centre. It was described as a plan for investment and reform which would eliminate geographical inequalities, improve service standards and extend patient choice. It outlined a vision of a health service designed around the patient.

It was released for the first time in March 2000 by the then labour government. The NHS Plan defined a programme of change, underpinned by 10 core principles, with the aim of tackling the systemic problems which have undermined the effectiveness of the NHS. Some of these principles are based on the original founding values of NHS such as providing a universal service for all based on clinical need and not ability to pay. Others are related to improving and modernizing the NHS. These include a commitment to respond to different needs of different populations and to work continuously to improve quality of services and to minimize errors. More recently Mrs May's government has come out with what is being called the NHS 10 year plan. Essentially the government has announced increase in NHS funding over 5 years, beginning in 2019/20 and has asked the NHS to come up with a 10-year plan about how best to use this funding."

Response Analysis:
This is a much better answer as it demonstrates an in-depth understanding of NHS plan. The candidate has clearly explained the origin and fundamentals of the plan. More recent developments have also been highlighted.

Overall:
It is a reasonable expectation that someone wishing to become a consultant in the NHS needs to have a good understanding of the key developments in the history of NHS, especially those linked to improving quality of care delivered to the patients. It is not enough just to be familiar with the jargon, rather one needs to demonstrate a knowledge about the impact of these developments.

47. How would you approach the problem of low NHS funding and treatment?

Resource allocation is a very important point of ethical debate in the NHS. Discussing it gives you an opportunity to show good reasoning abilities, an appreciation for the importance of justice as a principle in healthcare, and a strong moral compass. It also shows that you recognise that it can be challenging for doctors when treatments are available for patients that they are unable to offer due to limited funding. Explaining this to patients can be very difficult and potentially upsetting.

Bad Response:
I think the NHS funding should be increased by the government. However, I understand that this could be difficult in which case, the money should go towards treating those who need it most.

Response Analysis
A pragmatic albeit simplistic view on resource allocation. There is little insight into how treatments and procedures are funded by the NHS nor is there any mention of how the applicant would increase funding. Finally, there is no explanation as to what is defined as patients 'who need it most' and who would decide this. It also does not answer the question "funding and treatment."

Good Response:
A good policy for distributing limited funding is prioritisation so that the money is used in a way that produces the greatest possible overall benefit. A good way to quantify this is in Quality Adjusted Life Years (QUALYs) / £K spending. NICE analyses the average QUALY/£K for different treatments and produces guidelines on which treatments produce the most benefit. These guidelines are probably the best way of deciding how to spend NHS money. In the future, it could be necessary to suspend the free provision of non-vital treatments such as IVF. It is also important to ensure that the money is spent as efficiently as possible, e.g. by treating patients in the community instead of a hospital.

Response Analysis:
A much more comprehensive response that analyses the process by which treatments and procedures get approved and allocated. There is a good level of discussion regarding the multiple organisations that contribute to this and a valid plan of stopping non-vital treatments. The use of IVF as an example is well done though there is a slight danger that IVF is given as an option which is a wasted one and can be perceived as lack of empathy by some!

Overall
This question is also about understanding the interaction between beneficence, autonomy and justice, **and** rationalising treatment that is equitable. Whilst a treatment/intervention/procedure may be good for the patient (beneficence), it may be costly and, hence, limit its use in a large population. This would lead to finding means to restrict treatments to some (for the good of the mass) and that will not do justice. Governing bodies like NICE offer guidelines to ensure treatments remain equitable and fair to all. All patients in a similar situation should be treated similarly. Clinicians should ensure that the treatment options are cost effective and use resources correctly.

> **Top Tip:** Money follows patients. Be aware of service mapping, business plan and current money saving initiatives

48.Should NHS be free to all? (We pay for various commodities. Why should health care be free?) (Should NHS be privatised?)

This question is about having an informed debate about what is the best way of paying for the NHS. The NHS constitution declares that NHS belongs to the people so by default people should not need to pay when accessing any NHS service. Politically the broad principle of NHS being free at the point of use is supported by all political parties and most people consider a NHS a national treasure. That does not mean that a balanced discussion cannot be had and this question tests your ability to do so.

Bad Response:

"I don't think that the NHS should be free to all. Every day we hear about the NHS being cash-strapped, people abusing the NHS and lot of public money being wasted in senseless projects. Before the system collapses and dies on us we need to make changes. People should pay for health as they do for using trains or buses. Surely that will stop people spending their evenings in the Emergency department."

Response Analysis:

While it is true that there is genuine funding crisis in the NHS, this alone is not reason enough to suggest such a drastic change. The answer is obviously one-sided and presents a biased view on this very hot question. A much better way to answer the question would be to present a balanced argument based on the pros and cons of privatising the NHS.

Good Response:

"I have myself wondered if the NHS should be free to all. NHS services specially the Emergency department and ambulance services are often misused, clinic appointments are regularly missed with high DNA rates. People who take the least responsibility for their health are the ones who use the NHS the most, while people who have led a very responsible life still have to join a long waiting list when they need NHS. It is easy to get carried away by these arguments forgetting that the basic principle of providing free health care to all means that ill people get the help they need. Not only is this valuable for the health of individuals but also for the health of the nation.

The plight of the more than 45 million Americans who do not have health insurance is known to all. Thanks to the NHS such health inequalities do not exist in the UK. NHS may always seem to be short of money and health care costs continue to increase. It is well recognised that this publicly funded health system provides amazing value for money and the per capital expenditure in the UK is far less than in the US. People who smoke or consume most alcohol are the biggest users of health services. However, one can argue that they have already paid for it in the form of high taxes on alcohol and cigarettes. Having looked at the evidence I remain of the view that the NHS remains a unique and exemplary health system and its strength lies in the fact that it is free to the patient at the point of use. We certainly have to be prepared to spend more money on the NHS as a nation (as the population ages and newer treatments arrive) and we also have to actively look to make the NHS more efficient. However, that is not an argument to support privatisation of this much cherished service."

Response Analysis:

This is a much better answer which gives the impression that the candidate is aware of the difficulties facing the NHS and has taken the trouble to find out more about how different health systems are funded. The candidate not only presents his/her view but also a balanced logic for the reasons underpinning the view.

Overall:

This kind of question is a test of your ability to present a balanced argument on a very topical but controversial issue. You may well have quite fixed views on this topic founded on your personal experiences, however it is much more reasonable to present all sides of the argument at the same time demonstrating a good understanding of this this tricky issue.

49. What is the controversy re: the new junior doctors' contracts?

The new contract is supposed to lay the foundation for a 7-day NHS service that ensures good hospital care for all 7 days of the week. There are 3 main areas of change. The first involves safeguards that prevent doctors from being overworked by financially penalising institutions that do not allow for the contractually prescribed rest and break periods. The second set of changes involves the progress in salary. At the moment, the doctor's salary raises each year to reflect the increase in expertise due to increased experience. The new contract wants to bind pay raises to the reaching of new stages of qualification. The third area of change is aimed at core working hours. At the moment, these run from 7am to 7pm on Monday to Friday. This is supposed to change from 7am to 10pm from Monday to Saturday. This has a great impact on the work-life balance of doctors.

Bad Response:

"The main change to the junior doctor contracts lies in the payment structure. Doctors are expected to work more for less money. This is unacceptable as doctors in this country are already being paid relatively poorly in comparison to other countries such as the US. It is immoral to expect such a highly qualified profession such as doctors to work for such little money. Doctors maintain the health of society and as such should be appropriately compensated for their services."

Response Analysis:

This is a bad response as it falls short of the complexity of the contract changes. Whilst it is true that the changes will result in a decrease in pay, this is only part of the problem with the new contracts. Bigger issues lie in the poor work-life balance as well as in the removal of working time safeguards that protect doctors from being overworked in order to protect patients. Tired doctors make mistakes, which will endanger patient's health. It also fails to explore the impact of this contract on the NHS in the long-term, e.g. junior doctor's exodus to other countries.

Good Response:

"The new contract entails several changes that will have a great impact on the junior doctor's life, both professionally as well as privately. Changes to working time protection will remove safeguards in place that currently aim to prevent the overworking of doctors. This is essential to prevent mistakes that happen when doctors are tired. Another area of change concerns antisocial working hours. At the moment, core working hours for doctors run from 7am to 7pm on Monday to Friday. Anything else is defined as antisocial which amongst other things carries higher financial compensation. As part of the new contract, the core working hours are supposed to change to 7am to 10pm on Monday to Saturday. The final point of change lies in financial recognition of gained experience. At the moment, pay increases each year to reflect this gain of experience. This is supposed to change to a promotion-like system where pay increases upon completion of training milestones."

Response Analysis:

This is a good response as it aims to address the different changes suggested in the new contract and tries to put them into context with regards to their impact on the individual doctors. It is important to stay as neutral as possible as the question does not ask about opinions, but rather only about the changes suggested in the new contract.

Overall:

This is an important issue as it will eventually affect everyone in the medical profession. Given that this is a rapidly developing topic, it's absolutely paramount that you keep yourself updated by reading the news (BBC Health, BMJ, BMA website). Avoid getting drawn into a political argument about governmental health policies or critiquing the Health Secretary (Jeremy Hunt) – that's not the point of this question or the interview.

50. How would you control the TB problem in the homeless population?

This question has several components to it. On one hand, it tests the candidate's understanding of an infectious disease and on the other hand, it addresses the understanding of the interaction between health and population as well as ethical issues regarding healthcare. It is important to address each individual component of this question in part in order to gain maximum points. The more holistic the answer, the higher you will score.

Bad Response:

"In order to control the TB problem in the homeless population, if one exists in the first place, the easiest way is to ensure that every homeless person receive the TB vaccine. We could use police patrols/community matrons to force every homeless person they come across that has not had the TB vaccine and then give them the shot, whether they agree or not. In order to ensure that people are not vaccinated more than once, we can hand out pieces of paper confirming the vaccination status of the individual."

Response Analysis:

Generally, a bad response ignores parts of the question or only providing superficial and judgemental points. This answer is bad in several aspects. It shows very little insight into the complexity of TB and also some serious ethical issues. Detaining an individual and then forcing them to be vaccinated ignores with fundamental principles of freedom and consent to treatment. Consent is a particularly important aspect of this question with regards to a medical interview.

Good Response:

"TB represents an important problem in the homeless population but also for public health in general. Therefore, control of this problem has a direct positive impact not only on the health of the individual but also population as a whole. In order to control the problem, it is the most reasonable way to tackle it on several levels. Firstly, there is the TB vaccine. Whilst it has a limited effectivity of 60 – 80%, it still provides an important starting point for the control of the problem. Ultimately, though, the best way to control the problem is by getting the homeless off the street and into secure housing. This requires financial support from the government and establishment of necessary support structures providing general medical care as well as food and addiction support. Due to the general immunocompromise associated with alcoholism, poor nutrition and other drug addictions, providing help for this will also provide a good starting point."

Response Analysis:

This is a good answer that attempts to address all components of the question and also manages to remain non-judgemental. It also provides an idea of some insight into the interaction of infectious diseases with the individual as well as lifestyle and treatment. Also, points out the connection between individual and the population.

Overall:

A complex question always requires a complex answer as there are no easy solutions for complex problems. Making sure to consider the individual as well as the population and the impact of lifestyle choices will always improve the quality of an answer.

51. What is the EWTD? What is its significance?

The EWTD is the European Working Time Directive. Most of your answer should be based on the latter question; what is the EWTDs significance? In answering this question, it is important to show your understanding of the working environment of doctors, the importance of ensuring that working conditions do not compromise the work of doctors, and the significance of working hours of doctors to the quality of patient care. You should be able to identify the priorities of a doctors in accordance with doing the best job they can with respect to patient welfare and health. It is wise to recognise the unintended impact of EWTD on specialist training and continuity of care. You should aim to keep the answer to this question relatively short but specific. Be prepared to have a follow-on question on junior doctor contract (or vice versa).

Bad Response:

"The EWTD is the European Working Time Directive. It is in place to make sure doctors don't work too hard and a work-life balance is maintained. Doctors are placed under too much stress as it is. They have endless amounts of work and the work is often very emotionally draining. Doctors should not be forced to work for long hours without a break as this is risky causing doctors to burnout and consequently, they will be more likely to quit. The EWTD is an important directive that is a key factor of why many doctors find their jobs bearable."

Response Analysis:

The candidate provides an excessively pessimist viewpoint of the working life of doctors. The candidate fails to identify any reasons as to why working as a doctor is a valuable or rewarding job. This can cause the interviewer to question the candidate's belief in his/her own decision to study medicine. The candidate mentions the emotional toll of work on the doctor; this is an important and sensitive issue that should be addressed with caution. A doctor needs to be able to cope with the emotional stress that their job carries with it in a healthy manner so that they can process difficult situations without such experiences influencing their judgment or competency.

Good Response:

"The EWTD is the European Working Time Directive. It limits the number of working hours of doctors in the UK and specifies when rest periods and holiday periods should be given and how frequently they should be taken. The directive is in place to protect both patients and doctors in order to not overwork doctors or cause them to burnout. The importance of the EWTD lies in providing a legal basis for safe and fair working hours, in order to avoid excessive tiredness and consequent errors that might endanger patients and compromise their care. This will require careful considerations in light of new junior doctor contract negotiations. While EWTD has made a very positive change to the junior doctor's work-life balance, its impact on training has been reduction of hands on training time with concerns about the adequacy of training specially in surgical specialities. Also, there is a perception that introduction of new EWTD compliant rotas has had an impact on the continuity of care"

Response Analysis:

The answer identifies that the major issue here is the threat of long working hours reducing the quality of service doctors delivering to patients. Any risk of potential harm caused to patients is a very serious issue and something that must be avoided at all costs, and this is what the European Working Time Directive aims to avoid. The answer also recognises that every change almost always has some unintended consequences and presents this in a balanced format. It is interesting how the candidate is almost inviting for a follow-on question on new contract for junior doctors.

Overall:

The details of the directive do not need to be stated but you should have a good idea of what they are (see the EWTD page earlier in this book for more details).

52.Should a doctor need consent to be able to perform a procedure?

Consent is essential in medical practice as it is the basis of autonomy; one of the core principles of medical practice. In order to achieve appropriate consent, the patient has to be provided with all relevant and significant details of the procedure and be given all the relevant information related to the procedure. This includes the risks & benefits of the procedure and details about what the procedure involves.

Bad Response:

"Consent is just a formality. What matters is that the patient agrees verbally in a conversation with the doctor. Any doctor can get consent from a patient and he does not have to be able to perform the procedure himself. The doctor also only needs to give the patient a rough idea of what is going to happen during the procedure. Details are only necessary on a somewhat limited level, as long as the patient is happy to undergo the procedure. In general, consent needs to be achieved, but it is sufficient to give the patient a general overview of the procedure".

Response Analysis:

This response is inadequate as it has several inaccuracies and shortcomings. This puts the candidate in the bad light regarding his overall understanding of medical practice. Consent is one of the core values of medical practice and being aware of all the implications associated with this is vital. The candidate displays an overall lack of appreciation of the important information about the consenting of a patient.

A Good Response:

"Consent is vital for medical practice. Doctors can only perform procedures that have been given informed consent by the patient. Any violation of this is battery which is a criminal offence. When consenting a patient, a good understanding of the procedure itself as well as of the risks associated is important in order to tailor the information delivery to the individual patient. In addition to this, an understanding of the procedure will allow the doctor to answer any question the patient might have in full and with enough detail to allow the patient to make an informed decision about the procedure. Ultimately, that is the basis that needs to be satisfied in order for consent to be valid. In general, a doctor should only consent a patient for a procedure that he/she is familiar with, as only then will he/she have the necessary appreciation for the exact processes underlying the procedure".

Response Analysis:

This is a good answer as it gives a good degree of background information about the process of achieving consent as well as about the different factors influencing consent and its validity. The candidate demonstrates a good grasp of what it means to consent a patient for a procedure and the importance of valid consent for medical practice.

Overall:

The aim of this question is to analyse your ability to emphasise and think about medical core ethical principles in clinical setting. There is not really a right or wrong answer, but the you need to demonstrate an understanding of the relevance of consent in the overall practice of medicine and what place consent and the information provided holds within clinical medicine. It is important for you to know this as you will be responsible for training the future doctors. It also gives an indication of your approach to medical practice from a legal perspective and the implications this has on the delivery of care. The necessity of this is two-fold; on one hand, this is to protect the patient and on the other hand, this also protects the doctor from litigation. An understanding of the safety concerns associated with medical care is central for any prospective doctor.

53.Should the NHS be run by doctors?

The NHS is the supplier of the vast majority of medical care in the UK. Due to the nature of the NHS as a government institution, the input into the managing structure is very diverse and includes a high proportion of non-medical professions. In the light of the recent junior doctor contract conflict, the question of NHS leadership and management is very important.

Bad Response:

"The NHS should most definitely be run by doctors. Only doctors are able to understand the complexity of medical care and what it means to deliver this care every day. In addition, it seems that doctors would be more trustworthy than politicians with the latter only being out for power and control. Doctors do the job they do in order to help people and should, therefore, be put in charge of the organisation that was established to help people."

Response Analysis:

This response is a bad one as it is very one-dimensional and does not appreciate the complexity of the issue of leadership. Whilst a doctor may be a great physician or surgeon, that does not necessarily mean that he/she is a good manager with the ability to control and efficiently guide a large body of employees. The candidate ignores that. The comment on the morality of doctors may or may not be an appropriate representation of the truth, but most importantly, it does not provide a valid judgement of the ability of the individual to perform the specific task at hand.

Good Response:

"The NHS as an institution is very important and very high profile. It is the largest single employer in the world. This necessarily makes its administration very complex. This needs to be reflected in the leadership. Whilst the argument can be made that doctors are able to understand how medical professionals work and how healthcare is provided in the hospitals, this falls somewhat short of an appropriate justification for the superiority of doctors' leadership. Due to their special knowledge of medical realities, doctors should be involved in policy making and long-term decisions in the NHS, but so should nurses and other health care providers as they ultimately work in the same environment. It is also important to underline that only because somebody is a good doctor, they might not be good managers. And efficient management is centrally important in running an organisation as large as the NHS."

Response Analysis:

A good response as it is very diverse and attempts to address the underlying issues surrounding the administration of the NHS. The complexity of the NHS as an enterprise is very important to recognise, so is the appreciation of limited abilities as a manager. This answer also addresses limitations of the question by pointing out that there are more healthcare providers in the NHS than just doctors.

Overall:

This question is relevant at this moment in time as it addresses an important issue with the NHS. Due to its size, an efficient administration is very challenging and appropriate allocation of resources is as well. Having first-hand experiences of healthcare provision will facilitate an understanding of what areas need the most support in terms of money etc. and what aspects demonstrate the biggest shortcomings. It is vital for candidates to have an opinion on questions like that. Having an understanding and a founded opinion on the questions such as this one is an excellent way for a you to set yourself apart from the rest of the applicants and it will make for a very positive and mature impression.

54. What is the "obesity epidemic"?

Obesity is an escalating global epidemic and affects virtually all age and socioeconomic groups. It is no longer limited to developed countries and millions suffer from other serious health disorders as a result. Obesity poses a major risk for diabetes, hypertension, stroke, and certain forms of cancer. Its health consequences range from increased risk of premature death to serious chronic conditions that reduce the overall quality of life.

Obesity levels in the UK have more than trebled in the last 30 years and, on current estimates, more than half the population could be obese by 2050. Income, social deprivation and ethnicity have an important impact on the likelihood of becoming obese. For example, women and children in lower socioeconomic groups are more likely to be obese than those who are wealthier. The car, TV, computers, desk jobs, high-calorie food, and increased food abundance have all contributed to encouraging inactivity and overeating.

Bad Response:
"More people in the world are gaining in weight which is causing an epidemic. The US is a particular culprit. This weight gain is primarily due to our heavily sedentary lifestyles and high-fat diets."

Response Analysis:
The response itself is correct and contains all true information but it is lacking in detail. "Gaining in weight" is non-specific; a better answer would have included the Body Mass Index as an objective measure of obesity (BMI greater than 30 is classified as obese). The answer also discusses the US. While it is true that America is a key example of the obesity epidemic, it is important to remember that the UK is not innocent. Talking about the UK would be more relevant and could lead nicely into a discussion of the burden on the NHS. The last sentence is also scientifically correct but ignores factors such as genetics and epidemiological factors, e.g. socioeconomic background.

Good Response:
"The obesity epidemic describes the rise in cases of obesity globally. Obesity is defined as a BMI greater than 30. This rise is not limited to certain areas or ages; we are now seeing children as young as eight years old classified as obese. Obesity is associate with a variety of disorders, including diabetes mellitus, cardiovascular problems and some cancers. This is particularly troubling due to the increasing burden on the NHS which already faces multiple challenges. In the current political climate, the escalating obesity epidemic places great pressure on an already strained NHS."

Response Analysis:
This answer clearly defines obesity which shows us that they know this topic well. Obesity in children is a very hot topic in media and health so by mentioning it, the candidate has shown that they are aware of the key issues on this topic. The increasing burden this place on the NHS due to its various co-morbid conditions is also an essential part of this topic and shows that this is a strong candidate. The last sentence briefly touches on current news – "current political climate" clearly means Jeremy Hunt, the junior doctor debate, and the possible privatisation of the NHS. It also gives the interviewers something to grab onto so you can direct them to a topic you know a lot on (make sure you know about the Jeremy Hunt situation before you do this!).

Overall:
A good answer will look at the impact of obesity on the NHS and draw on current health news. Common follow-on questions to this would be: *"Should obese people be offered weight loss surgery?"* Or *"should doctors be obese?"*

55. What do you understand by the term "postcode lottery"?

The postcode lottery is shorthand for the countrywide variations in the provision and quality of public services. Where you live, defines the standard of services you can expect. So, if you live in the "wrong" area, you may get a poorer service than your neighbour or you may not get the service at all and have to pay for it privately. The postcode lottery is a big issue in the NHS.

In practice, there are geographical variations in almost all aspects of care. Recent examples include variations in charges for disabled people's home care; availability of NHS in-vitro fertilisation services; waiting times for NHS treatment; and access to NHS cancer screening programmes. Generally speaking, the lower the socio-economic background, the worse your care and access to it are likely to be. This is known as the "inverse care law". It also shows the variation in spending between GP Practices – both overall and on types of disease.

Although some variation is warranted because different populations have different levels of need, the postcode lottery highlights the need to impose basic minimum standards of acceptable care across the UK. The Government argues that rationing within the NHS is necessary to ensure that resources which could be spent elsewhere are not wasted and that patients receive only treatments which have real clinical benefits.

Bad Response:
"The postcode lottery means that some people do not get the same healthcare as others. However, it is important for the Government to regulate healthcare provisions to ensure the most healthcare is provided for the most people. This follows the "justice" principle in ethics."

Response Analysis:
The answer is the worst possible one. Be sure to research key issues in the NHS. It shows a poor understanding of what the postcode lottery is. Although the information is correct, the answer fails to grasp that the widespread inequality caused by the postcode lottery goes against the ethical principle of "justice".

Good Response:
"The postcode lottery describes the inequality in the provision of healthcare based on where people live. There are differences in access to NHS treatment throughout the country and this can affect the quality and availability of NHS services one can expect. The increase in rationing within the NHS has led to an increase in the effects of the postcode lottery, in determining which patients have access to certain treatments. This has affected waiting times, cancer treatments, and most notably, in vitro fertilisation therapies. I understand that it is important to ration healthcare due to limited resources but there should be a clear agreement on the basic standard of care across England, and even the UK."

Response Analysis:
This answer is very well constructed. It begins by succinctly defining what the postcode lottery is and how it can arise. "Important to ration healthcare due to limited resources" shows that the candidate clearly understands the justice component and thus the other side of the argument. The answer concludes with a strong statement using key information (included in the background) that shows the interviewer that they truly understand the topic.

Overall:
A good answer will show understanding of the topic. Begin your answer with a definition and then go into the causes. Be sure to give a balanced view to show you understand both sides of the discussion.

56. What health problems do doctors face?

As a doctor, looking after your own health is just as important as looking after your patients. Medicine is a challenging and stressful profession. While making care for the patient a priority, it is important to appreciate that doctors can be susceptible to health problems too.

Stigma: There is a large amount of stigma that surrounds illness in doctors. The expectations that doctors place on themselves is likely to contribute to the problem. The myth persists that good doctors do not make mistakes and that illness, particularly mental ill health, is a weakness. Taking time off work is letting colleagues and patients down; showing vulnerability may lose the respect of others.

Stress: Doctors report that stress has an impact on their ability to provide high-quality care, this can be reflected in GMC referrals. Medicine is a stressful profession; sources of stress may include: work pressure, poor support, high demand workload, investigations, complaints and court cases, and trauma of dealing with suffering. There is extra stress for some groups – for example, women with small children have to manage the competing tensions of work and home life.

Mental Health: A third of doctors have some kind of mental disorder. Yet for many, it is a shameful secret because of the deep prejudice towards mental illness that still exists in the medical profession. Doctors often have significant mental health problems before they seek help. Many doctors work long hours and have heavy workloads, which can cause severe depression and lead to suicide attempts. Suicide rates have also increased, particularly in female doctors, anaesthetists, GPs and psychiatrists.

Substance Misuse: Over 5% of doctors will have a substance use problem during their lifetime, using it as a way to cope with stress. Doctors' access to prescription drugs plays a part in their risk of substance use and suicide, as well as making it easier to treat themselves rather than seeking help.

Bad Response:
"Doctors are people too and they have normal health problems like everyone else. It is important that they seek help but this may be difficult due to their long working hours."

Response Analysis:
The response itself is good in that it mentions that doctors are human so can suffer illness. It also recognises the difficulty doctors face in seeking help. However, it fails to grasp the most complex details of this issue which shows this is a weak candidate. Mental health in doctors is a key issue and a hot topic in the news so would be fitting for this question.

Good Response:
"Doctors can suffer from poor mental health. Being a doctor is a stressful job which can predispose to mental illness. The personality of people can also lead to poor mental health. Media and doctors themselves place a great deal on doctors to act as an infallible guide to health, this can make doctors think they "are not allowed" to be ill. There may be alcohol misuse as a way of coping with stress or a lot of depression. I feel it is important that doctors know how and where to seek help."

Response Analysis:
This answer clearly grasps the most complex issues surrounding doctors' health and shows that this is a strong candidate. Mental health in doctors may be a sensitive topic but it is important to show that you are aware of the darker side to medicine. Any awareness of the pressure on doctors and the myth of the all-knowing infallible doctor shows knowledge of the current news. A better answer would have included the effect on patient safety.

Overall:
A good answer will show understanding of the more complex side of doctors' health. It will also include the potential negative effects on patient safety.

57. If you could propose one policy to reduce obesity in poorer communities, what would it be?

These kinds of questions are difficult to answer, especially if it's the first time you've seen them. Crucially, it's important to remember that there is not one absolute golden response or one concept that is considered correct. Rather, the key here is to present a logical and feasible solution to a serious problem. You are not a government policy maker and your interviewer know this. The point here is to engage you to see how much you really understand about current issues.

Bad Response:

"Fat children are a big issue. The link between diabetes and obesity is well known, and therefore, childhood obesity needs to be tackled. The easiest way to tackle this is to prohibit the sale of junk food and sweets to children. If children do not have access to unhealthy food, they are less likely to become obese. This would solve the root cause of the problem limiting the long-term implications of having too many fat children in our society. You could also have a policy where you make healthy foods cheaper so that more people buy them. That way, more people eat healthily so that they don't become obese. This would probably work because lots of poorer working people are obese because they eat a lot of junk food. So, if you made healthy food cheaper, they wouldn't buy so much junk food."

Response Analysis:

This response isn't actually that bad but it comes across as quite judgemental. The underlying point of making healthy food cheaper is a valid point. But here you'd have missed out on an opportunity to show that you have a greater understanding of how funding works, and why people in poorer communities are obese. It attempts to find a simple solution for a complex issue. Simply making the sale of unhealthy food to children illegal is unlikely to solve the problem and would come with significant challenges regarding the policy itself. It also does not tackle additional factors influencing obesity apart from unhealthy food.

Good Response:

"I'd propose a government subsidy of healthier food options, funded by greater taxation on less healthy foods. That coupled with the existing legislation that prevents junk food advertising aimed directly at certain communities should help. I think it would work because of the link between poverty and obesity. A lot of the time, parents will feed their children less healthy food, not necessarily kebabs every night, but foods that are high in salts and fat purely because they're cheaper than the healthier alternatives. If you have four mouths to feed on a really limited budget, it makes sense to buy the cheaper option just to make sure your kids get their caloric intake. It's not an active choice to be unhealthy but just a fact of the economics. If the healthier options were cheaper, this problem would be ameliorated."

Response Analysis:

This response is better because it shows a greater understanding of the issues. Now, you might not necessarily agree with the above argument, but at the very least it does sound feasible and is actually proposed by several political think tanks. This response shows a deep understanding of complex issues like the link between poverty and obesity, and a real-world approach to how people in tough situations might behave. It also shows an understanding of basic economics by acknowledging that money for making things cheaper doesn't just come from thin air, but rather from taxation of other products. This kind of holistic approach to problems is important to foster. Whilst the response does not "spell out" a specific policy, it gives solid thought processes that can be implemented.

Overall:

This is a very important question as child obesity is a big problem for the NHS. Don't be fazed if you don't have a unique response to this question. It's important to take a step back and think about this before you answer. Ultimately, if you can show an understanding of the issues (why people make certain food choices) and give details about the implementations of your policy regardless of the efficacy, you'll do well. It may be worth alluding to the sugar tax on fizzy drinks if you really want to shine.

58. What is public health and why is it important?

Public health is defined as "the science and art of promoting and protecting health and well-being, preventing ill-health and prolonging life through the organised efforts of society". This means that it aims to protect the health of populations. These populations can be as small as a local community or as big as an entire country or region of the world.

The National Health Service is a public funded healthcare system that provides healthcare for the UK, so has a vested interest in public health. A large part of public health is promoting healthcare equity, quality and accessibility. Public health professionals try to prevent problems from happening or recurring through implementing educational programs, recommending policies, administering services and conducting research - "prevention is worth more than a cure" – so it works to promote healthy behaviours. Public health also works to limit health disparities.

Public health is heavily influenced by a number of social factors and is, therefore, continually adapting. Although sanitation and vaccination are still key; it has now broadened to include smoking cessation, the harmful use of alcohol, nutrition, obesity and physical inactivity, and multi-drug resistant bacteria.

The work of public health professionals is important because public health initiatives affect people every day in every part of the world. It addresses broad issues that can affect the health and well-being of individuals, families, communities, populations, and societies—both now, and for generations to come. Public health programs help keep people alive. These programs have led to increased life expectancies, worldwide reductions in infant and child mortality, and eradication or reduction of many communicable diseases.

Bad Response:
"Public health is about the health of the public. It is concerned about the main diseases that can affect England. It is important because it works to reduce the incidence of disease in England."

Response Analysis:
It is important to remember that public health is a worldwide thing e.g. the Ebola epidemic was managed by the World Health Organisation which deals with global public health. The definition does not mention "specific populations" which is key in public health – different populations have different health needs. A specific example of a type of public health initiative would have demonstrated that the candidate had real knowledge on this topic, however, this is lacking.

Good Response:
"Public Health is concerned with looking at the health of populations and the different diseases that may dominate in a particular population. They look at prevention, which can include screening programmes, for example, the National Chlamydia Screening Programme (NCSP) is an NHS sexual health programme that forms part of public health initiatives, along with the provision of free condoms. The NHS is a public health service so public health plays a key part in its role."

Response Analysis:
This answer has a clear definition of public health. Vaccination is often the example of public health most candidates know so by providing something different this highlights the candidates as someone of interest. Some other examples could be smoking cessation, weight management e.g. exercise on prescription initiatives).

Overall:
A good answer will add detail and give an example of a current public Health measure, such as the National Chlamydia Screening Programme or smoking cessation clinics. It will also relate the question to the NHS and comment on the importance of public health.

59. Why is antibiotic overprescribing a problem?

Antibiotics are be useful in the treatment of relatively mild conditions such as acne, as well as life-threatening conditions such as pneumonia. However, antibiotics often have no benefit for many other types of infection.

Bacteria can adapt and mutate to become resistant to the effects of an antibiotic. The chance of this increases if a person does not finish the course of antibiotics they have been prescribed, as some bacteria may be left to develop resistance. This means antibiotics are losing their effectiveness at an increasing rate. With indiscriminate use of antibiotics, the chances bacteria will become resistant to them are greater and they can no longer be used to treat infections. Antibiotics can also destroy many of the harmless strains of bacteria that live in and on the body. This allows resistant bacteria to multiply quickly and replace them.

Using antibiotics unnecessarily would only increase the risk of antibiotic resistance, so they should not be used routinely. Antibiotic resistance is one of the most significant threats to patients' safety in Europe. It is driven by overusing antibiotics and prescribing them inappropriately.

Antibiotic resistance has led to the emergence of "superbugs". These are strains of bacteria that have developed resistance to many different types of antibiotics. They include Clostridium Difficile and MRSA which are large problems in hospitals. These types of infections can be serious and challenging to treat and are becoming an increasing cause of disability and death across the world.

The biggest worry is new strains of bacteria may emerge that cannot be effectively treated by any existing antibiotics. To slow down the development of antibiotic resistance, it is important to use antibiotics in the right way – to use the right drug, at the right dose, at the right time, for the right duration. Antibiotics should be taken as prescribed, and never saved for later or shared with others. Often doctors feel pressured to give in to a patient's request for antibiotics. Most infections physicians see in their clinics today are viral and do not require antibiotics. Instead, physicians should be willing to engage in dialogue with their patients and to not be afraid to say no.

Bad Response:
"Antibiotics are given to treat infections. If too many are prescribed it can lead to resistance so they are less effective. This can lead to disease that cannot be treated by antibiotic drugs."

Response Analysis:
The response lacks a key fact: antibiotics are given to treat BACTERIAL infections. The issue arises when patients ask for antibiotics to treat a viral illness, such as a cold, which is not cured by antibiotics.

Good Response:
"Antibiotics are used to treat bacterial infections. However, overprescribing can create a selection pressure that results in antibiotic resistance. This can create superbugs such as MRSA, which are a big issue in hospitals. It is important for doctors to explain this to patients when they demand antibiotics for viral infections. MRSA is a problem to the extent that the number of MRSA bacteraemia/year are nationally reported and trusts are assigned specific numbers above which they are penalised."

Response Analysis:
This answer explains why antibiotics are prescribed and their role in antibiotic resistance. By discussing the pressure patients place on doctors for prescribing, the candidate shows a great understanding of a key issue within the NHS. "MRSA" is always a topical issue in medicine and it highlights the candidate as a competitive applicant because it shows they are aware of this issue. Candidate very cleverly brings in the issue of MRSA bacteraemia and could have gone a step further to quote the number of reported MRSA by the trust and number capped for coming year for the trust you are being interview. That would demonstrate that you have done a thorough background research about the trust and shows keenness.

Overall:
A good answer clearly explains the proper use of antibiotics and how antibiotic resistance occurs. It will also relate the question to the NHS and comment on current health news, e.g. superbugs.

60.How have technological advances changed medical practice?

This is a question related to current affairs, and your awareness of and how much you keep up-to-date with advances in the medical world. There are many ways in which technology has impacted medicine; including more efficient methods of patient record storage, endoscopy, laparoscopic surgery, the use of simulators in training and advancements in scanning equipment used. Genomic sequencing also allows the identification of particular gene mutations in a patient's DNA, which is important in diagnosing patients and also tailoring treatment to fit their particular needs.

Bad Response:

"Technology has an important role in medicine, which can be seen in how much laparoscopic surgery has taken over when operating. This allows the surgeon to operate without completely cutting a patient open and therefore minimise scarring. A disadvantage of this could be how difficult it is to use, and there may be more errors when performing this type of surgery."

Response Analysis:

The candidate has not fully described what laparoscopic surgery is, how it is performed, or the contexts or types of surgery for which it might be used. Although they have presented both an advantage and a disadvantage, they have provided incomplete arguments for both. The disadvantage argument also comes across as rather weak as it is a guess and the candidate has not taken the time to read up on or briefly research the answer – are there really more errors when performing laparoscopic surgery? The overall impression given is one of incomplete knowledge and understanding of the procedure.

Good Response:

"I think something that is gradually changing the way medicine is practised is the smartphone. There are more and more apps being developed to serve as a quick and easy way to diagnose patients, such as apps to take blood pressure and ECGs (using an attached sensor), and also to interpret the results. Another example is insulin dose-recommending calculators for diabetic patients. These devices could take a load off the number of consultations health care professionals have to deal with daily. This could also have very positive implications in poorer areas of the world where more sophisticated scanning equipment is not available. Also, video consultations via laptop or smartphone are becoming more and more popular, and serve as a good way for doctors to communicate with patients who are too far to visit or to save a patient time if they are at work or unable to travel to a clinic. The subject has even been reviewed in literature (virtual clinics), showing how important it is likely to be in the future. A possible danger of this is patients relying too much on technology rather than seeing their doctor – perhaps the use of these apps should be regulated more. Another example that I can think of the use of IT systems for safe and effective handover e.g. nerve centre"

Response Analysis:

The candidate has chosen to talk about something very current and relevant, which is having an increasing impact on the day-to-day practice of medicine. The candidate has offered some relevant examples of how the smartphone can be used in diagnosing patients (although perhaps a bit more research/detail is needed) and has mentioned how these can influence the practice of medicine. The advantages are listed, and a disadvantage is also mentioned, as well as a possible way of combating this problem. The candidate has ended the question with the "cliff hanger approach." This is as if the candidate is inviting for a follow-on question in an area the candidate knows is very proficient with!

Overall:

Technological advances are designed to improve medical practice, so in all likelihood, you will be focusing on the pros rather than cons when giving an answer. Give examples of a situation where and how these technologies can be used rather than just listing. The more recent the advancement(s) you reference, the more up-to-date with the medical world you'll seem. Some other things to talk about are the ambitious IT programme that aims to create the NHS to a spine.

61. What can you tell me about the current NHS reforms?

Background Analysis:

The biggest reforms within the NHS currently are probably the attempted transition to a '7-day NHS' and the general move towards more privatisation – the outsourcing of NHS contracts to private sector companies. This is well worth reading about and there have been dozens of articles written about this on recent times. It is also worth having a general idea of the changes that came through the Health and Social Care Act in 2012, not just for interviews but because it involved changes in the NHS that are important for anyone working in NHS. Some other changes to choose could include referral to treatment target (RTT), choose and book, 2-week target (cancer waiting time), red to greed days etc.

Bad Response:

"There have been reforms recently in the NHS that means the NHS is getting closer to being privatised. This is a bad change because privatisation means the NHS is going to become much more unfair – like in the United States where the private health care system means that some people simply cannot afford healthcare."

Response Analysis:

While it is good that this candidate identified the issue of privatisation, they did not demonstrate any deeper knowledge of the process by which this is happening or the arguments for or against the reforms beyond a somewhat simplistic level. Despite these reforms, massive differences remain between the NHS and the insurance-based system in the United States. The changes since the Health and Social Care Act (2012) extended a market-based approach to the NHS, meaning that healthcare services could be more easily provided by private companies. While this is controversial with arguments for and against the changes, the Act made no overt moves towards any insurance-based system or upturning the principle of an NHS which is free at the point of delivery to patients.

Good Response:

"The most recent reforms that are trying to be made to the NHS are about introducing a '7-day NHS'. As I understand it, this is the ambition to extend current weekday services – such as access to GPs, specialist clinics and more senior staffing – over the weekend. These changes have partially been based on statistics claiming that there is a higher mortality rate for patients admitted into hospitals on the weekend, though, there have been criticisms that the original research for this is being misrepresented. There is significant resistance to these changes with critics claiming that there is no way they can be brought in without either significantly impairing the quality of care from the NHS or spending an unaffordable amount of money on even more doctors and other NHS staff. Meanwhile, the government says it has a mandate to pursue the changes and that they will ultimately benefit patients."

Response Analysis:

This candidate has shown a good understanding of the controversy surrounding the suggested '7-day NHS' reforms while maintaining quite a balanced standpoint. It can be good to express an opinion as this shows you have really engaged with the arguments and thought about them, but make sure you can support it with good reasoning and bear in mind that the interviewer is likely to have an opinion on the matter and it could well differ from your own so try not to be dogmatic with these controversial problems.

Overall:

NHS reforms are in the news almost daily, so interviewers are likely to expect you to have shown an interest in them and be able to discuss them briefly. Some of these reforms could be controversial, so when discussing them remember to show that you appreciate that there are two sides to the argument.

62. What would you consider the bigger challenge for the NHS, diabetes or smoking?

This question asks you to evaluate two big public health challenges and contrast their impact on the NHS. We need to consider the cost incurred due to smoking & diabetes as well the ethical issues such as stigma, especially because self-inflicted diseases can be seen as a burden on the general public.

Bad Response:

"Diabetes and smoking represent both very important issues for the NHS. For this reason, cigarettes should be made significantly more expensive through the use of taxes in order to make them less attractive to buy. If cigarettes are more expensive, fewer people will buy them and, therefore, fewer people will smoke overall. The increased income of the taxes can then be used to pay for other things like roads etc. The price increase would be particularly effective as smoking is most prevalent in lower social classes who will be less able to afford buying cigarettes when they are more expensive."

Response Analysis:

This is a poor response as it is judgemental towards specific parts of the population, i.e. lower income households. This is ethically unacceptable. The answer also does not actually address the question but rather goes into detail on how to reduce smoking in a population. Whilst this is an interesting concept, it does not have much to do with the question and will not provide any benefit in the interview.

Good Response:

"Smoking and diabetes both represent major challenges to the healthcare system. They both affect a significant amount of the population and they both have significant implications for the individual's health prospects. Before addressing them in some further detail, it is important to stress that diabetes is an actual diagnosis, whereas smoking is a lifestyle choice. An additional fact to consider is the fact that diabetes is limited to the individual, whereas smoking has a significant effect on the other individual as well through passive smoking. In general, both factors represent equally great issues for the NHS, though on different levels. Whilst diabetes is a chronic disease requiring continuous treatment, smoking has implications on the future health of the individual. Due to the inherently different nature of the two issues, it is difficult to make a judgement on which one of the two is more severe."

Response Analysis:

This response is good as it considers several different aspects of the question and also provides detail about the background of the question. This is important as it shows the individual's train of thought. The latter is particularly important as the student ultimately does not make a choice between either. If pushed to choose one, you can choose either and justify your reasonings with valid arguments.

Overall:

This question is very complex and addressing the complexity is essential. Any attempt to simplify the question will ultimately cause the answer to be insufficient. In general, being aware of public health issues such as this is very important for as this demonstrates awareness of medical developments and the impacts of medical care on the individual. There is always a chance that there might be a question asking about evaluations of impact on the whole of society and common public diseases such as diabetes offer themselves for this type of question.

63. How is the nurses' role in healthcare changing?

The NHS is increasingly training nurses to do some tasks that doctors have historically performed. This gives them more responsibilities and more opportunities for training and opportunity to some becoming Nurse Practitioners; an invaluable member of the team in GP practices and hospital clinics. Nurse Practitioners typically see the less complicated patients (e.g. routine check-ups) on their own but have access to a doctor if the patient's situation is more complex than anticipated. This reduces the burden of routine appointments on doctors' workloads. Nurse Practitioners are usually well-liked by patients as their extensive experience gives them excellent interpersonal skills. Nurses also teach and help patients learn about their disease, empowering them to manage it better. Working well with nurses is absolutely essential so this question is designed to seek out any underlying prejudices against the nursing staff or misconceptions about their roles and weather you value the input from different team members.

Some examples of nurses developing specialist roles are epilepsy nurse, colostomy nurse, pain specialist, diabetes specialist nurse, nurse endoscopist etc. Being aware of the nurses' role, responsibilities and the limitation is key to responding to this question.

Bad Response:
"Nurses are being given more responsibilities to the point where they are starting to take over the doctors' jobs. This means that people will be confused about the role of doctors and will lead to patients respecting the doctors less, and there will be fewer jobs for doctors."

Response Analysis:
Firstly, as outlined below, the roles of nurses and doctors remain different (and equally important!). This answer implies (by saying that people will respect doctors less) that patients think that jobs done by nurses must be easier, i.e. that nurses are less intelligent. The answer also shows a preoccupation with commanding respect as a doctor and completely misses the mark – whilst respect can be an important asset in communication skills, the priority should always be patient care. Does the broader role of nurses improve patient care? If so, that should be the overriding conclusion.

Good Response:
"In order to deliver cost efficient service and take pressure off the busy consultants, role of the nurses is changing. Nurses are being encouraged to train to be able to take on more responsibilities and perform more procedures, therefore, freeing up the doctors to focus on tasks that nurses aren't qualified to perform. This has led to some concerns over the nurses "taking over the doctors' jobs", but in reality, whilst there is beginning to be some overlap between roles, the nurses remain responsible for the daily management of the patient whilst the doctors provide more targeted intervention. This is a good allocation of resources – nurses have excellent practical and interpersonal skills from years of experience with patients, whereas doctors have good knowledge and understanding of pathology from studying medicine.

Specialist epilepsy nurses are able to adjust dosages of anti-epileptic drugs- they act as a go between patient and doctor. This reduces the amount of time doctors need to spend per patient. We are seeing a lot more where nurses are developing skills and even becoming nurse consultant and are able to prescribe (after appropriate training and mentorship e.g. diabetes nurse consultant). Whilst there are kinks that need to be worked out, better integration between healthcare disciplines results in good result for patient safety and care."

Response Analysis:
This response shows insight into recent trends in the NHS. The candidate also shows that they understand that nurses and doctors have different and equally important roles, skills, and abilities (and they could potentially expand later upon the important parts of patient care the nurses are involved with). The candidate acknowledges that the transition has not been perfect but more importantly looks at the big picture with the patient as the focus. This shows that the candidate has their eye on the most important person (the patient) rather than getting involved in interdisciplinary squabbling.

Overall:
As working with nurses is so important, candidate who carry prejudices against nurses or who have unrealistic expectations of their roles and responsibilities will find this doesn't help them in clinical practice. With increasing overlap between roles, understanding everyone's jobs and responsibilities is essential.

Top tip: Do not ridicule anyone. NHS has a huge skill mix. Every team member is important. Recognise them. Value them.

COMMUNICATION SKILLS

64. When can doctors break confidentiality?

As doctors, we have an ethical & legal obligation to protect patient information. This improves patient-doctor trust. However, there are circumstances under which doctors are allowed to break patient confidentiality like:

➤ The patient is very likely to cause harm to others, e.g. mental health disorder, an epileptic that continues to drive
➤ Patient doesn't have the capacity, e.g. infants
➤ Social Service input is required, e.g. child abuse
➤ At request of police, e.g. if a patient is suspected of terrorism
➤ Inability to safely operate a motor vehicle, e.g. epilepsy

Bad Response:

"Doctors can break confidentiality when they believe that it will benefit the patient. Confidentiality is an important aspect of medical care because it protects private patients' information from disclosure to the public. Confidentiality can also immediately be broken if a patient who has been advised not to drive is found to be driving as it causes a risk to the public if the driver is involved in an accident."

Response Analysis:

The first sentence in this response is a little vague; ideally, the candidate would expand on how exactly breaking confidentiality would benefit the patient. For example, is it because the patient in question is in grave danger from abuse, threatened by a weapon or details about them need to be disclosed in order to catch the criminal? The question does, however, appreciate the importance of maintaining confidentiality. To state that confidentiality can be broken immediately without first consulting the patient (as in the driving scenario) and advising them of disclosing information themselves is technically inaccurate.

Good Response:

"Patients have a right to expect their doctors to maintain confidentiality and doing so is very important to maintain a good patient-doctor relationship as well as maintain the public's trust in the profession. However, there are a number of circumstances under which doctors may break confidentiality. As stated in the GMC guidance, it may be broken if it is required by the law, if it is in the public's best interest due to a communicable disease such as HIV or a serious crime needing to be reported such as a gunshot wound. It is always important to ask patients first if their information can be disclosed and to encourage them to disclose things themselves. For example, if a person with uncontrolled epilepsy is driving, we have a duty to report it to the DVLA but we must give the patient every chance to tell the DVLA about their condition themselves. In this case, we can only break confidentiality if the patient refuses to inform the DVLA so that we can protect them and the general public."

Response Analysis:

The response identifies the importance of maintaining confidentiality. The candidate nicely references an appropriate source for doctors such as the GMC to state instances in which confidentiality is broken. This shows that the candidate has read guidance that doctors are expected to know and is able to apply their knowledge to answer this question. The examples are accurate.

Overall:

It is important to be familiar with key 'hot topics' in medicine such as consent and confidentiality and to carry out a little background reading on these prior to the interview in order to provide them with accurate examples. Whilst it is true that in your training towards consultant post, these things are bread and butter for you but often, simple question like this is handled very badly. Interviewers will indeed be impressed if you understand these core concepts and their importance to medical practice. The GMC website's 'good medical practice' is a very good site to visit in order to obtain further information on these topics and others that are likely to be assessed in your interviews.

> **Top tip:** Have one or two scenarios ready when you had to break patient confidentiality. E.g. Epileptic person that continues to drive, HIV positive person wanting to withhold diagnosis from wife

65. Why is it important for doctors to be empathetic towards their patients?

This is a really important question because it tests whether a candidate truly understands and appreciates what being a consultant is about. It would be useful to have a good think about what empathy means (in particular how it differs from sympathy), and why this might be important in the doctor-patient relationship. This question is based on the idea that a patient's ideas, concerns, and expectations must be addressed with as much diligence as their clinical symptoms or disease and is an important message to convey when answering this question. As a consultant, you will need to demonstrate empathy and train your team to do so.

Bad Response:

"Medical professionals have to show empathy to depressed patients to try and cheer them up. Patients need support when they are in hospital and empathising with them will help them to get better quickly. Empathy makes patients think that I am a nice consultant, which is an important requirement in this responsible post. It also gives you a good feedback rating, which would help me in ensuring I have no problems when it is time for revalidation, and make patients like me more than my colleagues."

Response Analysis:

This response states all of the wrong reasons for the importance of empathy; additionally, it confuses the term empathy with sympathy. It fails to address any of the reasons that empathy is actually important.

Good Response:

"To me, empathy means putting oneself in the patient's shoes and imagining how things must seem from their perspective, which I believe is really important as a doctor. Firstly, empathy is essential because patient's ideas, concerns, and expectations are just as important as their clinical symptoms and must be addressed with compassion. If we imagine what the patient is going through from their point of view, we might think of new ways in which we can improve their care that may not have seemed obvious at first glance. Additionally, if someone is caring and shows that they understand how the patient is feeling, the patient is more likely to feel at ease and be open about discussing their ideas and worries, which would ultimately help to deliver better care. Overall, I think empathy helps to break down the doctor-patient barrier, making patients feel more comfortable in an otherwise seemingly daunting and unfamiliar environment."

Response Analysis:

This is a good response because it explains briefly your understanding of what empathy to the interviewers (and demonstrates that the term hasn't been confused with sympathy) and then goes on to back up this idea with examples of how it is important. It mentions a variety of reasons for the importance of empathy, and uses keywords and phrases such as "ideas, concerns, and expectations," and "compassion" which are things that interviewers are likely to be looking out for to show that candidates understand the crux of doctor-patient interactions and have thought beyond simply solving the patient's clinical problem.

Overall:

This is a really important subject for candidates to appreciate and is likely to come up in some form at the interview, usually as a follow up question (ethics/situational questions). Knowing what empathy is, and 3-4 reasons that it is important will be helpful, not only for the interview but also for future careers. Easy pitfalls with this question are confusing empathy with sympathy, thinking that empathy is something that is only used when patients are upset to cheer them up, and believing that empathy is useful for personal gains and career advancement, which should never be mentioned in an interview as a reason!

66. Tell me about a time when you showed good communication skills

Communication is a very important part of a doctor's life. Most doctors work within teams and so need to be able to effectively convey important information to many different members of staff who have different expertise as well as patients and relatives. Communication is therefore essential for an effective integrated approach to patient care. Additionally, in order to ensure that the patient's autonomy is fully utilised, the patients themselves must be fully informed of all the details of treatment plans and procedures. This often requires excellent communication skills.

Bad Response A:

"Errm, in my last locum job, I felt that the take list was poorly managed and patients were simply recorded on a piece of paper. This may at times, caused missed patients and some patients may not get seen until the next consultant ward round. I sent an email to all the SpRs that it was their responsibility to ensure patients were correctly recorded in the take list. I think this simple communication solved the problem."

Response Analysis:

The answer starts with the filler word "Erm, a poor start. It can be tough under pressure but avoid filler words. It's better to take your time and speak a bit slower if it means not using so much filler. Filling is not good communication! It gives off a tone of a lack of understanding. Moving on to the bulk of the response, the anecdote is a bit weak. This response suffers because it lacks detail and it really sells the candidate short.

This candidate has identified a situation that they had where they potentially could have made huge difference to patient care by effective communication skills. Though, the candidate suggests that they have effectively communicated with their registrar, there is no evidence to show that, hence just a view point not hard fact. Additionally, it would have been far more impressive had they said that, instead of just emailing, they spoke to different SpRs to identify the problems and worked out a solution e.g. may be a software or integrating the take list to the existing software for tracking patients. This response is thus incomplete, lacks structure, example given is poor and seems to have been given as the candidate can't think of something or they lack this, making them unattractive in the future role as consultant.

Good Response:

"In my last locum job, I felt that the take list was poorly managed and patients were simply recorded on a piece of paper. This may at times, caused missed patients and some patients may not get seen until the next consultant ward round. I spoke to different registrars who were having the same issues. I asked SpRs to choose a "Take list champion" and we both worked with the IT department to get the take list merged with the electronic patient record. Thus, all patients that were admitted to the hospital were electronically recorded and the list was saved as pdf file which was accessible from shared drive.

We shared this with different specialities, presented in grand round and various teaching activities so all team members were aware of this. This way we communicated at various levels to ensure that the patients were not missed and all were seen without compromising patient care. The take list champion also gained from this as it required motivating, convincing at different levels and learned from the experience. I felt good as I effectively coordinate my team so that everything ran smoothly. We also conducted satisfaction questionnaire survey before and 6 months after the launch of the new take list which showed significant improvement in level of satisfaction and the missed from post take datix incidents also reduced."

Response Analysis:

This candidate has demonstrated an impressive ability to identify a simple issue but serious consequences in patient care/safety, has come up with a solution which has apparently entailed communicating with individuals from many different professions (junior doctors, IT, managers). The ability to maturely communicate effectively with so many different individuals to deliver a coherent and successful end product is very impressive. Being a consultant is not always about treating patient. It required skills to identify and rectify issues.

Change is not always welcomed and this required excellent communication to get people on board to engage with an idea. The example given is apparently not just about a clinical pathway, the candidate has effectively demonstrated that they hold fundamental communication skills that are widely applicable for the rest of their life, including their future medical career.

The key is also specificity. This is a good point to ensure that the anecdote you tell is actually true! The candidate goes on to show that they did something of value and added to patient care/safety. Giving the specificity of the above response, it is believable. It's important to pull from real experience and the confidence of pulling from your actual experience will be evident in your own body language, and will yield a better outcome.

Beyond the details of the anecdote itself, this response is good because it actively highlights what the candidate actually did as far as good communication skills are concerned. The bad responses did not do this. The points about going at an appropriate pace and observing body language are absolutely essential to get across in your response because it shows that you actually know what the interviewer means by good communication skills.

Overall:

Whatever the example you use, make sure that it shows you have developed or are developing good communication skills. At the end of your example, it would then be useful if you could demonstrate an awareness of why communication is so important in your role.

Ultimately, this question is all about the details. Both the good and bad responses used similar anecdotes, but the good response has the level of detail necessary to succeed. There is, of course, a balancing act between giving enough detail to sound reliable and going so far as to become esoteric and alienate the interviewer. Crucially, it's important to highlight what actually counts as good communication skills. Don't fall into the trap of just assuming that both you and the interviewer know what good communication skills are. It's a nebulous term, so going out of your way to specify what qualities it includes is a valuable thing to do.

67. Do you think communication skills can be learned?

Effective communication is a key skill for doctors to possess. Good communication leads to more satisfying interaction with colleagues, enables better time management, and it also makes you a more effective team leader and member. Communication can be verbal and non-verbal. This means that communication skills can be fine-tuned, if not learned. We may be great at explaining things to patients in simple terms and communicating with our friends and family, but there will be certain circumstances which we may never have faced such as breaking bad news- which has its own format to approach and a skill one can be taught and improve with experience.

The number one reason for complaints in the NHS is due to poor communication. The interviewers here, therefore, want to ensure that you have had a little think about the importance of communication in clinical practice and in your role as consultant. When communication is in settings outside of patient care, it requires fine tuning by learning to avoid negative phrases, avoiding "attacking/aggressive writings in emails/letters." This comes with experience and can be learned.

Bad Response:

"Communication skills cannot be learned. It is something that an individual is either good at or not. It is not like science or maths where you can learn facts and apply them to practice. And isn't that why the interview process takes place? To see if you have the ability to communicate effectively- this should sieve out the applicants who are weak at communication and only hold on to those who show good communication skills. This then leaves you with people who only need to concentrate on developing other skills such as analytic skills and presentation skills."

Response Analysis:

Whilst it is entirely appropriate to state that communication skills cannot be learned, this candidate was rather harsh in his/her approach to answering the question and the candidate could have followed on by stating that there is scope for improvement. The candidate may, therefore, be followed up with a question asking them about why they think communication sessions are arranged for NHS staff. The counter-answer to that may become difficult.

Good Response:

*"Communication is a very hot topic in medicine and I am glad you asked me this question. I think that whilst many components of communication such as body language and eye contact are difficult to learn and be taught on, I think people can definitely improve the way they deliver information. We know that it is important to deliver information at an appropriate level to our audience. This is because we have been **taught** this. This way, we are being taught and subsequently, learn how to communicate effectively. Furthermore, whilst eye contact and body language cannot be learned, if people pick up subtle things about how we communicate non-verbally and feed this back, one is more aware of it themselves and will make a conscious effort to modify it and improve."*

Response Analysis:

This response understands the importance of communication. The candidate also provides a comprehensive answer by discussing verbal and non-verbal communication. There is an element of open-mindedness as the candidate has taken on board what the candidate has learned and the feedback received about non-verbal communication, utilising the information as a means to improve communication skills.

Overall:

Interviewers will want you to understand that communication is central in your role. They will want to know how you think/do not think communication skills can be learned. Using personal experiences where you improved/couldn't have improved on your communication skills will strengthen your answer. The BMJ has published a number of articles on communication skills and whether they can be learned and it is advisable to read some of these prior to your interview. Quoting a prestigious journal is a good way to show that you are well read.

68. How would you tell a patient they've got 3 months to live?

This is a very testing question; it tests your ability to cope well under stress. It is important that you do not panic. When you enter an interview, you should be expecting the unexpected and be broadly prepared for everything and anything! To answer this question well you will need to think logically and work through your answer step-by-step. As a senior clinician, the bucket stops with you and you are expected to know any formal protocol on how to deliver bad news to a patient. You will be teaching this to your juniors and it is important that you have the skills to do this comfortably in an empathic manner without being too emotive. You should be aware that the interviewer will be looking to see evidence of your empathy skills, your problem-solving skills and your ability to think on the spot. A good answer will be based around the keyword in the question – "tell"; i.e. how will you articulate, communicate or disclose this information?

Bad Response:

"I would ask the patient to sit down. I would then use a very serious tone of voice. I would try not to show any emotion in my facial expression and be very factual with the information I was passing onto the patient. I would not keep the patient in suspense; I would tell them as soon and as quickly as possible."

Response Analysis:

This answer is too short and not enough thought has been put into it. The candidate has not explained the intended impact of his actions of the patient. If he had, he may have realised that he would have come across as rather cold. The answer also suggests that the candidate would rush this interaction with the patient rather than taking his/her time to deliver the news. The candidate has not identified why the information he is disclosing to the patient is important and seemingly skirts around the fact that he is revealing to a patient that he/she has a terminal illness. The interviewer needs to know the candidate is able to talk about difficult issues in a mature and sensitive manner. The answer above does not demonstrate this.

Good Response:

"I would be very aware of the patient's current position; the level of awareness and understanding the patient currently has about his condition, available sources of support for this particular patient – for instance, family and friends, religious circles, specific support groups – and the current anxiety and distress the patient is feeling as a result of their poor health. I would adapt the specifics of what I would say as appropriate for an individual patient. But most fundamentally, I would use clear and simple communication and a very professional manner. I would give a thorough background explanation of what has led the doctors to reach this conclusion. I would check throughout the conversation that the patient has understood what I have said before I move onto the next point. I would openly show my empathy and sympathy to the patient by letting the patient know that I am terribly sorry that they are in this situation and by offering my support and patience, and inviting them to ask any questions they have."

Response Analysis:

The candidate shows exceptional empathy skills; they seek to understand more about the patient to understand more about how they will feel and how they can potentially cope with the information they are about to receive. The candidate understands that this consultation is a very personal and sensitive interaction between patient and doctor. This response shows awareness of the importance of good quality communication and understanding of context to help the patient make sense of what is helping them and how they can cope with this life-changing event.

Overall:

The interviewer will want to see that you realise you are doing much more than simply communicating a fact to a patient. They will want to see that you understand the significance of this information to the patient and hence the significance of the style of (well-informed) communication you use.

69. Your consultant colleague turns up on Monday morning smelling strongly of alcohol. What do you do?

Situational judgement questions aim to assess your approach to complex scenarios which you may encounter in your workplace. They are designed to test your potential across a number of competencies. In this case, this question tests your ability to deal with a colleague whom you suspect is drinking alcohol and has turned up to work smelling of alcohol. There is usually a pattern to follow when answering these questions: try to approach the person in question to gather a bit of information- are they, in fact, drinking alcohol? You may have been mistaken and it would, therefore, be wrong to take any further action. Next, you should try and explore the reason behind their behaviour- is it a transient and short-lasting event that has caused the consultant to drink? If so, hopefully there shouldn't be a long-term issue here. Thirdly, the interviewer would like to hear that you are taking steps to ensure that patients are safe. This may involve asking the consultant politely to get some rest and go home- clinical errors or prescribing errors due to alcohol consumption is dangerous. Lastly, you may want to suggest the consultant seek some help.

Bad Response:
"Smelling strongly of alcohol at your workplace is, in my opinion, unacceptable. The consultant, although a senior figure, should know better and I think his behaviour should be reported promptly. The consequences of having a drunken consultant in the clinical area are unsafe and it also tarnishes the doctors' reputation as a whole. I would therefore ask my fellow consultant colleague to have a word with the consultant and hopefully, the matter will be escalated to the medical director who can then decide the best course of action."

Response Analysis:
This candidate is rather rash in his/her approach to the situation. Firstly, there is only a suspicion that the consultant is drinking alcohol- it is thus better to sensitively explore this first before discussing the situation with anybody else. Reporting somebody without first getting the facts straight is inappropriate. Lastly, whilst you can seek help from another consultant colleague. The answer here sounds more like you are passing the buck to another person and asking him to sort the situation out rather than seeking advice and acting on the advice yourself; interviewers will appreciate you being proactive and sorting matters out yourself.

Good Response:
"This is a complex scenario. As there is only a presumption here that the consultant has been drinking (he smells of alcohol only), I would tentatively approach him and politely ask him if he has been drinking any alcohol. I would next offer to explore his behaviour by asking him what has led him to drink alcohol and be so out of control that he still smells of it when he comes into work. I would then suggest he takes the rest of the day off after ensuring his shift is covered by explaining that patient safety may be compromised if he practices medicine under the influence. Lastly, if I believe that this may be a long-term problem, I would suggest to him that he seeks further help, either by going to his GP or going to occupational health. I would also consider involving his line manager if appropriate."

Response Analysis:
This answer takes a calm and measured approach to the situation by following the 'usual' steps (mnemonic **SPITS**: Seek information, *Patient* safety, *Investigate* at your level, *Team* involvement and offer *Support*) for this type of scenario. The candidate is information gathering rather than reporting the consultant straight away. There is also an awareness that patient safety may be at risk, and the candidate provides a solution to tackle this and understands the need to be sensitive here.

Overall:
Situational judgment questions can be difficult and the key is to take a measured and calm approach to the situation. Reporting individuals straight away before attempting to resolve the situation between teams is often not the right approach, but interviewers would rather you to talk to the person in question yourself and take it from there. But remember that patient safety is the most important aspect here and if the consultant were to refuse to go home and continue seeing patients under the influence, you may then need to escalate the situation to someone more senior to you to ensure that patients are not in danger.

70. What do you think is more important, spending money on hospital beds or on community care? Why?

One of the biggest challenges in hospitals these days is the discharge of medically fit patients into the community. This is particularly relevant for the elderly that are not able to care for themselves but have no medical conditions requiring hospital care. As they cannot be discharged into an unsafe environment, it is not uncommon for patients to spend a long time in the hospital, even though there is no medical need for them to do so. This binds important hospital resources, is very expensive for the health service, and also puts the patients at risk of acquiring further morbidities, including but not limited to infections by multi-drug resistant pathogens.

Bad Response:

"Hospitals are more important than community care. Waiting times in A&E are ever increasing and this is in large part due to the overall lack of hospital beds. The provision of more hospital beds is essential in alleviating this. This is particularly true as the patients presenting to the hospital are generally ill and in need of actual medical care whereas the cases in the community are less relevant. Therefore, money should go to hospitals."

Response Analysis:

This answer fails to appreciate the connection between hospital care and community care resulting in vital shortcomings in the answer itself. It furthermore fails to appreciate the complexity of hospital admissions and presentations. Whilst it is true that some people presenting to A&E will be very unwell and needing hospital care, a proportion of people presenting will not. Effectively, it is not possible to judge one more important than the other as there is a very close interaction between both spheres.

Good Response:

"Availability of hospital beds represent a great challenge in the NHS. In the view of bursting A&E departments that are unable to find space for presenting patients, this message is particularly obvious. It would, however, be wrong to assume that a simple increase of hospital beds at the cost of community care will necessarily alleviate the problem. There is a very fluent exchange of patients between community care, in particular, care homes and hospitals. It is not uncommon for patients that are medically fit for discharge to remain in the hospital occupying beds simply because they have nowhere else to go. This, in turn, produces other issues such as increasing rates of hospital-acquired infections as well as an overall poorer long-term prognosis due to prolonged hospital stay. Not to mention the high cost associated with an occupied hospital bed. In the light of this, it is, therefore, important to spend money on the improvement of both factors: the amount of hospital beds available as well as community care."

Response Analysis:

This response is well-balanced and well-argued, providing a good overview of the complexity of the issue of hospital beds and community care. It gives a precise and justified answer and makes intrinsic sense. It also provides an additional perspective by addressing the consequences of unnecessarily prolonged hospital stays.

Overall:

A very relevant issue to be aware of, especially considering the overall limitations in availability of hospital beds in the UK in relation to the population (237/100 000 in 2011). In the prospect of ever shrinking social care budgets and increasing amounts of council budget cuts, it becomes an even more pressing issue. Furthermore, a good answer to this question demonstrates an understanding of the interaction of different levels of healthcare and the interface between these levels and the patients. Different healthcare environments have different requirements in regards to funding, but all are highly relevant for the overall delivery of care that in the end spans all levels of care provision.

71. You are doing a ward round and you notice your colleague – another consultant is doing ward round, but wearing a watch; what would you do?

This question is testing your knowledge about the on-going current issues, infection control the various policies which the NHS is implementing such as 'bare below the elbow policy'. This is also testing your skills on communication and dealing with a colleague who is in a similar position you yourself.

Bad Response:

"The consultant is my colleague and it would be very inappropriate of me to go and confront him. At some point, later on I might jokingly point out that we need to follow hospital infection policies and he should not be wearing a watch."

Response Analysis:

This response is very short, it totally overlooks the patient safety issue as well as not using the opportunities that can be used; for example, this is an opportunity to talk about governance, patient safety, policy awareness – such as infection control bare below elbow policies. This is also the opportunity to bring out topical issues e.g. anything that you may have read in the hospital report such as Clostridium difficle infection rates for the Trust or something that was mentioned in the CQC rating about the MRSA bacteraemia. All those opportunities are missed and, hence, it is a bad response.

Good Response:

"NHS Trusts are following a 'bare below elbow' policy to minimise the risk of hospital acquiring infection. I note that these infections are not only opportunistic but the risk can be minimised by the appropriate hand washing techniques, bare below elbow policies, proper isolation techniques. If I am in a situation where my consultant colleague is wearing a watch I would politely ask the consultant to have a quiet moment to politely point out that maybe he should remove the watch; offer to keep it in a locked cabinet in one of the lockers in the ward matrons office so that he can collect it later on. I would expect no 'face off' or confrontation because the consultant will also show some maturity. It is important that implementation of such policies will minimise hospital acquiring infection; we know that some of the Trusts – for example – this was an issue in our local Trust where we were slightly over the yearly allowed C. Diff. numbers. Therefore perseverance of hospital policies is of paramount importance."

Response Analysis:

This is a good response; it is not hesitant, it shows the assertiveness of the consultant, awareness about the policies as well as highlighting the issues involved about the breach of the policy. Not only is the candidate happy to go and talk to the consultant colleague, he does it politely and offers a solution about how to handle a watch by keeping it secret.

Overall:

The response is good; it includes the various topical issues as well as uses the opportunities about the CQC ratings, the NPSA different policies. Be prepared that this question can be followed on and you may be asked "Tell us about the C. diff. rate that the Trust had, what is the minimum allowed for our Trust, what did the CQC say about infection control regarding our Trust. You should have gleaned this information from the minutes of the board meetings that are publicly available or from the pre-interview visit.

72. A patient with a needle phobia needs to have blood taken but is very nervous. How would you go about persuading them to have it done?

This patient is afraid to have their blood taken although it is necessary to test their blood, perhaps to check if they have an infection; if their body is responding well to an infection; if they have anaemia etc. This is a test of your ability to remain calm and empathic towards a patient and not lose your patience, and also your ability to communicate and persuade. It is important to be able to ensure patients are fully informed when it comes to what kind of treatment they should receive but also to acknowledge you can't force a patient to undergo treatment as they need to provide consent.

Bad Response:
"I would tell the patient that the procedure is absolutely necessary for them to get the care they need and that it won't hurt very much. I would tell them that even little children go through it and end up fine so it can't be that bad! I would tell them it would be best just to do it now and get it over with."

Response Analysis:
The candidate is quite pushy in convincing the patient to have the blood test. The candidate tries to reassure the patient, although saying the procedure doesn't hurt 'very much' is subjective and not very helpful. Also, the comment about children going through the procedure may be reassuring to some, although it could also be interpreted as belittling to the patient, implying that they are acting worse than a little child in refusing to have blood taken. The last point about just getting it over and done with is not bad, although it is phrased in a way that is rather pressurising to the patient.

Good Response:
"I would start by asking the patient why they are afraid – sometimes verbalising fears helps rationalise them. Also, it is important for a patient's fears to be listened to and not dismissed. I would then explain why the blood test is needed and how the hospital staff can't provide the best care possible without the blood test. I would say that it would be over very soon and I take the utmost care over the procedure – if I wasn't the one doing it, I would say I would be there the whole time to offer support if needed."

Response Analysis:
The candidate starts by just talking to the patient about their fears, showing empathy towards them and taking them seriously. The situation is explained to the patient in a way that isn't pushy or coercive, with attempts made to reassure the patient. Further empathy and care are shown in how the candidate promises to do the procedure as best they can, as well as willing to stay and offer support if the patient needs it; making them feel valued as a patient.

Overall:
Show empathy and kindness to the patient and persuade them without being pushy. Don't belittle their fears but talk to them about it and help reassure them. If you bully the patient into it and they have a bad experience, they may not return for future treatment.

73. You're on a busy A&E call with your registrar who tells you that he feels 'fed up and just wants to end it all'. You know he has gone through a difficult divorce and is on anti-depressants. What would you do?

This is a situational question which aims to assess your ability to take the correct steps to effectively deal with a complex scenario. Approach this situation like the other situational questions in this booklet (see previous question): discuss the person in question's feelings, ensure patient safety is maintained, and advise the person to seek help.

Bad Response:

"This is a rather tricky question- I'm not sure exactly what I would do- perhaps I would like to ask my fellow colleagues what they would do if they were in my shoes. I am quite concerned that the registrar wants to 'end it all', but it is a busy A+E shift. I think he should have called in sick if he didn't feel like working today. I could speak to the consultant about him because he is in charge and, therefore, should be able to deal with the situation effectively. Or perhaps his medication has not been titrated enough? Maybe I can advise him to increase the dose of his medication and see if that makes him feel better?"

Response Analysis:

It is important to support your colleagues through difficult times and act compassionate towards them, just like you would with any patient. Therefore, try to listen to them and help them out rather than worry about how busy A+E is. Whilst asking fellow colleagues for advice is good practice, it may be that the registrar has come to you in confidence and would not want you to discuss his situation with others. Also, remember that it is better for you to suggest for the registrar to raise the issue with their clinical/educational supervisor too, consultant rather than you raising it- the registrar will be in a much better position to explain his/her situation than you will. The risk here is that again that you may come across as "passing the buck" hence this should be followed with clarification. It is dangerous of you to ask him to increase the dose of his medication- this should be left to the person who prescribes the medication, as they will have information about his other medical conditions and know if it is indeed safe to increase the dose. In this way, it may have been more appropriate to ask the registrar to seek help from his/her own doctor.

Good Response:

"This is a difficult situation but this is how I would approach it. I would firstly suggest to the registrar to move to a quieter room to explore his feelings further. Before doing this, I would ensure there is adequate staff cover on A&E and inform the nurses of our temporary absence. From the scenario, it seems as though his low mood has been poorly controlled on the current medication and I would, therefore, advise him to book an appointment to see his GP. Furthermore, I would advise him to discuss his issues and concerns with his educational supervisor, as he will be experienced in dealing with pastoral care issues. He should also see his GP or get an appointment with our occupational help. I would also point out the confidential support line from BMA or counselling service from the trust."

Response Analysis:

This answer demonstrates a good understanding of the necessary steps to deal with a complex scenario. It shows that it is important to discuss the registrar's feelings with him, not only to provide colleague support, but also to understand how severe the low mood is in order to establish whether he is able to continue with work and not compromise patient safety. It also nicely highlights that communicating with the nurse and ensuring the shift is covered is very important. The answer also provides longer term management options and offers the registrar further advice on who to turn to for further help. It also demonstrates your awareness of different resources/help available to people in this situation.

Overall:

Situational judgment questions will be difficult and the key is to take a measured and calm approach to the situation. Try not to discuss sensitive issues with your peers but rather try and discuss it with the registrar. If you cannot find a solution, then ask him/her to escalate to the consultant in charge. Remember, patient safety is very important here and if the registrar is too depressed to work, he/she will need to step out of the clinical area. Lastly, remember there are a number of people in the hospital which are present to help doctors with these types of issues.

74. You are faced with a patient's angry relatives. The patient is sleeping poorly and complains staff are ignoring her; she is very tearful. What do you do?

Sometimes hospitals can fail in their care and complaints are made. This is more common than you think and a normal part of working in the NHS. Lack of time and attention paid to patients means that serious mistakes can be made. Medical staff may not have enough time to deal with them so patients' full medical and emotional needs may not be met. Patients are left in a high state of anxiety because staff do not talk to them enough. Patients can be very tearful after surgery and they need emotional support and staff need the time to deliver that.

It is important to take a holistic approach to patient management (this mean developing the whole person including physical, emotional, mental, and, at times, spiritual); there is a whole person sitting there - not just a medical condition. It's also easy to forget that patients frequently suffer from numerous medical problems and that treating one of them might exacerbate the other.

However, hospitals are under huge pressure to deliver a service. Pressures include understaffing, an increasing number of inpatients and emergency admissions, and the financial constraints on the NHS. Hospitals often struggle to cope with the increased number of elderly admissions, especially in winter. The key skill needed for dealing with angry patients or relatives is communication. It is important to listen to concerns and receive feedback to improve future service.

Bad Response:
"I would apologise profusely and make time to spend with the patient. "I can understand why the relatives were angry. However, I would explain that the staff are very busy and would assist the patient as soon as they were available."

Response Analysis:
In the first answer, the candidate does not understand the workings of the NHS. To simply say they would "make time" misses the complex nature of the situation. Doctors are often time-pressured and carving out time is not that easy. The second answer is almost the opposite. It is likely to anger the relatives. The lack of apology and the rush to defend the service gives an impression of lack of empathy. Empathy is an essential quality in a doctor and it is important to acknowledge and address the relatives' concerns.

Good Response:
"Good communication skills are key to fulfilling a doctor's role. This includes listening. I would first listen to the relatives concerns and try and find out more about the situation – is the patient more concerned about the lack of attention or the reduced sleep? I would then work with the relatives and patient to address the patient's primary concern – partnership between healthcare professionals and patients is important in order to produce a patient centred culture in the NHS."

Response Analysis:
This answer is very well constructed. It begins by very quickly getting to the point of the question – interviewers want to know about your communication skills. By acknowledging this early, the interviewers know you are aware of the key issue in this question. The candidate also shows a caring and reflective nature by realising that there may be more than one reason for the patient's emotional state ("is the patient more concerned about the lack of attention or the reduced sleep?"). Using the phrase "partnership between healthcare professionals and patients", shows the candidate is aware of the need for patient involvement in their healthcare which is essential in the modern-day NHS.

Overall:
A good answer will show empathy and showcase your communication skills. It is important to remember that healthcare professionals work together with patients to deliver optimum care.

75. You are on call and an elderly patient comes to you saying they are suffering and want to end their life, and they have heard of a place in Holland where they can do this. They want your help to refer them. What would you do?

When approaching this question, you need to be aware of several things. Firstly, you should understand what euthanasia is the act of deliberately ending a person's life to relieve suffering. Secondly, you should be aware that euthanasia is illegal under English Law, hence, you cannot advise or help patients in ending their life. Thirdly, regardless of whether you know the previously mentioned facts, your main focus should be on the fact that you have a patient in front of you who is considering ending their life; thus, they need serious help. As a doctor, your role should be to protect and promote the health of patients with a focus of ensuring a good quality of life for all patients.

Bad Response:

"I would express my sympathy for the patient and try to understand how they are feeling. I would listen to them and try to dissuade them from carrying on with their intended plan. If I were unable to change their mind, I would make it clear that they still have a full right to decide and I must agree with whatever they decide to go ahead with. Hence, should they still wish to end their life, and though I disagree with euthanasia, I would write the referral letter to the clinic in Holland."

Response Analysis:

This answer involves being empathetic but still referring them or giving advice on how to access the facility in Holland. Many candidates make the mistake of going through some initial steps of trying to dissuade the patient, but then stating that it's the patient's decision at the end of the day and you have to agree with what they wish to do, hence, would refer them to the service in Holland. Whilst this would apply to many other situations, in terms of end of life care, due to the law, you cannot refer them to the service in Holland. This answer is poor because the candidate is not aware of the law for euthanasia.

Good Response:

"I would attempt to explore the issues around why the patient wishes to end their life whilst respecting their privacy. I would try to understand and empathise with the patient whilst remaining sensitive and sympathetic. I would make it clear to the patient what my role and capacity is, and ensure they are aware that I am not legally allowed to offer any advice or referrals regarding this. However, I would make it clear to the patient that there are other options that may improve their quality of life such as pain-alleviating medications or referring them to specialists such as counsellors/pain management team. I would state that I'd be willing to work with them and I would treat the patient with respect and try to gain their trust. I would end the consultation reviewing what we've discussed and offer to refer them to a counselling service and arrange a follow-up appointment if they are willing."

Response Analysis:

When answering this question, it involves you being aware of the law on euthanasia. You are expected to know this in your position. This answer involves being empathetic, considerate and aiming to understand the reasons behind the patient's feelings whilst making it clear that you are not allowed to refer them to the facility in Holland.

Overall:

In summary, in questions regarding difficult or sensitive issues such as end of life, it is always important to realise and think about what you can do in the moment to help the patient, i.e. aim to relieve suffering and increase their quality of life. Realise that you have a patient in front of you who needs help and act sensitively and considerately. It is wise to learn about the laws regarding topics such as euthanasia, abortion, and disclosure of patient information as these are likely to be asked about in interviews, as they are very topical.

76. You were minding your neighbour's dog when it ran away, got hit by a car and died. How do you break the bad news?

This question may appear to be slightly out of sync with consultant interviews but that is not the case. This is to see how you are able to handle difficult situations as well as being able to admit to your mistakes and deal with the consequences. You are likely to have patients who are angry/upset at a mistake you have made. Also, you may have to explain to someone that a relative has died while under your care. It is a test of your empathy and ability to communicate. Some trusts now adopting OSCE style interviews where you are in a role-play situation where an actor will play your neighbour.

Your neighbour is likely to be angry/upset; make sure you are as tactful as possible when speaking to them. It is important to remain calm; never say "I understand how you feel" unless you actually do, as this can anger people further. Don't be too blunt as this is fairly heavy news, but break it as gently as you can.

The answers below are just guidelines; in the case of role play, there will obviously be a dialogue with the actor or with the interviewer if they ask you to role play the situation with them. Otherwise, you would just have to relate how you *would* take on the situation.

Bad Response:
"I would try and say as calmly as possible that her dog had died. I would say that I did the best I could but the dog ran away from me when I wasn't looking. I would offer to help buy my neighbour a new pet to replace the old one I was partly responsible for losing. If she got angry, I wouldn't shout back but would keep quiet and say that I understand. I would stay with her until she had stopped crying."

Response Analysis:
The candidate does not fully accept the blame, saying they are 'partly' responsible and partly blaming the situation on the dog. Although they perhaps think they have come up with a solution to the situation, the candidate shows very little tact in offering to buy their neighbour a new pet when their old one has just died! Saying "I understand" does also not necessarily show empathy – the neighbour may get very angry ("No you don't! How could you understand?"). This phrase is, therefore, best avoided unless you actually have been through the situation yourself.

Good Response:
"First, I would make sure she was sitting down. Then I would try and break the news to her slowly so she could prepare herself: 'Mrs Jones, I'm afraid I have some bad news. It's about your dog. When I wasn't looking, he got hit by a car.' Mrs Jones is likely to be angry or very upset; I would admit that it was my fault as I was responsible for looking after him and that I feel terrible about it. I would tell her I had stopped the driver and gotten his details if I could have, and I would ask if there was any way I could make up for it, e.g. by helping with the gardening for a month. I would ask her if she needed anything right then, such as a cup of tea, though, if she just wanted me to leave her alone, I would understand."

Response Analysis:
Shows foresight and prepares the situation well by making sure the neighbour is sitting down. The neighbour is prepared for the bad news rather than being told bluntly, showing empathy. The mistake is admitted to rather than passed off, showing the candidate is not afraid to take responsibility. A sense of actually caring and a real desire to deal with the situation is shown in chasing the driver up and in offering to help in some other way to make up for this mistake. Kindness is shown in offering a cup of tea, but the candidate is not pushy in their need to be forgiven, understanding that how the neighbour feels is more important.

Overall:
Be tactful and empathic, showing care for your neighbour. Admit to your mistake and try and come up with a solution to the problem (that isn't buying a new pet!). Work your own experience in if relevant to show empathy ("my pet died last year and I know how devastating it can be").

77. If you had a patient who only spoke a foreign language, how could you improve communication with them to ensure they had a good understanding of your explanations?

This question is examining your ability to take initiative and be aware that each patient is individually unique and has different needs. When approaching this question, you should acknowledge the fact that patients who speak another language may require more assistance and help to ensure that they reach an equal level of understanding as an English-speaking patient. Think of a variety of ways to help the patient. Many cities in the UK are home to people from a range of ethnic backgrounds, especially in cities such as London, hence it is important to demonstrate the ability to communicate with all patients. Communication skills are very important in medicine and often, medical interviewers will try to examine your ability to demonstrate good communication skills.

Bad Response:

"I would speak in very slow English to see if they can understand the basics of what I am saying. If this does not work, I would request for the patient to come back with someone who spoke English if possible so that I could explain everything to this other person to ensure the patient received all the necessary information. Similarly, if there was a doctor fluent in the specific language, I would try to transfer the patient to this doctor."

Response Analysis:

This answer involves attempting three different methods in trying to improve communication with the patient. Whilst some are good suggestions, most of the options involve trying to utilise someone else to improve the communication. Whilst beneficial, the use of translators has been shown to reduce rapport built up between doctors and patients. It would be beneficial to suggest other methods that also involve yourself. Furthermore, sending the patient home and telling them to return with someone who is English speaking shows poor commitment and determination, and also it may jeopardise the patient's health and decrease their trust with you as a doctor.

Good Response:

"Patients who cannot speak English may not receive the same quality of care as those that do speak English. It may affect the doctor-patient relationship if the doctor is unable to communicate with the patient. I would request the help of a translator, but ensure that I take an active role in still trying to build rapport with the patient by using visual cues for example, and with the help of the translator, finding a way to check the patient's understanding such as showing a 'thumbs up'. This would allow me to create somewhat of a relationship with the patient to ease their comfort." I would also try and keep additional time for this consultation as the use of a translator increases the overall time needed for a satisfactory discussion. There will also be times when a translator is not readily available and the only satisfactory option available will be the use of language line.

Response Analysis:

Though similar to the poor response, this response suggests several methods involving the doctor such as finding a way to check the patient's understanding or using visual cues. The answer also starts off by stating the effects of language barriers between patients and doctors and their awareness of the difficulties language barriers can pose. This answer is better as the candidate tries to build rapport with the patient and make them feel more comfortable.

Overall:

This question aims to test your creativity and patience with patients. This kind of scenario may be commonly encountered as a practicing doctor in various cities in the UK and abroad of course. By suggesting a variety of ways to help in improving communication with patients who cannot speak English, you will demonstrate your ability to take initiative and consider the fact that patients may have different needs.

78. What do you think about the use of statistics when discussing treatment options with patients?

This question has no right or wrong answer. These kinds of questions are asked to test your ability to create a balanced argument by looking at both sides of a question, for and against, and coming to your own conclusion. You will not be marked down for your opinion as long as you can show an ability to rationalise and think from different viewpoints.

Bad Response:

"I think the use of statistics when discussing treatment with patients is good as they give the patient an approximate idea of the success of various treatment options or the chances of risks occurring. Giving statistics to patients makes options easily understandable and comparable. Without statistics, patients may understand the use of phrases such as 'very good' or 'high risk' differently. Therefore, I think the use of statistics is beneficial and necessary when discussing treatment options with patients."

Response Analysis:

This answer discusses reasons for the beneficial use of statistics when discussing treatment with patients. The reasons are valid and good, however, a balanced argument has not been demonstrated, and no points against the use of statistics have been stated. It would be a better answer if a balanced argument was created and points for and against the use of statistics were discussed.

Good Response:

"There are several reasons why the use of statistics when discussing treatment with patients may be beneficial. Firstly, they give the patient an approximate idea of the success of various treatment options or the chances of risks occurring. Giving statistics to patients makes options easily understandable and comparable. Without statistics, patients may understand the use of phrases such as very good 'or' high risk differently. However, there are some reasons against the use of statistics. Firstly, patients may take the statistics literally. If a patient is told that their treatment has a 90% success rate, they may be certain that their treatment will work. However, they may be less aware of the fact that there is still a slight chance of treatment failure. Using statistics may give patients a false sense of hope or worry. Overall, I think the use of statistics is beneficial for patients as it gives an approximate idea of success or risk, however, doctors should ensure patients are aware that statistics may not guarantee certainty."

Response Analysis:

This answer is much better as it demonstrates an ability to create a balanced argument. Though the candidate has their own opinion, they mention several points for and against the use of statistics when discussing treatment options with patients, and then conclude with their own opinion. This demonstrates the ability of the candidate to rationalise and think from various viewpoints. The reasons for and against the argument are also valid and well thought of.

Overall:

In summary, in any interview, it is common to get asked questions that require your own opinion about a topic or ethical scenario. Interviewers tend to look for your ability to generate points for and against a topic, as well as demonstrate your ability to form an opinion. It is common in the practice of medicine to have to think from different viewpoints and answering a question in the structure mentioned above would show the interviewer that you are capable of this.

79. Whilst on call, a 16-year-old patient comes in, accompanied by her mother. You wish to speak to the patient alone as part of the consultation, however, the mother refuses to leave. What do you do about this?

When treating children, the majority of the time you will have to also communicate with their families and interact with them as they may play a key role in their care and decision-making. A question like this may be asked to test your ability to act politely but, in the patient's, best interest too. In medicine, you may be faced with difficult circumstances where you may be worried about being rude or offending someone, with both patients and relatives of patients. It is important to find a balance between being polite and also doing what you believe is right for the patient with their best interests in mind.

Bad Response:
"I would ask the patient what their own opinion would be, whether they would like their mother to leave the room or not. If the patient wishes for her mother to leave the room and her mother still does not comply, I would tell the mother that even if the mother refuses, her daughter has the right to be consulted alone and that I am suggesting this because I think it would be beneficial for the patient, in their best interest.

Response Analysis:
This answer is poor, firstly because it involves asking the young patient what they would want. Though this can be beneficial, if the patient is withholding information by saying they would like their parent to leave the room, it may draw attention to this, hence they may refrain from agreeing with their parent leaving. It may put the patient in an uncomfortable position. Also, the way in which the mother is dealt with, by forcing her to leave may create a bitter relationship with the family, especially if there are other children in the family and this may deter the mother from returning for further management.

Good Response:
"In a calm manner, I would suggest that according to standard protocol, I would like to see the patient alone. I would say that I am simply following protocol and this is not unusual with patients of this age and that I believe it is in their best interest. I would allow the mother to discuss her concerns with me about leaving the room and offer her the chance of also having a separate discussion afterwards to allow her to discuss her own concerns about her daughter's health. To prevent this from happening again, I would begin my future consultations by telling patients of a specific age and their parents about the standard structure of consultations with a joint discussion to begin with, followed by a separate discussion with the patient and then with the parent alone should they wish."

Response Analysis:
This answer is much better as it shows the ability of the candidate to be polite whilst taking initiative and simply stating that it is standard protocol with patients of this age to be seen alone as well as with their parents, should they wish. Offering the mother, a chance to be seen alone is also a good idea as it shows concern for both the patient and the parent. This answer finds a good balance between being polite and doing what you believe is right for the patient.

Overall:
In summary, when asked these types of questions, it is always important to demonstrate politeness and avoid actions that may damage rapport built between the patient/parent and the doctor. It is important to acknowledge that this is in the best interest of the patient and that no offence is intended to the parent.

80. You are a doctor and your patient requests to be seen by another doctor instead for an unspecified reason. What do you do?

According to the NHS, unless you require urgent or emergency treatment, the patient has the right to be able to see any consultant-led team, or be treated in a specific hospital of their choice for a procedure (provided the team provides this treatment). This choice is offered at the point of referral and is a legal right. If the patient does not wish to be seen by a particular doctor, then they can choose to be seen by another. This question is asked to assess how well you approach the scenario and whether you are able to handle the situation in the most professional manner possible. It's important not to take their refusal personally.

Bad Response:
"Firstly, if I have been assigned as the doctor to a particular patient then I would have to explain to the patient that I am their doctor and they must be seen by me. However, I would make sure I understand why the patient wants to be seen by a different doctor in the first place."

Response Analysis:
The statement is factually incorrect and is not the best way of handling the situation. The patient has a right to be seen by another doctor and you must respect their wishes. If they have been referred from A&E, then this may not be possible and the answer would somewhat apply. However, in other circumstances, e.g. wards and clinics, this is not the case. The only redeeming quality of this answer is trying to understand the reasons for the patient wanting to see a different doctor.

Good Response:
"It is my understanding that the patient has the right to choose their consultant-led team and the hospital in which they receive their treatment, given that this treatment is provided by that team. If a patient was referred to me from A&E, I would have to explain to the patient why their request would not be possible. However, I would try and understand the reasoning for why they would like to change doctors and address their concerns. Additionally, I would ask whether there is anything I can do to make them feel more comfortable. If they have been referred to me from their GP, then I would once again try and understand their reasoning but oblige their request and ask a colleague (my consultant) to examine the patient instead."

Response Analysis:
This is a much more in-depth response and has a good insight into the rights of a patient. It also gives an example of a diplomatic method of handling the situation. The bad response involved stating that you would understand their reasoning, but the good response has a much more *active* approach and attempts to address their concerns. The ultimate solution, in this case, is to ask a consultant to see the patient instead as this is what the patient requested. These sorts of questions have a scenario and must be approached in three steps: action, reason, and outcome.

Overall:
The important part of this question is to address the patient's concerns in an active manner. Simply stating your action without a reason and why you chose it is insufficient and requires further depth. What distinguishes between a good and bad answer is not only what you say, but how you say it. The bad response is blunt and lacks empathy. On the other hand, the good response promotes an element of understanding (by asking what the problem is) as well as addressing the problem if it cannot be rectified.

81. A leukaemia patient is refusing stem cell treatment on religious grounds. Without the treatment, he has a 20% chance of survival. How would you use your communication skills to deal with this situation?

Paternalistic medicine (the attitude that the doctor always knows best) is falling out of favour. It's important to recognise that sometimes, certain lifestyle decisions are even more important to patients than their own health. It would be inappropriate to dismiss these choices even though the doctor's focus is on health. From a communication skills perspective, this question is asking you to demonstrate creativity in how you would use your own interpersonal skills to try to resolve the situation. Reaching a compromise between the patient's values and the physician's goals is a frequent conundrum in medicine, so being able to listen to the patient and figure out what is most important to them is an absolutely essential skill.

Bad Response:
"I would override his refusal by getting a court order as he clearly lacks the capacity to make a rational decision about his own care. Therefore, I should act in his best interests as I know from my medical training what is best for the patient, and it would be irresponsible of me not to do my best to treat him."

Response Analysis:
Whilst this at first seems like a good answer, the response shows a lack of willingness to engage with the patient on their own terms. The court order is unlikely to lead to treatment being enforced either, especially if the patient has the capacity and is over 18. Whilst it is indeed true that doctors should try to do the right thing for their patients, this paternalistic view would be frowned upon in interviews as it assumes that the treatment is what is best for the patient overall. This opinion suggests that the patient has a 'problem' to be 'fixed', rather than a complex combination of ideas, concerns, needs, and expectations. For example, this patient may suffer severe psychological distress from being forced to act against his beliefs. Therefore, is the stem cell treatment really the best option for his health?

Good Response:
"I would firstly understand the religious grounds behind his refusal. If there are conflicting opinions within his religion, it might be worth asking a religious representative (e.g. Chaplain or Rabbi) to visit him and discuss his options sensitively. If there is genuine concern that the patient lacks capacity, there may be grounds for going to the court to get permission to treat him. However, at the end of the day, respect for patient autonomy must be paramount. If the patient has capacity and refuses the treatment, we must support his decision and instead treat any symptoms and problems he may have as a result of the refusal of treatment."

Response Analysis:
This is a good response. The first part demonstrates a desire to understand the patient's point of view, an open mind to learn about different cultures and backgrounds, and a willingness to use communication (even via a third party) to work through problems and issues. The second part demonstrates knowledge of the process of consent for minors, but interviewees wouldn't be expected to have an in-depth knowledge of the laws and processes involved in this. The third part of the response is the most important point – respect for the patient's decision also involves treating any problems they may have as a result of their (informed, consented) decisions. This is an essential aspect of medical care that many doctors struggle with.

Overall:
Being sensitive to the patient's motivations and concerns is an important part of being a doctor. This sort of question makes sure that the interviewee has the right attitude towards care that is expected of a modern doctor, and that they understand that 'acting in the patient's best interests' and giving the most efficacious treatment are not necessarily the same thing. It's also important to recognise that if a treatment is rejected, the doctor should give their best efforts to support the patient medically through other means, even if the patient experiences problems as a result of having rejected the therapy.

82. What is more important for a doctor– good communication skills or good clinical skills?

A doctor must, of course, be equipped with both communication skills (e.g. bedside manner) and clinical skills (e.g. phlebotomy). This question is asked to make sure that the candidate understands why both sets of skills are important – the decision made doesn't really matter as long as the response is thoughtful and appropriate. As with any question, a knee-jerk response (particularly one that comes across as lacking insight) shows bad listening skills, so consider both sides of the question carefully. Use this opportunity to show that you can carefully consider a question without immediately disregarding certain points. The temptation is to immediately conclude that clinical skills are the most important, but it's worth considering why good communication skills may be even more important, and in which situations.

Bad Response:

"Good clinical skills are more important; communication skills won't fix medical problems."

Response Analysis:

This response shows a lack of understanding of the role of communication and potentially belies poor bedside manner. Good communication skills can be an essential part of treatment – for example, over half of prescribed medication is not actually taken in the manner prescribed. Ensuring the patient understands why they are taking their medication can often produce a sudden improvement in their blood pressure. The short and blunt answer also shows a closed mind – the candidate hasn't taken the time to step back and reflect on the question before answering. Thinking about the question is an essential skill for a doctor. If an answer such as this is given, the interviewer may prompt the interviewee to reflect on the role of communication skills as a follow-up question.

Good Response:

"Good clinical skills are obviously required to diagnose the problem and treat the patient. However, communication is also essential as about 75% of a diagnosis is made from the clinical history, which relies on the quality of communication with the patient – for example, a clinical examination can't tell you about the patient's family history of a genetic syndrome. Without good communication, the patient may be non-compliant with medication, meaning that despite good clinical skills, the patient would still not get better. Sometimes symptoms that defy diagnosis can be resolved with good communication skills, such as in the case of Functional Syndrome, where psychological issues manifest as physical symptoms – in the case of this disease, neurological symptoms (which can be severe) can be cured through psychological therapy."

Response Analysis:

This answer successfully shows not only the value of both skills, but also discusses how they relate to each other and how communication sometimes succeeds where clinical skills fail – an important and often overlooked point, even by qualified doctors. Non-compliance is also a huge problem as discussed above. The examples given are very insightful and show off some good knowledge of the diagnostic and treatment processes.

The candidate could then nominate which skill they think is overall more important – but again, reiterate that both skills are essential in a doctor. By addressing both parts of the question, the candidate demonstrates good listening and analysis skills in addition to however they have actually answered the question.

Overall:

In conclusion, an excellent answer to this question can be achieved by playing the skills off against each other to show how they interact and are both essential. The question also tests the knowledge of some underlying aspects of holistic care of the patient, and recognition that 'fixing' the physical symptoms may not be enough in all circumstances. Additional knowledge of situations in which communication skills become more important than clinical skills adds an extra 'edge' to the answer.

83. You are on call Consultant and an elderly lady attends the A/E with osteoarthritis. She explains that she feels her current course of prescribed medication is not effective and her friend has recommended herbal remedies that she would like to try instead of her prescribed medication. How would you respond?

This question tests for effective communication skills, and variants of this frequently crop up. It's important to remember that how you convey your message is just as important as what you say.

Bad Response:

"Don't be silly now, this herbal stuff doesn't work at all. You're far better off sticking to the medication you've been prescribed. If you don't like it, we can try something else, but it's pointless spending money on this kind of stuff. You'll probably feel a bit better at first, but it's just a placebo effect. Whoever tried to sell you this is taking you for a fool. They're just preying on your vulnerability."

Response Analysis:

This response is a situation where the candidate is literally speaking their mind. The individual points themselves aren't wrong, but the way they're being conveyed is poor. Saying "Don't be silly now" isn't a good start. It sounds patronizing, which is exactly what medical professionals must try to avoid. We want our patients to see us as their equals, that way they can confide in us without fear of being judged so they can be honest with us. This is what we mean when we talk about moving away from the medical paternalism that dominated the last century of medicine. It also trivializes the patient's concerns. This patient probably wasn't making this decision on a whim, but rather had taken the time to think about this before approaching you. The fact that she's asking you as opposed to just neglecting your treatment shows that she genuinely believes this may be of benefit to her, and by trivializing her concerns you undermine any respect she may have had for you. The rest of the response actually has good underlying points, but poor delivery. It lacks any sense of empathy for the patient's situation and comes across as being short with her. A lot of this is to do with how it's delivered, but generally, a more considerate response is ideal.

Good Response:

"I would try to explore the reasons for trying the herbal medicine. "Well, what seems to be the issue with your current medication?" "If you're willing to try another treatment, we can help with that." If she seems adamant that she wants to pursue the homeopathic remedies, it's important to address this directly. "Why do you believe this treatment will work?" In response to her concerns, an explanation of evidence-based medicine is useful. Explain that our drugs are tried and tested. We know with a fair degree of certainty that these drugs are relatively safe and do work, however, that safety isn't guaranteed with these alternative treatments. We can keep an eye out on her prescribed medications to ensure there's no conflict, but we can't do that with the alternative therapies because we don't know what's in them. Our concern is finding the right combination of medications to make her feel better. The herb provider is only trying to get her to buy as many herbs as possible. Finally, if I still haven't convinced her and she takes the herbs, she should still come in regularly for appointments to make sure things aren't dangerously wrong."

Response Analysis:

This is a good response for a few reasons. It comes across as far more empathetic with probing questions showing that you've listened. Notice that the core message is the same as in the bad response, but rather than being short with the patient, this response takes the time to actually explain why our drugs work and doesn't trivialise the patient's legitimate concerns. The final remarks about coming in regardless are also important to prevent the patient from becoming disillusioned with modern medicine.

Overall:

This question actually represents a common scenario you may have already encountered in real life. It's important to have a good response here and keep in mind that situations like this are increasing in frequency, at least partly due to the profession moving away from medical paternalism and the internet increasing patient access to information.

84. You are called to an urgent situation. A patient is angry and is violently threatening the nursing staff. How might you calm this angry patient down?

This question focuses on how you can use your communication skills on the spot and under pressure to bring a difficult situation to a positive conclusion.

Bad Response:

"There are several things that can be done to calm down an angry patient. Firstly, you could use communication techniques to show that you are not a threat. Secondly, you could use hospital security. Finally, you could explain to the patient that they should calm down as it will not benefit them to be angry. People often fail to realise that their anger only acts as a detriment to the care they might receive in hospital, so it is necessary to explain this to them."

Response Analysis:

This answer is flawed in many ways. Firstly, the question asks you to put yourself into the situation, so it makes for a significantly stronger answer if it is delivered in the 1ˢᵗ person. Secondly, the points made are very weak. In questions that involve dealing with some kind of difficult patient, it is paramount that you put yourself in the patient's shoes and try and understand their emotions. Omitting to do this shows a lack of communication skills. In addition, this answer only talks in vague terms and doesn't describe what the student would actually do/say.

Good Response:

"The most important thing that must be achieved in this situation is to assess what is causing the patient to act in such a way. Is there something they are worried about? Something they are scared about? Or do they think that some kind of wrong has been done to them? To do this, it will be necessary to begin an effective dialogue with the patient. It is crucial that I give off a calm and confident persona both through speech and through body language. For similar reasons it is also key that the patient knows who I am, so I would be sure to introduce myself and explain why I had been called. For these reasons, I would begin by saying: "Hi, I'm Dr Brown, Consultant on call, I understand that there are a few things that you're not happy about. Could you tell me a little bit more about these so that I might be able to help?"

I would make sure that I did not stand in a way that would block the exits and would check that the patient did not have some kind of weapon before I went any closer. If he did have a weapon, I would contact hospital security not only to ensure my own safety, but also for the safety of staff and patients. Upon initiating a dialogue, I would constantly remind the patient that we were there primarily to help the patient and that he/she could leave at any time. After finding out the reason for the angry outburst, I would seek to solve this issue. I would keep in mind that the first concern that the patient raised might be something that was actually mundane which could be masking the real issue."

Response Analysis:

This is a very strong answer. It makes key points and covers all key bases including; identifying the cause of the anger, identifying the need to protect yourself, and ensuring that you identify yourself to the patient. A strong answer should include all of these. Furthermore, the answer uses the first person and illustrates the points with a demonstration of what would actually be said.

Overall:

In questions like this, it's essential to demonstrate that you can put yourself in a patient's shoes and can think on the spot about how to deal with any situation that requires your communication skills.

85. What issues might arise when using a translator to mediate a patient consultation, and as a doctor, how might you overcome these issues?

This question asks about a part of medicine that is rarely discussed but is of increasing importance to clinical medicine in this country. 'Translators', in this case, could mean official in-hospital translators or could also include multilingual family members who are used for the purposes of translation. Make sure you define this in your answer.

Bad Response:

"It is bad to use a translator in a consultation. For example, the translator might not be able to translate things fully and so information will be missed. Also, time might be wasted trying to find the translator in the first place and this is especially important for busy doctors. There is a chance that the translator might not know medical terminology and so could struggle to relay all the correct information between the patient and doctor."

Response Analysis:

This is a terrible response for several reasons. Firstly, there is very little structure to the answer. The opening is weak, there is then a list of points that are poorly illustrated, and there is no conclusion that brings the points together at the end. Finally, this candidate has made the grave error of not answering both parts of the question. This is a mistake that is often made in the pressure of an interview setting. If you are in an interview and hear an 'and' that is joining two questions together, make sure in your head that you set out to answer both parts. You might structure this as two separate answers or combine answers to both into a single argument.

Good Response:

"In our increasingly multicultural society, the use of translators in medicine is increasingly common & necessary. Many of the usual communication skill/techniques used by doctors are rendered useless when the patient does not speak the same language, and a strong patient-doctor relationship can be difficult to establish. Furthermore, in a profession in which strict confidentiality is essential, the use of unofficial translators may be open to abuse and any medical professional should do everything in their power to prevent such abuses.

There is a distinction between in-hospital official translators and when family members are used as translators, as is often the case in clinical medicine. A consultation that requires the use of a translator may not be ideal for either party, however, there are several things that the doctor might do to improve the situation. Firstly, before beginning the consultation, it is crucial that both the patient and translator understand the format of a translated consultation and are happy to proceed. This is especially true when a family member is used as a translator.

Secondly, it is key that all information is correctly conveyed across the language barrier. This can be achieved in several ways. For example, the doctor might use simple language and easily phrased questions. He/she should also only use short questions and wait for the translator to translate each portion. Finally, the doctor could regularly check and confirm throughout the consultation that the patient understands what is being said and indeed that the doctor has understood everything that the patient has said. Furthermore, there are several pitfalls that might occur during a consultation when using translators, and these pitfalls have the potential to be highly detrimental to the patient's welfare. One potential issue is presented by the identity of the translator. If the translator is a family member or knows the patient personally, something which is quite likely if they come from the same community, then the patient might be embarrassed to present certain pieces of information that may be of critical importance to the consultation. In addition, the same could apply to the translator through their own embarrassment or ulterior motive. For example, if they are wanting to present their community in a positive light, they might not correctly translate information. If any of these possibilities are suspected, then the doctor should seek to repeat the consultation with a different translator.

In summary, there are multiple important issues that arise through the use of translators in medicine. However, translators are an absolute necessity in our multicultural society, and therefore, doctors should be well educated on the possible pitfalls that might arise and should know how these can be avoided."

Response Analysis:

This candidate's answer starts with a strong opening that describes the importance of the issue. It then goes on to define what exactly the term 'translator' includes in this context. There is a strong structure with each point being well signposted. As opposed to having two separate answers to the two parts of the question, this candidate has decided to combine the two answers into one narrative. Either is acceptable.

Overall: Always ensure you answer both parts of a question.

86. You have to take consent from a patient for a procedure. What do you need to consider to ensure that consent is achieved?

Undertaking any procedure without due consent from the patient is unacceptable. As a consultant one needs to have a good understanding about how to take consent correctly as recommended by GMC guidance.

Bad Response:

"Consent is very important in modern medicine; without consent, a procedure cannot go ahead. Consent is achieved when the doctor explains what the risks of a procedure are and has checked that the patient is happy to proceed. The issue of consent has many ethical implications. The Hippocratic Oath states that a doctor should do no harm and should act in the patient's best interests. Modern medicine relies on the fact that patients trust the medical profession to provide the very best service. If this trust is undermined, for example, by not following the Hippocratic Oath fully, then the medical profession cannot as effectively serve the population."

Response Analysis:

The key fault that this candidate makes in their answer is that they go off on a tangent about the ethical implications of consent. It is easy to fall into this trap as you may have a confident answer to something very much related to the question being asked, so it is tempting to talk about that even if it is not a direct answer. Always make sure that you structure a very relevant answer to the question that is being asked.

Good Response:

"Consent is a fundamental prerequisite of any procedure in an ethical healthcare system. Before visiting the patient, it is essential that you yourself understand the procedure, why it is being performed on this particular patient, and what the possible risks of the procedure are.

I think that there are four key criteria that must be met to attain consent. Firstly, it is imperative to make sure that the patient fully understands what the procedure involves. For this reason, any explanation of the procedure given by the doctor should not involve medical jargon and should be at a level that the patient can comprehend.

Secondly, the patient must know about the risks involved. Even if a procedure is perfectly explained, this might imply that there aren't possible risks to the procedure and so the patient would not be able to give effective consent. Finally, it is crucial that the patient understands what will happen if they do not have the procedure. They may not wish to undertake a daunting procedure, but this might be by far the better of two options. Therefore, to be able to give true consent, it is necessary that the patient understands this.

However, before one can assess these different criteria, it is necessary to check that they can properly process information and that they can actually retain information. This could be done by asking the patient to repeat what you have said so far at various points during the consultation. Furthermore, we must consider the patient's mental state, for instance, if they are not corpus mentis then consent cannot be obtained. This is because a patient who has a psychiatric condition may be able to appear to give consent but this cannot be accepted from an ethical standpoint."

Response Analysis:

The candidate gives an excellent answer to the question. There is a strong opening, followed by three clearly structured key points that are a direct answer to the question. The candidate then goes into further detail by explaining pitfalls that could arise if we just followed the basic formula of consent.

Overall:

A key learning point in this example is to always make sure that you directly answer the question. This is a question about what informed consent is – not an ethical dilemma!

87. A patient is adamant that they will refuse your treatment and use homeopathic medication. You believe that due to the seriousness of their condition, it is best that you persuade them to follow your treatment plan. How might you go about doing this?

This question is not asking for an ethical argument, instead, it is questioning communication skills and techniques that would be used in the situation to reach the desired outcome for the patient.

Bad Response:

"I would make sure that I convinced the patient. To do this I would talk to them rationally and would set out in a logical manner why it was necessary for them to have my proposed treatment. I would also show that the benefits of the procedure would outweigh any possible risks."

Response Analysis:

This is a poorly answered question for several reasons. Firstly, most of the narrative is delivered in the first person (notice how there is lots of the use of 'I') and this creates a patronising outlook and shows that the candidate cannot put themselves in the patient's shoes. Furthermore, they have not considered what they would do in this scenario if the patient was still to refuse treatment. This is very important, as again, it shows that the candidate is not putting themselves in the patient's shoes and is not planning for different outcomes.

Good Response:

"A key pillar of the Hippocratic Oath is patient autonomy. However, if the practitioner strongly believes that a treatment that the patient will not consent to will give the best outcome, then it is his/her duty to try and persuade the patient of their preferred plan.

If I were the doctor in question, before going to the patient, I would read up on the case including the exact treatment option being declined as well as any alternative options. On seeing the patient, after building a rapport, I would try and assess the reasons for why the patient was refusing to accept the suggested treatment. Blunt logical reasoning is unlikely to be constructive in this type of scenario. It is important to show to the patient that I accept and register their beliefs. I would be trying to assess whether they had an emotional reason to turn away from modern medicine. This might be an underlying fear or anxiety, or possibly even a previous bad experience.

Next, I would explain to the patient in the simplest language possible why I thought that their homeopathic treatment would not be effective and why the treatment that my team are proposing is going to be effective. I would then proceed to address the possible risks/benefits of the treatment and crucially explain why I thought the benefits outweighed the risks.

Finally, I would address any specific fears or bad memories that I felt the patient might have. It would be key throughout the whole consultation to ensure that I let the patient speak whenever they wanted to raise a point and that I was never overbearing, but instead, always courteous and understanding. I would hope that by doing this I could persuade the patient to accept the treatment. However, if the patient still refused to accept the treatment I would respect their wishes. I would also offer to arrange a second opinion to discuss this further."

Response Analysis:

This is a strong answer for several reasons. There is a strong opening set out for why it is an important situation. There are then several good points that are laid out in a structured manner and are well signposted. In addition, this candidate considers a plan B in case the patient still refuses treatment. Finally, this candidate has gone into extra depth to consider what might be driving this particular patient's beliefs.

Overall:

When answering a question such as this, always try and imagine yourself in the scenario as this helps you to consider what you'd have to say and also what other factors you might have to think about, for example, what to do if the patient continued to refuse treatment as these could be explored in follow-up questions.

PERSONAL ATTRIBUTES

88. Which 3 skills are most important to possess to be a Consultant?

A variant is when you are asked on "the most important skill". This is a very common interview question, to have some idea as to how to approach this question prior to the interview. This will ensure that you deliver a clear and logical answer. This interview question attempts to evaluate your understanding of what makes a good consultant whilst also assessing your ability to prioritise the 3 main skills, as the list can be quite lengthy. Candidates who list 4, 5 or 6 skills will be marked down for not following the brief. The key to answering this question is, therefore, to clearly state the 3 skills which you **feel** are important and expand on why you think they are important. Adding personal experiences/scenarios can help in supporting your answers. Being aware of your own strengths and weakness and using them here is a good strategy. Job description usually includes essential and desirable criteria. You can use attributes from the job description. For example, it may include "good team player or "audit/research" experience. This way, you can use your time keeping/organising, IT skills, audit experience, working with people or a variance of these as the most important skill(s).

Bad Response:

"Doctors should possess a number of skills which include good communication skills, empathy, and the ability to listen to patients. This is key to ensure good patient care and also patient satisfaction. They will often face having to give patients what is complex information in simple terms. In that way, doctors need to be able to avoid jargon. Patients may also present with pain or anger about what happened to them and, therefore, doctors need to be empathetic towards them and try to stand in the patient's shoes. This will improve patient care as doctors will better understand how their patients feel and tailor what they say and do to reassure anxious and angry patients. Finally, it is important to listen to patients attentively. This will enable doctors to understand the patient perspective and ensure that no important information that the patient has said during the consultation has been missed."

Response Analysis:

Whilst the candidate has identified 3 important skills, the answer could have been better structured. In fact, the ability to listen to patients will likely fall under the communication skills category. Nonetheless, these 3 skills were well-discussed as the candidate highlighted why they were important. However, talking at length about communication skills may begin to sound repetitive and show that you have not considered the whole spectrum of skills that doctors should possess.

Good Response:

"No single characteristic makes a good doctor. The 3-most important skills, include good clinical knowledge, good communication skills, and good patient care skills. The skills that doctors learn during anatomy, physiology, pharmacology lectures are core to understanding disease and its treatments. Good clinical knowledge is key to ensure safe treatment with the best medical care possible. Good communication is important and can be achieved by actively listening to the patient. This ensures correctly gathered clinical data during history taking and it also achieves a therapeutic effect as patients can express their feelings. Doctors should deliver information in an appropriate manner to patients as it benefits both patients and doctors; studies have shown that good communication improves patient-doctor relationships, improves patient compliance with treatment, and also improves the job satisfaction of the doctor. Furthermore, patient skills are perhaps the most important for patients themselves; patients want their doctors to be empathetic, caring and patient. This will further enhance the doctor-patient relationship and patient satisfaction."

Response Analysis:

This answer is clearly demonstrating a good understanding of the necessary skills required to be a good doctor. It opens nicely with a statement acknowledging that a doctor requires a number of varied skills but is able to pinpoint 3 skills. It cleverly groups the 3 skills into 3 broad groups; e.g. communication skills rather than good listener which enables the candidate to cover most skills that doctors require whilst also further expanding on the answer. Lastly, the candidate understands the importance of each skill in clinical practice.

Overall:

It is important to have thought about what you think doctors should possess as skills and try and group them into broad categories if you can.

89. Is there any question that you wished we had asked you?

This question underlies the attitude interviewers will expect you to have when you come to interview. When you are preparing for consultant interviews, you should have three underlying themes you continue to refer back to:

➢ Knowing what your strengths are as an applicant. For instance, do you have experience from which you gained a lot of experience in a niche area (e.g. transplant work, immunotherapy) or an experience of having a high level of responsibility, or an independent project you have completed (guidelines, national project)?

➢ Knowing what makes you stand out compared to others – this is slightly different to the previous question. Here you are focusing on your individual skill set and attitudes rather than your experiences. For instance, proactivity, empathy, leadership and the ability to listen well. You should have examples ready to prove that you have these skills.

➢ Knowing what the interviewer wants to hear – you need to be in the interviewer's head, knowing what he/she is really asking you and the underlying tone of the question. Ultimately, the same common

➢ Questions are asked in interviews but are asked in many different ways to throw you off.

If you are asked this question, this is a golden opportunity to refer back to these themes. Open-ended questions are the best type of questions to be asked.

Bad Response:
"No, I think I have given you a good idea of who I am and why I want to take this job."

Response Analysis:
To answer "no" to this question is a missed opportunity to show yourself off to the interviewer. If you have a good answer to a standard question that you have not yet been asked, then you could state this or a more general question that shows you to be a very competitive candidate where you summarise your strengths.

Good Response:
"Yes. I would have liked to answer the question: 'Why do you think you have the potential to work in this busy academic tertiary referral centre as consultant?' I would answer this question by reflecting on my training in the similar unit in London as well as the work I carried out whilst being a research fellow at the Stanford University on the immunotherapy for rheumatoid arthritis. I worked as part of a team to develop protocols and pathways for people with Rheumatoid arthritis requiring immunotherapy and implemented the change. This was my first experience in a large setting but was very rewarding as it was a steep learning curve. I was required to adapt and problem-solve in response to a role of responsibility I had never held before. I learned a great deal through this experience.

I believe I am an individual who is able to adapt very well to new and challenging situations and I am passionate about ensuring the best quality of care while understanding the importance of good communication, teamwork and empathy skills in doing this. I would be able to use this in my new role."

Response Analysis:
This answer shows a constructive reflection of how the candidate has developed and have considerable experience in a very specific area which he feels confident in using to the greater good in new role.

Overall:
Always try and relate your answers to questions back to your understanding of the job, local needs, your role in your future organisation.

90. Is there anything that we need to know but you are not telling us?

Think fast if you have not thought about this. Do not get trapped and start telling all the sob stories, your break up and rehab. They want to see your reaction to questions, clearly designed to put on the spot.

Bad response 1:
"Ummm.... I guess you could know about my depression after the death of my father. I was so attached to him that once he was gone, I could not bear the thought of living in the world without him. I was really lost. Beside this, I think I have covered everything in my application"

Bad response 2:
"Well, there was this time, when I was arrested for drink driving as I was coming back from a Christmas do"

Response analysis:
Both the responses are knee jerk responses to a question that the candidate has not thought of. It is clear they have been surprised and rather than thinking logically, just rattled out what they are thinking or what came first to their mind. Whilst its perfectly acceptable to have a grief reaction to a traumatic event it also shows candidate's inability to deal with stress. Such response may make future employers tread cautiously.

Good response:
"I am not sure how to answer this question? I have submitted my applications giving details of everything asked. I have also met some of you and you have my references. I am not sure without knowing what you know about me, I can answer this question. I follow good medical practice, follow evidence medicine to provide clinical care to my patients that is governance safe, fully trained with good team working skills. I can assure you that there is nothing that I am hiding from you that would impact on my abilities to work as a consultant in the organisation"

Response analysis:
This is a well measured response. The candidate has not been surprised and has given a balanced reply and not spilled any beans! He has also highlighted and drawn attention to his application and attributes and gently eases in some essential attributes leading the interviewers to probe further. He goes on to assure the employer that he is capable of working independently and has the maturity to deal with the unknown.

Overall:
Such questions are less common but a mature response in this type of questions can be the job clincher. A response given with a maturity would just ensure the employer that you have what it takes to deal with the unexpected. Do not start talking about how a break up with a friend made you suicidal (unstable personality) or your time spent in rehab for drugs.

91. What are your top three skills?

This question is assessing your understanding of the skills required to be a consultant and your suitability based on those skills. In other words, think of all the different skills you need to be a good consultant and then pick the three skills which you can most easily demonstrate that you possess. Ensure that you provide evidence and state how these skills will help you to become a successful consultant. On surface this sound very similar to previous question. But there is a fine distinction.

Previous question is asking *"what are the top three skills"* whereas this one is about *"what top three skill do you have"*. A clever candidate would have thought about this question and use the same skills in both question with correct phrasing as it is unlikely that you will be asked both questions. You may be asked do you have as a follow on to what are and all you need to do is smile and say yes!

Bad Response:

"I am a brilliantly talented pianist and performed my first solo concert at the age of 15. My teacher used to say that she had never taught someone with as much natural musicianship as me before so I would have to say that is my number one skill. In achieving my dream of becoming a concert pianist, I have had to remain extremely motivated in order to fit in rehearsal time amongst my other commitments, I would, therefore, rank my time management as another one of my top skills. I also enjoy musical composition and have received high praise for my work so I would rank my creativity as my third most impressive skill."

Response Analysis:

Whilst this answer demonstrates some remarkable achievements, and even skills which would be very useful for a doctor, e.g. time management and creativity, it seems to miss the point of the question by solely discussing the candidate's passion for music. It does provide good evidence to back up the candidate's claims but it should explain why these skills are useful in medicine.

Good Response:

"I would say my top three skills are my communication skills, my interpersonal skills, and my ability to work under pressure. I have demonstrated and developed excellent communication skills through my years of working in different teams during my years of medical and specialist training. Also interacting and relating to patients who are often at their most vulnerable, has helped me to develop patience, and an ability to explain things in a simple way, along with an ability to understand the concerns of others, and skills to build a rapport quickly.. These skills have been immensely helpful in my day to day interaction with patients and working with multi-disciplinary teams.

I have always considered myself a people person and show a range of important interpersonal skills. I am a naturally caring person, I take interest in other people and find it easy to be empathetic. I interact confidently with people from lots of different backgrounds. I have further developed these skills over the years while looking after so many unwell patients and sharing their stress and grief. I have become a better listener in particular from this experience. Again, these skills are vital for any doctor and help me to treat patients holistically rather than just treating their disease. Finally, through my years of dealing with medical emergencies and increasingly of leading teams through difficult life and death situations, I have improved my ability to work under pressure and am confident in making decisions quickly and effectively."

Response Analysis:

This is an excellent answer that shows a clear understanding of the skills required to be an effective consultant. It promotes the candidate's suitability for a place by providing convincing evidence that the candidate possesses these skills and that they can demonstrate the practical benefits of honing these skills.

Overall:

If you are lucky enough to be asked an open-ended question like this, make sure you take full advantage of it. These types of questions give you huge freedom to display your understanding of the qualities required by a consultant and give you an invaluable opportunity to sell yourself to the interviewer. Make sure you back up everything you say with evidence and continually demonstrate why your skill-set would make you an excellent consultant.

92. How to do cope with stress?

Stress is a normal response and "not getting stressed" is practically unheard of. People react and respond to stress in different manner and gets stressed about issues that may sound very trivial to others. Questions like this are also attempting to see more human side of you, to see that you are like them and can fit in.

Bad Response:

"I am extremely resilient to stress. Whenever I feels stressed I try to avoid it an actually try to avoid the circumstances that can cause stress. Stress is not very good and I feel bad when I come under stress and try to take all precautions – eg. ensuring that I meet my deadlines; if someone behaves inappropriately I do not react to that; in a situation of conflict I try to ensure that the way I react is not adding fuel to fire. This way I avoid stress and, hence, do not have to worry about my stress busting mechanisms."

Response Analysis:

This is not a good response because it is very unnatural for someone not to get stressed. Stress is a common day to day occurrence; people may have different coping mechanism but otherwise stress on a day to day life is unavoidable. The candidate is trying to show that they do not get stressed and try to impress but, actually, the effect could be counterintuitive.

Good Response:

"Stress is a normal reaction and in day to day life it can be encountered in a multitude of ways. I try to avoid a situation where stress may occur but if I am ever in such a situation first of all I try to stay calm. I also have a good circle of friends and good family support whereby I can discuss a situation which could cause me stress, worries or anxieties. This way I can discuss my situation and can find a way out of the stress. I also have a mentor so that if the situation is related to work I can talk it through and identify any problems or issues so that I can avoid similar mishaps or get out of the stressful situation. In addition, I also have hobbies such as scuba diving, photography, dancing etc (insert as appropriate) so that if there is a situation I can disengage and enjoy my hobbies which offers me some relief and respite."

Response Analysis:

This is a good response; it demonstrates that the candidate is human. It also helps the interviewer to like the candidate because they can feel that what is being said is something that has affected them at some point. The candidate then goes on to enumerate the stress busting mechanisms and support that he has available – which is good because having a stress mechanism ensures that the stress will not continue. It also shows insight as well as the candidate's ability to deal with stress.

Overall:

It is unlikely that someone does not get stressed. Stress can occur in various forms – a conflict at work, stress about being late, stress about someone else being late to work and we need to be able to handle those situations and show maturity in dealing with such situations. Stress could occur in various forms and can affect in a variety of ways. One should have a coping mechanism, develop some hobbies, could be team working or could be one to one – anything that gives pleasure.

93.How do you handle emotional issues at work?

This question is asking you to show that you have the ability to overcome and cope with stressful situations. In answering this question, it is important to identify specific coping strategies you have used and describe how they have enabled you to cope well with stress. You need to provide evidence of self-discipline and conscientiousness. It is important to constructively analyse how you dealt with your emotional issues and describe what you learned from this experience. Note: the question is slightly open as it does not clarify if the emotional issues are to yourself or someone else. In this situation, one can take either route i.e. dealing with emotional stress to yourself or dealing with emotional stress of others and show the maturity to handle with strategies to reduce anxiety/stress.

It is better to be prepared for this kind of questions as it can come up in different ways. Structure of the answer remains the same and it is the example given that varies, i.e. putting yourself or someone else'

Bad Response:
"When on call, I often have to deal with aggressive and disrespectful family/patients. I sometimes get annoyed, aggravated, and angry with this. To handle these emotional issues, I have learned to focus my attention on my work, where I worked faster and did not interact with angry family/patients so much."

Response Analysis:
The emotional issue described here is very valid but the coping strategy is not. The candidate is ignoring the underlying cause of his emotional issue rather than trying to find an active solution to it. The answer can be improved slightly by rephrasing as shown below:

"When on call, I often have to deal with aggressive and stressed family/patients. To handle these emotional issues, I have tried to understand why the family/patients could be rude or angry. I started interacting with them and would ask them the reasons of their annoyance. I offered to talk to them, to listen to any issues. I learned that understanding their reasons offering some form of assurance to them, thus being able to come up with something to reduce their anxiety/stress made them, and myself, feel better."

This response is better than the one given as it shows that you have the maturity to deal with stressful situations and can remain calm under difficult scenarios (something that can often happen with angry patient or relatives in your medical career). This response shows that rather than being angry in retaliation or shying away from the situation, you feel confident and can look for resolutions of the problem.

Good Response:
"As a clinician we encounter a number of situations that we have not anticipated. Often, we see patients with serious underlying conditions or terminal illness with frailty; it feels like that the things that made them human has been taken away from them. Occasionally, I have felt a sense of hopelessness at seeing such patients. It seems to me as though the patients have lost their sense of dignity. I have learned with time that the illness and getting over (or not) is part of the life of an individual and I am playing a small part in this journey. I ensure that the role I play is the right one. I have developed my coping mechanism where I do my job and learned to keep the best interest of the patient foremost, involve them/family in the decision-making process, to make them feel involved as much and do as best as I can. I follow good medical practice, I have learnt to keep myself detached from patients as the monitoring and ongoing treatments are necessary whilst ensuring provision of the delivery of the best quality of care and prognosis for the patient."

Response Analysis:
The response above talks about an 'emotional issue' very much in the context of the sort of emotional 'issues' or 'challenges' that a consultant will experience in their day-to-day life. The coping mechanism here is not particularly structured or formalised but it is clear and fundamental. It highlights how the candidate identifies the perspective of the doctor and patient as being important to understand the situation.

Above response can be improved by adding some qualifying statements adding individual stress bursting strategies to be something like:

"As a clinician we encounter a number of situations that we have not anticipated. Often, we see patients with serious underlying conditions or terminal illness with frailty; it feels like that the things that made them human has been taken away from them. Occasionally, there is a sense of hopelessness at seeing these patients, where it seemed to me as though the patients had lost their sense of dignity. I have learned with time that the illness and getting over (or not) is part of life of an individual. I am playing a small part in this journey and I ensure that the role I play is the right one. I have developed my coping mechanism where I do my job with the best interest of the patient, involving them/family in the decision-making process to contribute the best, as I can. Following the good medical practice, I have learnt to keep myself detached as the monitoring and ongoing treatments are necessary to ensure delivery of the best quality of care and prognosis for the patient. I have a good circle of friends and family that I interact frequently. I have number of hobbies (art, cycling) which gives me a sense of fulfilment and keeps me rejuvenated to look forward to the next day at work!"

Overall:

It is very important to reflect on what you learned through your experience and the success of your coping strategy. Give a true-life example to answer this question and modulate the analysis of your chosen example accordingly. It might be useful to comment on the advantages and disadvantages of the coping strategy you used and what you would do differently next time. Be ready for a follow-on question asking you to give an example. You should be able to come up with one from your experience in the past.

94. When you have time off, what do you like to do to relax?

This is a common question is asked usually towards the end. This question is supposed to help the candidate to calm down by thinking about their favourite past times, it can elicit a knee-jerk response in over-prepared candidates! Use this question to focus on portraying yourself as an interesting and well-rounded person. Talking about an interest or hobby should be fairly straightforward if you enjoy it enough, so take the opportunity to get on top of any nervous energy.

This question should reflect on you as a person – any made-up answer will come across as unconvincing, or worse, that you don't particularly enjoy your hobby. Show that you have a multifaceted personality, are prepared to work hard, and you are not just a boring academic. Extracurricular interests offer respite from work and an opportunity to meet people outside of medicine. Regardless, ensure you only tell the truth. There is no point saying that you do scuba diving but not know about altimeters! Your interviewer may have the same interest as you and it will become very obvious and look bad if you have been less than honest, is a probity issue and you lose all your credibility you have developed so fare, and the job with one slip.

Bad Response:
"When I finish a long day of studying hard, I like to read the latest BMJ before I go to bed. I also like to watch TED talks about medical topics for a bit of light relaxation."

Response Analysis:
This is exactly the response the interviewers do not want to hear. Interviewers don't expect much in-depth knowledge – they are looking for the right attitudes and qualities that will make a good consultant with the resilience and character to succeed. This question is about "how you relax". Whilst you may be trying to impress them, it has the opposite effect. People do need to find time to recuperate and hobbies are a great way to do so. Even if you don't have a hobby, something like walk in the garden, gym/swim is better than reading BMJ. If reading is your hobbies, quote books that provoked you or inspire you. A subject book is never classed as relaxation method as it is just an extension of your normal work.

Good Response:
"I really enjoy painting. I'm currently in the middle of a large commission of landscapes, but I mostly enjoy doing my own art, especially painting people- I'm really fascinated with people's stories. I also use painting and art as a way to process challenging situations and circumstances in my life."

Response Analysis:
This kind of response is often warmly received. If the interviewer is intrigued, they may ask more questions which can put the candidate at ease since they are talking about a topic they (presumably!) know a lot about. In terms of choosing a hobby to talk about, most people are musical to some degree, so standing out from the crowd may be difficult unless you play an unusual instrument or have achieved a lot.

Conversely, choosing a hobby that is too niche may confuse the interviewer and set the interview off to an awkward start, unless you can show real passion and enthusiasm which may intrigue the interviewer to find out more. In addition, mentioning enjoying pseudoscience hobbies such as homeopathy is not advised due to the obvious conflict between medicine and alternative therapies.

Within any hobby you mention, figure out how you can apply the skills involved in that hobby to medicine. For example, in this response, the candidate shows that they enjoy a dextrous skill (useful for surgery!), that they are good at it (talking about gaining a large commission), and far more importantly, that it's a useful emotional outlet for the stresses of life. This question is essentially making sure that the candidate is not all about medicine and that they have a way of dealing with the distressing and challenging situations they will find themselves in and can healthily process their emotions. This answer also has the bonus of implying one of the candidate's main motivations – their love of people – which they may be able to link back to later in the interview. For this reason, being genuine (rather than reciting a prepared answer) for this kind of question is essential.

Overall:

A consultant with a healthy way of processing the stresses of medicine will be far more successful than one who lives and breathes all that is medicine! Remember that medicine is more than scientific facts and figures, and in fact, the most challenging aspects are often dealing with patients and bad situations. Knowing that you can cope with the stresses makes the interviewer more likely to invest in you as a candidate. NHS trusts are looking for well-rounded individuals. Pursuits that require a lot of practice (sport, music, and drama for example) are a good way of demonstrating diligence. Furthermore, life as a doctor can be hugely physically draining (from hours and hours of running up and down wards, standing in an operating theatre, etc.) and so playing some sport helps show that you have the fitness to handle this. However, you don't have to stick rigidly to interests like these. Any hobbies outside of medicine can be important in helping to deal with the stresses of a medical career. A question like this is an opportunity to let some of your individuality and character shine through.

95. Tell me a weakness you have.

This is a fun question. It is checking how you react to unexpected, how you handle criticism and weather you have an insight. There is nothing like a perfect person and it is absolutely fine to admit a mistake. Yet, be careful. It could be fatal to admit that you are a shy person and that you don't do this or that.

Bad Response:

"I think I get very angry when things don't go right or don't go the way I have planned; this just makes me feel very upset and sometimes I just don't react the way I should and this can cause a bit of stress to myself and, maybe, the people around me can become distressed as well. I do try to reduce this by trying not to let it show to other people but I am recovering from it and plan to attend a course."

Response Analysis:

Getting angry is a normal human reaction – but this is something that should not be communicated in an interview setting. While this is a normal emotional response - and everyone goes through it - in a consultant post being angry and getting upset about a situation and causing a stressful situation is not something that is expected or desired from a consultant. It can cause a team break-down or organisational insufficiency. It could be sugar-coated in a slightly different way giving a different example to make it look better.

Good Response:

"I am human like everybody else and I am very punctual and keep to time. Therefore, if things are not running on time there is the potential of me feeling stressed. However, I understand that delays can happen because of factors beyond my control (e.g. excessive traffic) and have taken measures to avoid such situations.

Whilst I can't change my personality of being punctual – I have said that whenever I have a deadline to meet or a meeting to attend I allow another 10 to 15 minutes extra for myself so that if I am stuck in traffic I still have time and do not allow it to stress me out."

Response Analysis:

This is a good example where a strength is given as a weakness. It is short and avoids faffing. Being punctual is good and clearly preferable to being late and wasting someone's time. It also gives a positive spin to the weakness in that the candidate has thought about it and actually taken steps towards improving it.

Overall:

When you are asked a question that could put you in a negative light, it is always nice to think of something that can be presented in a positive way. Making statements like "I can't tolerate fools" can sound rude and convey the message that you are full of yourself and not a team worker. A humorous response if delivered well can be quite acceptable, e.g. where a candidate says 'just look at me – I love food!' this was coming from a candidate who had a high BMI. The panel members just laughed (thinking "me too").

96. What is your biggest weakness?

This question often catches candidates out. A careful balance needs to be struck between not coming across as arrogant and demonstrating a dangerous lack of insight (nobody is perfect!). It is also important not to identify a weakness that may make the examiners worry about who they are recruiting to the post. The answer needs to identify a weakness and then demonstrate how you are attempting to rectify this.

Avoid the urge to give an answer that is not really a weakness, e.g. "I'm a perfectionist", as a more profound degree of self-criticism will be appreciated more. Instead, by simply changing the phrasing and customising it to yourself, you can say something very similar, e.g. *"my time management can be a weakness, often because I spend too much time concentrating on minor details in my work".* You would need to develop this by showing what you've learnt from reflecting on your weakness, e.g. *"...so when I am working on a project, I set myself strict targets to meet and try to get the bulk of the task done before worrying about the finer details in the early stages.".*

Showing humility when answering a question such as this is a good way to make you appeal to the interviewer as a person. Some candidates may be tempted to answer this with a joke, however, this is not advisable as it is a very important question.

Bad Response:

"My biggest weakness is that I'm sometimes quite arrogant. I've always been very successful at most of the things I try and do and so have an awful lot of self-belief. I rarely feel the need to ask for help as I know that I will likely be OK without it. When I fail at something, I get very angry with myself and will often feel down for several days afterwards."

Response Analysis:

This is a dangerous response. Many medical applicants will indeed be very good at lots of things; however, saying that this has made them arrogant is not good. The candidate states that they rarely seek help for things and have an innate belief that they will be good at anything they turn their hand to. It is not possible to be good at everything from the offset, and knowing when to ask for more senior help is an absolutely critical part of being a doctor. In medicine, it's not just that your ego will be bruised if you fail, but a patient's health may be severely affected.

Good Response:

"I consider myself a natural leader and so my instinct in many situations is quite often to lead the team and exert my authority in coordinating others. However, I appreciate that quite often during my career I will not be the most appropriate individual to lead a team. Therefore, I'm working really hard on my skills in working effectively within a team and not necessarily as the leader. In order to improve on this, I've recently started working at my local carpentry shop with little experience, and am therefore very reliant on senior advice."

Response Analysis:

This candidate identifies a valid weakness that, if too extreme, would be a problem in medical practice. However, crucially the candidate has demonstrated insight into this problem and how this could be an issue as a future doctor. Impressively, they've even shown that they are being pro-active in trying to address this weakness (working as part of a carpentry team).

Overall:

Medical practice is quite rightly very keen on quality control and ensuring best practice. It is essential that those that practise medicine have sufficient insight to identify where they are struggling and when to ask for help. Be this a surgeon who is struggling with a new procedure or a doctor who fails to consider the opinions of his team sufficiently. A good doctor will identify their flaws and adjust these so as to prevent the quality of patient care being affected.

97. What is your biggest strength?

To answer this question will requires a good sense of self-awareness. First and foremost, your answer should be honest. Your biggest strength does not necessarily have to relate to medicine, although it would be advisable to relate your strength back to how it would enable you to be a better doctor. For example, your biggest strength could be creativity, which is very useful in terms of problem-solving and developing and adapting methods of communication to specific patients with special needs, to give but a few examples.

Bad Response:

"My biggest strength is my ability to think quickly on my feet. I think this is a very important skill for a doctor to have. Doctors think on their feet every day using both their clinical and scientific knowledge and can also be required to rapidly assess the ethics of a situation as well as using past experiences to inform judgement. If an emergency situation arises, there is no time to panic, you simply need to be able to act in the most appropriate manner and think clearly and logically."

Response Analysis:

This response sounds fake. The candidate gives no evidence to support what he is saying. The candidate needs to demonstrate to the interviewer either how he has developed these skills or an example of how he has used these skills. The question is asking for details about the candidate's strength and not about the way in which this strength is useful in a medical career, and hence this answer is lacking much detail. However, this response does show good insight into the role of the doctor which adds value to the answer.

Good Response:

"I think my biggest strength is probably my leadership ability. I have a lot of experience in leading a range of people and groups in different situations. I really enjoy getting to know the strengths of the members of a team, define and set aims and objectives for a team, and lead a team efficiently to secure the best possible outcome. With my theatre group, I directed a cast of 20 young people in a performance of an adapted, classic fairy-tale. Last year, I took on the "red to green" days project to facilitate early discharges and reduce bed blocking, I worked with staff, discharge coordinators, flow managers and social services to get a facilitated early discharge. We communicated the roles and goals for different team members and were able to achieve early discharges by prompting junior doctors to do TTA the day before and the ward team to book transport in the early half of the day. Effective communication, better team organisation, were key to success. I also appreciate the value of reviewing and constructively criticising my performance as a leader in a given situation to enable me to develop and improve my leadership skills."

Response Analysis:

This response is focused on a single strength and goes into specific detail to provide evidence that the candidate possesses this skill. Two examples are given to demonstrate the leadership experience of the candidate. The candidate shows knowledge and understanding of what good leadership is and promotes a good reflective attitude towards the way in which he/she works. The candidate also demonstrates a good understanding of his or her own personal development.

Overall:

It shows insight and maturity to have thought about ways in which you can bring your strengths to good use in your potential future career as a doctor, do take some time to do this.

98. How would you motivate a junior doctor to embrace your speciality?

There is a staffing crisis in NHS and number of junior doctor posts are unfilled. Recruitment and retention are important to ensure safe staffing level. Think what is involved here. This question is about convincing junior doctors by act, experience to choose the speciality.

Bad Response:

"If I am working with them I would ask them to come and attend the clinic. When I am teaching or doing a ward round with them they would obviously see that this is a good speciality. I would show them the positive side of the work where they could see that this is a good speciality; I would explain that it has potential, there is a lot of private practice, it keeps me busy and I get more recognition. Hopefully they would also notice and get enticed to enter the speciality."

Response Analysis:

This is a reasonable response but it is not something that would be liked by the panel – the main reason being that this talks about private practice, it is not giving any idea about leading by example, it is not putting the positive side across of the speciality.

Good Response:

"When I work with the Junior Doctors I obviously would like to ensure that they have a positive experience of the speciality. Some specialities such as paediatric emergency department is interesting for the juniors. For this I would like to get them to have a feel of the speciality, I will be showing them the good aspects, challenges and how rewarding the work is. Sometimes it is useful to show them the research work that is coming out and how the patients benefit from it. Once they have had a positive feel of the speciality they would be interested and would like to continue training in that speciality."

Response Analysis:

This is a good response; it talks about the clinical aspects, it also talks about giving a positive response, giving them some responsibility.

Overall:

This response is basically casting your educational and motivational skills; it is checking whether you have the ability to shape and what it takes to convince someone else to hopefully change their mind – more so if they are undecided. Giving them 'positive experience/feel' is the way forward to get someone to take a speciality on board.

99. If I asked your friend, what would they say your weakness is?

This is another way of asking the same question as the previous one but also checking on your ability to take this on board and improvise. Remember that what one thinks as a weakness, may be strength for someone else or in different circumstances. It is an opportunity for you to sneak in "team working, taking feedback, demonstrating that you are a learner." It also shows that you have friends that can be honest and open: a huge plus.

Bad Response:

"My friends would possibly say that I don't like criticism; I get upset very quickly. Otherwise a good friend of mine shouldn't be telling you my weakness – particularly if they know that I have applied for a job."

Response analysis:

Short, sharp and lacking insight is what comes to mind. As a consultant, one feels challenged for various reason and must demonstrate the ability to take criticism on board. If this is a weakness that your friend would give, you should work hard on this. Above response shows no remorse and candidate's anger is almost palpable in the response.

Good response:

"My friend would say that I am too easy on people always accommodate their needs and get taken for granted. I understand that this can be a significant drain on my time, I still feel that a desire and commitment to help people is my strength. My take on this is that if people come to me in times of their need, I should offer my support. If it eats into my time I have to deal with it by better time management as time given to someone else is a friend gained for future. Despite my reservations on my friend's views, I have taken them on board and am a bit more cautious on how and how much time I devote and rationalise the needs."

Response analysis:

A better version, good example. You may be probed further to give an example. You may even get asked to give another weakness.

100.   How do you deal with stress?

This question is a particularly important one as consultant job could be very stressful and that might not be the right thing for everybody. Having good mechanisms to cope with stress is essential to function well as a doctor in the long run. This includes two types of stress, the underlying stress when there is a lot to do in little time, and the acute stress of being in an unexpected or particularly challenging situation.

Bad Response:

"I do not get stressed, so I do not see the need to cope with stress."

Response Analysis:

Any answer that goes in this direction is inadequate. The practice of medicine is stressful and challenging. For this reason, it is essential to have appropriate mechanisms to deal with stress. Even if you have not felt stressed up to this point, it is very likely that consultant post will put you in a situation that you have never experienced before which will be very stressful. You need to be able to demonstrate that you have thought about ways on how to cope with situations like that.

Good Response:

"Medicine can be very stressful and I will have to make quick decisions as the final bucket holder. I have developed techniques to keep a clear head in heated situations. I have found that focusing on the task at hand and breaking my duties down in small, logical steps helps a great deal to make a situation more controllable and manageable. I also have a good network of friends that I can rely on and I like to play the Piano which I find very relaxing."

Response Analysis:

This response is a good one as it provides clear examples of situations experienced as well as techniques used. This answer addresses the acute type of stress, but a similar principle can be applied to the general underlying type of stress of being very busy. Providing exact examples of coping mechanisms is important as anything else will remain superficial.

Overall:

Whatever your individual coping mechanisms for stress may be, provide examples of where you have applied them. It will make them look a lot more valid as they are tried and tested and not just made up. Sources for coping mechanism can vary. Competitive sports can be one, playing an instrument can be another. Remember, though, this mainly applies to the underlying stress of being very busy.

101. Who should I phone/speak to have an honest opinion about you?

Don't get perturbed with this. This is to check whether you have friends and family that you can trust and hence would be able to support you in times of crisis. This is one time where your sense of humour can be played well.

Bad Response:

"I would be very reluctant to tell you who you should speak to; however, you could call my mother or my husband who can tell you all about me so they can tell you how I behave when I am angry or how honest I am and how hard I work."

Response Analysis:

This is not a good response; it completely misses the point and misses the opportunity to make a witty response. The question is not asking who they should contact, it is checking what your knee jerk reaction would be. Offering your parents number – who would usually be considered quite guarded or protective – is not the best approach.

Good Response:

"A number of people can give you an honest opinion about myself; it also depends on what area of my personality that you need to explore. If you would like to talk to someone regarding my personal life then in that case either my spouse, best friend or neighbour as they would give more insight into my behaviour and personality, whereas if you need to know more about me in a professional capacity then possibly my education supervisor or the clinical director from my last post would be the best person to give an opinion regarding how I work, how I work under stress and my resilience to stress and that I am not just a 9 to 5 person."

Response Analysis:

This candidate has thought about the question and was able to divide his life into two sections – personal as well as professional. It also leads the panellists to see that you can compartmentalise your life and have the ability to distinguish both parts.

Overall:

This type of questions is usually asked either towards the end of the interview or as a follow up question. Handle with confidence and you are a winner!

102. Considering the proposals for seven days service, do you think that career as a consultant is the right choice for you?

The difficulty of this question is in striking a balance between demonstrating that you have a realistic understanding of the challenges of a seven days service (staffing, resources, rota implications, EWTD etc) set by Mr Hunt's suggestions (brain drain). Remember, by discussing what you perceive as the advantages of a seven-day service and challenges of its implementation you are giving a reflection on what it is, it shows that you're aware of the impact and have thought of both sides of the argument.

In this question, there is the opportunity to show that you have thought about how you personally would deal with these challenges and what approaches you might employ to cope with them. A good response should probably give at least two disadvantages, link with positive qualities to demonstrate why the negatives are actually good for you. People have different people strengths, values, and priorities. Whilst some people may not feel that they can meet the challenges of being a Consultant (more so in the changing environment), despite the challenges, career as consultant is the right choice as you have the ability and attributes on what it takes to be a consultant and will continue to work towards excellence!

Bad Response:
"I read in the news that the government is planning to change the contract for new consultant. I am not too sure of the changes being suggested but sure it will not be implemented to make life easy for Consultant! It is definitely a disadvantage, but I still reckon the Consultant life is still cool. So still think it is worth it."

Response Analysis:
There are several reasons why this is a bad response. Firstly, it is too short to start with. Whilst your interviewers not expecting to hear an essay, the answer above is a missed opportunity. Secondly, even though it may not actually be the case, the interviewers could easily infer from the answer that the candidate is mainly motivated by easy life/money as a motivational factor to be a consultant. This is partially because the candidate failed to either clarify what they meant or offer other disadvantages which are more important to them. Seemingly being motivated mainly by money can be frowned upon by interviewers, who may suspect that those motivated by money may be more likely to move into private sector or may not be motivated to work to their best within the organisation.

Thirdly, while it is certainly good to demonstrate awareness of current developments in medicine, the controversy to which the candidate is referring has other elements that are more important – such as changes that are claimed to risk patient safety. Finally, this answer has shown no appreciation for any other challenges of a career as consultant, nor any evidence that the candidate has thought about how they would handle these challenges. This would not be a good way to convince the interviewer that you are the right person for the trust.

Good Response:
"The duties of the consultant require them to be conscientious, they must prioritise the welfare of their patients and juggle up efficiently between social and work life. This can often mean that sometimes they have long hours (on call) and may have to make personal sacrifices, such as missing social events because they need to work late or taking phone calls/getting out of bed to go back into hospital in the middle of the night when they are on call. While this is a disadvantage one often wouldn't get in other jobs, I feel that it is an inevitable result of the special level of responsibility as a consultant and reflects how being a consultant is so unique. It is a way of life and not just another job! Being a consultant is an exhilarating feeling, it motivates oneself when things get so hopeless or demanding. I don't think I will have to think twice about being a consultant!

Being a consultant is a responsible job. It requires the skill mix of sound clinical knowledge, experience, as well as mental agility to be able to deal with different kind of situations. The proposed seven days service is a good initiative to ensure patient safety is not compromised though implementation of this should be a well thought process. This will require looking at resources, impact on training of junior doctors as well as the various regulations e.g. EWTD. Seven-day service would ensure that the patients are seen every day, it means we need to look at expansion of our work pool"

Response Analysis:

This response is by no means perfect, but it demonstrates some good features. Firstly, it shows a realistic understanding of what it means to be a consultant! The candidate has clearly thought about these challenges and how they could handle them. It also shows an appreciation of some values that are important in medical practice such as conscientiousness, diligence, and empathy. It also gives the interviewer and opportunity to ask more about the candidate's view (as follow on question, as that will invariably happen in such type of open questions). This candidate should be ready to justify their claim that they are a resilient person, as this is something the interviewers might pick up on. This candidate does well to show that he learnt well during training, has reflected on the challenges of medicine and his own motivation/ambitions.

Overall:

You can see how a question like this can be used to give the interviewer more information about your understanding of your reasons to take up a job as consultant. It is testing your motivations, your values, your skills learned during training and much more. It can be worth taking a second to pause before answering and think about exactly what you are going to say so that you give a clear and well-structured answer that can incorporate some of these elements. Go further than simply listing the potential disadvantages of being a consultant or advantages of being one. Show that you have given thought to what motivates people (and yourself) to take on the final plunge and be a consultant and whether this is based on a realistic understanding.

This question is a double-edged sword. A badly phrased response can convey that you are choosing to be a consultant due to reasons other than your dedication, (e.g. money). Alternatively, if you are not open and honest about the obvious factors (i.e. hard work, long hours, and the ongoing need to make work-life balance), this means you have not really given the career enough thought and don't understand the challenges of being a consultant.

103. Tell us about a mistake you learned from?

This question often catches candidates out. A careful balance needs to be struck between not coming across as arrogant, incompetent, negligent and demonstrating a dangerous lack of insight (nobody is perfect!). It is also important not to identify a weakness that may make the examiners worry about your safety as a doctor – therefore do not give an answer that can be interpreted as medically negligent. The answer needs to identify a weakness and then demonstrate how you are attempting to rectify this.

Avoid the urge to give an answer that is not really a weakness, e.g. "I'm a perfectionist", as a more profound degree of self-criticism will be appreciated more. Instead, by simply changing the phrasing and customising it to yourself, you can say something very similar, e.g. *"my time management can be a weakness, often because I take on too many projects at the same time"*. You would need to develop this by showing what you've learnt from reflecting on your weakness, e.g. *"...so when I am working on a project, I ensure that I know exactly what the timeline is to completion before taking on more work."*.

Showing humility when answering a question such as this is a good way to make you appeal to the interviewer as a person. Some candidates may be tempted to answer this with a joke, however, this is not advisable as it is a very important question for medics.

Bad Response:

"My biggest weakness is that I'm sometimes quite arrogant. I've always been very successful at most of the things I try and do and so have an awful lot of self-belief. I rarely feel the need to ask for help as I know that I will likely be OK without it. When I fail at something, I get very angry with myself and will often feel down for several days afterwards."

Response Analysis:

This is a dangerous response. Many applicants will indeed be very good at lots of things; however, saying that this has made them arrogant is not good. The candidate states that they rarely seek help for things and have an innate belief that they will be good at anything they turn their hand to. It is not possible to be good at everything and knowing when to ask for more senior help is an absolutely critical part being a consultant as often specialist opinion is needed. In medicine, it's not just that your ego will be bruised if you ask for help or fail, but a patient's health may be severely affected.

Good Response:

"I consider myself a natural leader and so my instinct in many situations is quite often to lead the team and exert my authority in coordinating others. However, I appreciate that quite often during my career as consultant, I will not always be the most appropriate individual to lead a team. Therefore, I'm working really hard on my skills in working effectively within a team and not necessarily as the leader. In order to improve on this, I've paid significant attention to the (good) feedback that I received during my Team Based Assessments, looking at specific areas of my team working skills that I can improve. I have also attended a course that illustrated several different types of personality within teams, and how to ensure my personality adapts to the specific team environment. The work I have done has let me become a much more successful member of the teams I have been a part of throughout my time as a doctor so far."

Response Analysis:

This candidate identifies a valid weakness that, if too extreme, would be a problem in medical practice. However, crucially the candidate recognises this and shows insight and working towards improving.

Overall:

Try to be realistic. Avoid giving examples where clinical mistakes occurred (wrong site surgery, wrong medication) as this can potentially make you look negligent/careless. Use a mistake that occur due to team dysfunction or system breakdown, where lessons can be learned disseminated and risk minimised for future recurrence.

TEAMWORK

104. You are just about to finish your work for the day when the ward nurse asks you to talk to the angry sister of a patient who is admitted under a different team. You have a dinner date with your fiancée and drive to the restaurant. What would you do?

This question is about dealing with an angry relative as well as a nurse who may be left to handle the relative if no one can pacify the relative. It also tests your commitment to medicine and patients, as well as your time/people management skills. Your response to stress will also be assessed. If you don't leave in time, you will be late. Do you get stressed in this situation?

Bad Response:

"I would say to the nurse that I had finished for the day and as this was not my patient anyway that she should call someone else to speak with the relative."

Response Analysis:

The candidate comes across as someone who shirks from responsibility and has a lack of empathy. They fail to actually find out what the problem is from the nurse. This is important because simple issues could be quickly resolved, e.g. prescribe analgesia if the brother was in lots of pain. This would mean that the ward nurse wouldn't have to deal with the angry relative. Although it's important that you take your breaks as a doctor and leave on time, it's also important not to neglect your duties.

Good Response:

"This patient is not on my team but is being managed by Dr Smith's team. What is the problem anyway? If it is something quick maybe I could talk to the relative, and if it requires more discussion I'd advise her to make an appointment to see Dr Smith who is the responsible consultant. I can also bleep someone in Dr Smith's team so that they can explain this to the sister. If this is clinically urgent, I am happy to stay behind but I'll need to make a quick call to my fiancée to explain that I'll be late."

Response Analysis:

Answering this way, you have demonstrated that you are a hard-working doctor that will work well in a team, does not get stressed with unexpected situations, empathise well, and are able to take that extra step for patients' welfare.

Overall:

You will come across this type of situation in your life as a doctor. In such scenarios, it is useful to ensure that your actions don't compromise patient safety (in life and death situations you can't walk away). If someone wants to know about the progress of the family member, you should be able to spend a few minutes if it is a quick discussion to diffuse the situation and offer to get someone else to have an in-depth discussion. It is irrelevant that the patient is from a different team as the on-call doctor may also not be from the same team.

105. How can a team avoid making mistakes by using good communication skills?

This question is worded difficultly but don't let it put you off. The focus of this question is identifying how mistakes might be made as a result of a breakdown in communications and suggesting ways in which such mistakes could subsequently be avoided. Furthermore, it is key to have a strong structure when answering a question like this, as any answer is liable to becoming simply a list.

Bad Response:
"One way that stops mistakes being made when communicating is to use simple language. Another way is to ensure you speak slowly and clearly. By doing these things you can save lives in medicine. Another way is to make sure that things are checked over."

Response Analysis:
This candidate does seem to have the basics for some ideas but has presented them in a very poor manner. They do not illustrate their points at all and have not included any explanations or examples. In addition, there is no structure to the answer and it is obvious that the candidate rushed into the question and did not have their answer clear in their mind prior to answering. This is evidenced by the fact that they add in a further point after their summary.

Good Response:
"Medicine deals with human lives and so mistakes in conveying information, which may be hardly noticed and completely benign in normal everyday interactions, become magnified by the nature of the profession and can lead to dire consequences. Thus, it is paramount that teams of doctors avoid such mistakes.

This can be achieved in two key ways:
One way is to check and confirm that the information is correct and is understood by anyone who receives an important communication. An example of how this can be done is to make sure that the recipient of information repeats back what they think they heard. It is easy to see how doing this can avoid such a crucial mishap as mishearing a decimal place over a poor telephone line.

A second way in which communication errors can be avoided is to make sure they are not made in the first place. One way in which this can be done is to highlight when something important is about to be conveyed. For example, by starting a sentence with 'I have an unusual request and it is important that you take this in'. This will instantly bring a colleague to focus their full attention on listening to what you need to say. This avoids communication errors due to lapses in concentration and due to the making of assumptions about what information is contained within a piece of speech or text. Another way in which mistakes can be avoided in the first place is to avoid the use of complicated jargon and ensure that all speech/writing is at a level that is appropriate for the person you're communicating with. In summary, it is imperative that those in the medical profession do not make errors when communicating. As mentioned above, these errors can be avoided in two key ways; firstly, by repeating and checking information; and secondly, by using techniques that avoid or reduce the number of errors made in the first place."

Response Analysis:
This answer has a very strong opening. They immediately relate their answer to medicine which is clearly what the question was getting at. Furthermore, the introduction powerfully outlines the important implications of their answer.

Overall:
By comparing these two examples, we can see how a strong structure and several illustrative explanations can turn a few basic ideas into a formidable answer. A key learning point is that these 'furnishings' are often formed in the crucial several second pauses between hearing the question and starting your answer.

106. Do you think specialist nurses are important?

This can be the leading question or a follow-on question, more relevant in speciality where the nurse consultant or specialist nurse's role is well established or evolving (Epilepsy nurse, stoma nurse, diabetes nurse specialist). The answer to this question is obviously yes (you would be both foolish and disillusioned to answer no), but we must answer it in a way that distinguishes yourself from other candidates. The best way to do this is to bring in specific examples. The role of the nurses has evolved with time and they are taking on more diverse roles, e.g. educating the patients, researching, and acting as a go-between patients and doctors.

Bad Response:

"Nurses are very important to the NHS and play an integral role in the day to day running of the health service. I have always found it nice to have the nurses around. All of the patients in my clinic really liked talking to the nurses and although they were not as important as the doctors, they made a real difference to the care of the patient."

Response Analysis:

Nurses in the UK must undergo a rigorous training program before they qualify followed by further training on the job, so it is wrong to dismiss them in this peripheral manner. Senior nurses are qualified to prescribe certain drugs, and furthermore, certain nurses are available to do initial checks at GP surgeries. We are now seeing nurse led endoscopies. The statement that "it is nice to have the nurses around" further worsens this. It gives the wrong impression that nurses are serving no real purpose and just happen to be around the hospital. Although this may not have been the intention of the candidate, it certainly comes across in this manner and will not impress the interviewer. The final mistake is stating that nurses are not as important as doctors; this is definitely not the case and we will see how to correct this in the good response.

Good Response:

"Nurses are very important to the NHS and play an integral role in the day to day running of the health service. Senior nurses (nurse consultant) are able to examine and prescribe treatment to patients; the patients can be sent to a doctor if the nurse thinks it would be beneficial. This means that they help alleviate the strain of resources on the NHS and play a critical role alongside doctors. Furthermore, it is nice to have the nurses around, as the patients always found it easy to communicate with ease with the nurses. The doctors may only visit the patients for a short time to see if everything is going well, but it is always the nurses who remain with the patients throughout the day; it is the nurses who often help the patients with their daily needs. Nurses also act as a go between, educate the patients. We are seeing more of the nurse consultant, nurse prescribers these days. This frees up Consultant time to get more involved in other activities like research, service development"

Response Analysis:

This response is much better than the previous one, although note the level of similarity. Firstly, some of the specific roles of nurses is addressed and the factual errors of the previous answer have been corrected. Secondly, the rather loose statement that "it is nice to have nurses around" has been justified with a specific example. Finally, the equal but different roles of doctors and nurses are acknowledged. The response shows that you are aware of the changing NHS, limited resources, and different strategies that are being used to deliver cost effective services and the use of skill knowledge framework.

Overall:

This is a very standard question that may come up in a lot of consultant interviews, more so in specialities where nurses are taking more and more responsibilities. There are lots of small traps in the question that are shown by the bad answer, but, providing specific examples will help you stand out from the rest and demonstrate a respect for your colleague and team working spirit.

107. What is the difference between a senior registrar and newly appointed/junior consultant?

Be careful when answering this question. The question is assessing if you understand the roles that the consultants play (besides clinical work). Conveying this correctly will be a win-win.

Bad Response:

"I don't think there is a difference as a Senior Registrar – after completing their exit exam – would be eligible to act or work as a consultant as soon as they finish training. I therefore believe that a Senior Registrar who is finishing their training is as good as a newly appointed consultant although there will be less salary and less responsibility but they will be carrying out more nights – hence not being available on a 9 to 5 basis or a whole day which the consultants are".

Response Analysis:

This analysis does not look at the roles and responsibilities of a Registrar as well as the consultant. Although the consultant may be newly appointed or doing their first job after finishing their Registrar training there is a clear definition and role change. Consultants have the final responsibility for any difficult decisions made on the clinical floor. In addition to the clinical responsibilities they have more managerial input and they are responsible for the education supervision of the junior doctors – which is not alluded into this. This response is very superficial, it does not touch on the transition from a Registrar to a consultant.

Good Response:

"A Senior Registrar is almost finishing their training and has taken/passed successfully their exit exam. This means that they are now eligible to take on the consultancy. A newly appointed consultant has actually gone through the stage and has taken either their first job or they are doing the job in the first few years after finishing their training.

Although it can be said that both the Senior Registrar and a newly appointed consultant do not have much difference in terms of number of years, the transition between a Registrar and a consultant is a huge one. While the senior Registrars usually have increasing responsibility and independence they will be doing part of their work under the supervision of the consultant and are expected to seek advice and support in challenging circumstances. Consultants on the other hand are fully trained and able to work independently, not requiring supervision and, in fact, are providing supervision to the junior doctors – including Registrars. Consultants are also burdened with managerial tasks; they have service development issues and, in addition expected to act as the leader of the team and maintain a harmonious environment within the team. This way, while a Senior Registrar and a Junior Registrar do not have much difference in terms of clinical competencies there are other roles that the Senior Registrar is not able to play which a Junior Consultant is expected to play".

Response Analysis:

This response makes a finite distinction between both these roles; it alludes to the managerial responsibilities that the consultant plays. It also stresses upon the team working and maintenance of the team spirit which – although both do – the consultant has to play a major role at being the team leader or, at least, a senior member of the team. This response could also be improved by including other areas which consultants are expected to contribute to such as clinical governance and patient safety.

Overall:

This is a good response; it covers both aspects of the service commitment as well as the clinical commitment and the other roles that the consultant plays. Such types of questions are asked to see whether you have made that distinction. A Senior Registrar who has just become a consultant would have the clinical skills but may need support including a mentorship program for a newly appointed consultant, and this could be included in the response.

108. What are your views about locum consultants? Are they useful to the NHS? What are the problems in being a locum consultant?

This is assessing your team working spirit, your attitude and weather you respect your colleagues as well as understanding the manpower resource implications of not having the locums in place. A good candidate would demonstrate maturity, value the input from locum consultant and give both sides of the argument to justify before concluding, either way. Locum posts are taken as short-term experience gaining exercise e.g. an SpR just finishing training. This way, being a locum is a useful step up and prepares them for life as a consultant.

Bad response:

"Locum Consultant are needed to fill the gap. These jobs are essential to continue to run the service. Locum doctors are usually not as responsible and are not reliable. They also do not get the respect they deserve. They do serve a purpose but they are not very useful in long term planning and the uncertainties exists with them so locum consultants are not very good for organisation beyond a short-term gap filler!"

Response analysis:

This is incomplete and only giving one sided view. It can be perceived as bordering on "insulting" attitude towards the locum consultants. Locum consultants are needed and do have an important role. One should avoid expressing very strong views in the interview situation and certainly not exhibit negativism towards anything. It can easily be given a positive spin. There is no structure (think, analyse, body sum up) and does not answer the question at all.

Good response:

"Locum consultants play an important role in the NHS. Serving as long/short term gap fillers, they provide continuity of care keeping the service safe and running avoiding service disruptions. They often don't get the respect they deserve which may partly be due to the short time they spent in a job and miss out on an opportunity to get established and contribute in other ways beyond clinical care. Locum consultants have made a choice for reason. It is often taken for granted that the locums get paid a lot. Often this is not true (no pension, extra money needs to be spent on travel/accommodation/external revalidation fees etc). Some time, people choose to take up locum posts whilst waiting for the right post in their preferred location. The challenges of having locum consultants are mainly centred around the uncertainties that come with these jobs (for both parties). There is no long-term commitment, they can leave at short notice and they may feel less engaged at times. It is however unfair to criticise them as they have the same skill sets as substantive consultants. They just have chosen a different career path and may be travelling more distances or staying away from family. I know some locum consultants that have contributed very positively and are well respected team members"

Response analysis:

This response covers issues that the locum consultants face (nature of the job, short term contract, need to review at regular intervals, uncertainties in terms of long-term future, their inability to get settled. It even explores the social impact on their lives (travel, staying away). The answer has a depth and understand the issues. This is not criticising them and value the contribution of the locum consultants.

Overall:

Try not to ignore the contribution by locum doctors and not criticise them. NHS is plagued by the staff shortage at multiple levels. Without locums, consultants' posts could remain vacant (new post, maternity/sick ness cover) or simply expansion of the service and await substantive options. The locum posts are not always about more money and this is being reduced as most trusts are capping the money they spend on locum. There are downsides of being a locum job such as short-term job, no pension, revalidation, not eligible for certain roles e.g. The Royal college examiner or not eligible for clinical excellence awards. Understanding of this and conveying it in your answer makes it a mature response.

109. What is success? How do you define/measure it?

This is a question to throw you off. It is a very generic question and testing your life values. There is no right or wrong answer here but try not to appear very materialistic. They are also not interested in knowing if your idea of success is owing a Ferrari. The best way to approach this question is given an example.

Bad Response:
"Success is being able to achieve what one wanted – which could be variable as people may have different measures of success. For some it could be as simple as being able to walk when they were not able to after sustaining an injury. It is quite an ambiguous term with no specific definition but the measure could be what we couldn't do before and if we are able to do it now - then we are successful."

Response Analysis:
The candidate has briefly touched upon what success is, how to define, and why it is not definable together with an example on how to measure it. But structure is missing. There is no framework to it and it is bit jumpy – going between three sub-questions built within this.

Good Response:
"Success is quite an abstract term – although we all need success in one form or another to keep us happy. I would say that success is about achieving a goal or a target that we have set up for ourselves. The definition is variable because we need to know what our goals are. A measurement of success is, again, dependent on the goal and task; therefore, whilst the success could be measured in statistical terms e.g. were we able to achieve 70% of the task target – e.g. if we used course attendance in a specific course as our target, then having all places filled is achieving 100% of the target.

In other areas of life defining and measuring success can be very ambiguous e.g. if an elderly person who is unable to walk to the toilet without having an accident, is able to do so after treatment, it would be classed as success. We can therefore see that success is a variable term with the definition dependent on the task, goal and measurement also depends on the task. It is important that we are able to measure what it is so that we can achieve targets."

Response Analysis:
This is bit better though long and can be reduced by trimming the waffling. Goes from definition to measure and exemplifies. It is worth noting that the examples are same but the presentation is better on the second occasion. The candidate has brought in success by linking to the course attendance rather than money achieved from booking.

Overall:
Keep the answers short. Go straight to the point, avoid appearing materialistic and avoid mentioning money.

110. If you could choose, would you choose to have better clinical skills or better communication skills?

Do not walk into the trap of choosing one of these skills. You should know that both are important. Communication as well as clinical skills are both important and choosing one over the other is not the right tactics.

Bad Response: (Clinical skills):

"If I could choose I would like to have excellent clinical skills. I am here to do a job and my job is to treat patients. If I do not have the clinical skills I would not be able to treat my patients to the best of standards which is expected of me. My patients require the best care and no mistakes should be made. I will ensure that I am fully trained, fully competent and am able to provide the care that they need and deserve."

Bad Response: (Communication skills):

"If I could choose I would like to have good communications skills as, even if I make a mistake, I can communicate with my patients and my team and therefore not be penalised for having made a mistake. Therefore, although I may only be partially trained, if had the communication skills I would be able to escape or get by the situation."

Response Analysis:

We have chosen both the above examples as they happen in real life. The point of this question is to see whether you understand the importance of two integral components of your role; competency as well as communicating efficiently. If this is lacking, then patient care is going to suffer one way or another. Both the above responses show a lack of maturity whereby they have chosen one over the other and ignored the fact that both are related and necessary.

Good Response:

"A Clinician needs to be properly trained and have the skills to face all sorts of clinical challenges. One should be able to diagnose and manage conditions and also recognise when help is needed and be able to ask for it without hesitation. Good communication is vital for clinicians; people need to interact at various levels – emails, telephone calls, one to one consultation, group meetings or meetings where discussions can get heated. It is important to have the good communication skills to be able to interact appropriately in the most challenging of circumstances such as breaking bad news. Having one good skill at the cost of not having another skill would be detrimental because any breakdown in communication can jeopardise excellent care being given or excellent care – if not communicated well – will possibly result in sub-standard care (missed appointments/procedures). I would have to choose, to acquire both excellent communication and clinical skills."

Response Analysis:

This response may appear slightly ambiguous because it is not committing to either a clinical or communication skill. However, this question is not about you choosing one over the other, this question is probing what you feel is important. If you feel one aspect is more important than the other then you are oblivious to the fact that both are related. Hence, neither is inferior and both need to be given equal importance so that the clinical work does not suffer. Mistakes can happen at any level; as long as we have the clinical skills to recognise the mistake and are able to communicate in an open manner and follow the duty of candour, mistakes can be corrected and lessons learned. Hence, it is extremely important to have both aspects of work, clinical and communication.

Overall:

This question is not seeking your views; in fact, this is checking what you feel – whether one component is important over the other. A mistake can be made by choosing one over the other and that could be quite fatal as it just shows your lack of insight in understanding that both components are integral.

111. What is a good team? Give an example where you contributed to the team's success.

A good team is a group of individuals that are like minded, have a common goal and are working together to achieve a common goal for the betterment of patient care of to achieve a successful completion of the task. It does not always have to be patient care but if it is in the context of the NHS then this would be the case.

Bad Response:

"A good team is a collection of people that are working towards a common goal. I have had the opportunity of working in a team and when I was in my last post working as a Locum Consultant we were organising the surgical skill exams and I was one of the teachers. The exams went very well and I felt that we had achieved something great in that process because the feed-back of the whole process was fantastic."

Response Analysis:

This response cannot be criticised for being incorrect, however it is incomplete. It does talk about what makes a good team but it does not mention the attributes of the team. It is also giving an example which is mainly a participation of the candidate in something that was happening. This is just a task where the candidate contributed but is possibly is a small task, it is a small success but it could be elaborated in a better way.

Good Response:

"A team has different people and personalities with different skills with the common attribute being the common task that needs to be achieved. People put their own issues and views behind them and work towards the success. That is a good example of team working. I once participated in a surgical skill examination where I was asked to act as a teacher; this was a course which was organised by the local Trust for surgical training and there were a number of issues i.e. getting the patient right, circulating the program, getting people interested in the program, and being on the same hymn sheet when we were talking about the structure and the delivery of the matter. We had a number of meetings and I saw that by participating in those meetings and participating in the surgical skill examination for our trainees I contributed positively. There was a freedom for people to contribute to as per their ability and everyone's views and contributions were respectfully accepted. There were no personality clashes and people understood their role and responsibilities and had dedicated tasks to perform. My task was to contribute to the teaching activities on the day and I feel – because of the whole team working – that the task went very well."

Response Analysis:

This is a good example where the candidate talks about what a team is, what the attributes of the team are and how they contributed to the team's success giving specific examples; he also talks about the obstructions in the common goal such as differing personalities and views, and how these can be handled in a mature way.

Overall:

This is an example where you are being questioned to explore if you understand the key elements which make up a successful team and if you as an individual possess those attributes. It is also an opportunity to show that you understand the factors which hinder good team working and to demonstrate that you have the ability to handle such obstructions in a mature and balanced manner.

112. Give an example where your leadership skills avoided a major crisis?

Consultant job is a multifaceted job. You will often be working with a team and it is essential that a harmonious environment is maintained. This will require skills and experience.

Bad Response:

"Leadership is extremely important because we work towards a common goal. Different individuals have different roles. I feel that when I was working in a Trust we were setting up a new service where different people needed to do a specific task but, because of a weak leadership we were failing on that as different people were going about doing what they were doing due to the lack of directions from a weak leader. People were not being advised of their role and responsibilities and this was causing a defragmentation of the team and unhappiness prevailed. I spoke to the leader and asked them to take on some responsibility or maybe pass on the leadership to someone else so that the other person could take the tough decisions and work could continue. Eventually this happened and we were able to achieve our target – in fact we were able to deliver a better service in 3-months of it being started."

Response Analysis:

The example given is correct & commonly seen situation where there is a new service, new team members and the joining of new team members can cause a fragmentation within team with potential of a personality clashes. Where this answer goes wrong is that it is advising the previous leader to step down and allow someone else to take on this role. This approach can be perceived as being quite extreme and people may feel that a person with such views may actually challenge their leadership. This response can be improvised as shown in the good response.

Good Response:

"When I was recently acting as a Locum Consultant I was responsible for developing a urology service aiming to reduce the length of stay (LOS) for a minor urological procedure. Because of the National Tariffs, we were trying to develop this as a day-care surgery. The Trust funded the new appointments and when the new team members came in, it caused a personality clash because there was a feeling that the new people were taking the credit for the hard work that was done, whereas the new people felt that they were doing a good job of service moving forward; - they were doing what they were appointed to do. I worked and communicated with different team members and met team members individually hearing different people's views from both sides. I was able to get the ideas across to both of them that no one was being undermined and all team members were valued and important pillars and were essential in the delivery of the task that we were doing.

Once that idea was perceived and people felt that no-one felt threatened and that no roles were being taken away, things settled. We avoided a major crisis (Newly employed staff were feeling undervalued and were planning to leave and the older people were not getting engaged and were trying to withdraw)- hence there would have been no one delivering the service. This way we continued to achieve and set up the service where we were able to undertake day care surgery for patients and achieve our best practice."

Response Analysis:

This is a good response; it talks about personality clashes, it talks about changing team dynamics which is quite a common occurrence when new team members arrive and a flare up occurs or new services are planned. It results in an increased work load which obviously can cause stress to settled people or can be perceived as an extra work load by new people if the old team members cannot contribute or support them. The technique demonstrated here is off record communication, settled meetings which were not perceived as meetings but rather just some quality time where people were talking to each other in an off-guard situation and were relaxed. This approach did achieve the task and therefore is a good example.

Overall:

Questions on leadership skills are always challenging; they are trying to judge your skills, your attributes as to whether you would be a good leader. In a position such as a consultant, being a leader is a seamless unrecognised role that you play and you need to demonstrate this. For that you need to be able to understand what a leader is, what the qualities of a leader are, how to understand tension and how to dissipate this. It would be essential to do this without adding fuel to the fire. A good leader would demonstrate this, would assign roles and responsibilities based on skills, would be a good 'go-between' when there is a problem and also try to resolve any issues without allowing them to escalate to a dangerous critical level where the goals becomes secondary or threatened. Always be wary of these kinds of questions and try not to be very negative or critical of any task, person or leader.

113. Tell us about an initiative that you took and implemented the change

You will be working as consultant for long time. You will come across situation where things are not right or need exist to adept to newer/better ways of working. This will require an ability to identify the need for change and bring change. It will require team working, ability to convince others to embrace the change and implement the change.

Bad Response:

"When I started in a new role as an emergency Locum Consultant I felt that all patients presenting with abdominal pain were being bounced between medicine, surgery, obstetrics etc. depending on the scenario. I felt that we could improve on this service so I had a meeting with various clinical leads and we agreed that all patients presenting to E.D would be initially seen by the ED doctor and, based on the investigation, the consultant would decide which speciality the patient would be referred to if requiring admission and then, once the patient is referred, there would be no bounce back. This resulted in better patient care and we were able to implement this within a short period for which I felt satisfied."

Response Analysis:

While this is a good example where the candidate actually identified a problem – which is quite unique in a short period as a Locum Consultant and they were actually able to bring about the change. What this response lacks are the detail. For example, the candidate could have elaborated a little bit more about the processes and logistics, could have discussed the practicalities of implementing the change so that it demonstrates that he is aware of bringing about a change as demonstrated in a good response below.

Good Response:

"When I was a Locum Consultant in the emergency department we felt that there was lack of clarity in the pathways on management of patients presenting to the ED with abdominal pain resulting in time wastage and patients being bounced between specialities. The junior doctors or the team would then have to talk to a different team member. This was not good patient care and was not governance safe. I audited different times and followed patients' journeys from the point of their patient entry to final speciality destination. We identified unacceptable delays between the speciality transfer which was unpredictable. I met clinical leads in different specialities – mainly medical and surgical – and we came up with different pathways and processes – for example a pathway for abdominal pain due to stones and pathways due to biliary problems. We developed guidelines which were agreed and approved at the Trust's guideline committee. These guidelines were then put on the Intranet so that people were aware of the guidelines and we were able to bring about a big change in the whole process. This ensured safe patient journeys without major conflict within the department and unhappiness at various levels. The process was governance safe demonstrating good practices. A re-audit showed better outcomes."

Response Analysis:

This example is good, detailed and goes through the process of bringing about the changes; it talks about the hurdles that needed to be faced - audit to identify the scale of the problem, meeting with different service leads, writing the guidelines that require a consensus and agreement for approval from the Trust Board and, finally, to take it up to the Trust Intranet and dissemination of the guidelines to various levels. This is a very comprehensive response and shows that the candidate is aware of implementing changes. It also talks about the governance issues regarding delays and hence it is an all-round response.

Overall:

Questions which ask about initiative or about implementing changes are not just about whether you are able to bring about changes but also about how the change was brought on and its effectiveness. A change is not something that everyone likes, people are mostly not comfortable with change – this could be because either they are comfortable with what currently exists or they are not able to cope with change. It is important to get these people on board and convince them that change is embraced by everyone affected. In addition, the need for change needs to be established by some processes QIP or an audit and any change needs to be done with a consensus for the people who are going to be affected. Once the change is made it is extremely important to ensure that the change has not caused chaos and is acceptable and results in better patient care. It is a good idea to look at this from a conflict point of view; there are opportunities taken well to demonstrate your awareness and abilities to deal with conflict, team working, governance, audit, QIP activities in this kind of a response.

114. What do you think about change? Why people resist change?

Over period of time, people get set into a routine. Sometime, change is required for number of reasons (improve efficiency, financial reason, technology, new research etc). This means people need to adept to change. This question looks simple on surface but this is testing your abilities to see whether you can bring out a change without causing a commotion and getting confrontational. This is an opportunity to show your knowledge/awareness on team working, managing conflict and vision.

Bad Response:

"Change is a process whereby a shift from current to something which will happen in future. I think people resist change because they usually become settled into what they are doing; they have found their way to get around to whatever is expected or their way of doing things. A change means a change in lots of things and can cause either chaos, discomfort or people will have to adjust to whatever change is being implemented."

Response Analysis:

It is quite a reasonable response; it is not bad, it gives a bit of a rationale behind why people don't like change but again, it does not give the impression that the candidate is thinking in terms of NHS culture and it would be useful because change needs to happen, things need to change and people need to show adaptability because that is the only way to learn from mistakes and improve care.

Good Response:

"Change is a process where we find out any idea or a way of doing something which needs to improve for a better way or anything that needs a way forward. Change could be as a result of a response, a mistake that we need to learn from or to implement a better technique, innovation – something that we have found out is useful for better patient care. It could also be just a means of changing how we react; it could be a personal, institutional, organisational change or it could be based on technology. Therefore, change is part and parcel of our life, it is something that we have to be able to adapt to, learn from and continue to evolve. For example, a mistake made in clinical practice – while we work in an NHS 'no blame' culture we still have to ensure that no patients are affected in a similar way, so a root cause analysis (RCA) to fully demonstrate and find out what actually caused the mistake will also be a recommendation; these changes need to be implemented to ensure similar mistakes do not happen.

It is essential. People resist because, when change is implemented, people who have gotten used to a way of working, a way of doing things – it could affect their lifestyle, it could affect their travel, it may mean that they have to move to a different location – some people are simply unable to cope with technology. So, there are a number of reasons why people resist change but it could be implemented if change is brought slowly, if people are made to understand the reason and rationale behind the change the resistance would be less and we can avoid any conflict arising as a result of this. Change is therefore essential for continuous provision of better care."

Response analysis:

This is a good response; it covers multiple aspects and references root cause analysis, conflict, change in technology etc. This example could include the National IT programme and the big change that was initiated but never completed for various reasons.

Overall:

I think this is a good opportunity where candidates have the opportunity to demonstrate the need for change, the rationale behind it. They can even discuss governance, show their experience of any change they were able to bring in (QIP). They can show that team working spirit can go out of the window if change is not handled properly but results in all round happiness if managed correctly and with consensus.

115. When you have an idea that many are against, how do you implement it?

As discussed above, change is resisted by many. People can react in many ways (obstruct the change, criticise and negatively influence creating a situation of conflict. Implementing a change is a skill and become more so when many are averse to the idea.

Bad Response:

"If I have an idea which I feel is important and will improve patient care I will just try to convince people that this is going to be good for patient care; I will meet with them, I would try to speak to my bosses, my managers and I will demonstrate that the idea is great, it is going to improve, it has been done before and, hopefully, I will be able to convince people and the change will be implemented."

Response Analysis:

The candidate needs to understand why the idea is opposed by so many people. There could be a multitude of reasons and unless there is an understanding of why people are against it, it would be very hard to implement this. The candidate therefore needs to show more in-depth response to demonstrate this.

Good Response:

"When I have an idea, I will first float it to the people that it is going to affect to see their response. If I feel that they are against it, I would take a step back. I will look at the idea, I will analyse it from different perspectives, I will look at the evidence and look at places where the same idea has been tried. If it has happened before I will try to understand how the change was implemented and what the barriers were to implementing this idea. If the idea could be a simple thing an understanding of the resistance against the idea would help me in implementing it.

Sometimes I may need to think that maybe the idea is not so good actually, it may be my idea and I may be very passionate about it but if I feel that lots of people are against it, then in that case I would have to think again by possibly shelving it for the time being until I can convince people as to why the idea is good and how it is going to improve patient care. There is no point implementing a change, bringing out an idea or forcing it on people because it will not be implemented and will in fact may be counterproductive to patient care and that is the least thing we need."

Response analysis:

The candidate shows insight, he shows that he is prepared to take a step back and not force the idea on people. It shows maturity, it also shows the processes that the candidate would take i.e. share the idea first, take in the views of different people, doing a retrospective assessment of the idea, finding out the resistance to the change, answering queries and then implementing or holding for the time being until a resolution to all the challenges is found. This way the patient care is not compromised, which the candidate has alluded to as well.

Overall:

A question like this is just basically trying to see your thought process. An idea will eventually lead to a session of some change and if people are resisting or are against it then it can create a situation of conflict. One needs to be able to demonstrate this in that one should also be aware of the conflict, conflict resolution, implementing changes and the barriers to this. It needs to be linked with team working and governance so as to give a total good response.

116.   Tell us about a situation when you have been involved in a conflict? How did you resolve?

Conflict occurs when two people have different views on a something e.g. a change being suggested. Conflict is a behavioural reaction and can be obstructive in task achievement and may risk failure. Conflict could be due to different views, means to achieve or simply due to personalities of the individual. A team works less efficiently in such situation and must be avoided at all costs. NHS Improvement has suggested tools to manage conflict (see link).

Bad response:

"I try to avoid conflict. This is not something anyone is comfortable with. It can break a team and put task at risk. I am a cautious person and I avoid all situations where conflict can occur. I remember being in a situation of conflict when I was involved in a car accident and there was some argument re: who was at fault. I left it to the insurance people to decide the outcome."

Response analysis:

Conflict is part and parcel of life. It is not something that can be avoided as there would always be a situation where two people do not agree on something. It is hard to believe that the candidate has not been in a situation and if so, make one wonder if the candidate does make any assertive statements at all! The example given of a car accident and the solution left to someone else is not right. It can be taken as an escape mechanism and the inability of the candidate to stay firm on ground which is necessary at times.

Good response:

"Conflict is a situation that should be minimised for better experiences. Yet, it is not completely avoidable. I was involved in rota change discussions with the rota coordinator where we were looking at a rota to reduce number of people on shift at a time. There were a group of us who did not disagree as the rota change would have affected after we left the trust (we were not affected) but myself and some others felt that as we were making decisions for our colleagues we had to ensure that the rota was fair, did not compromise patient safety and we remained EWTD compliant. We also had to ensure that the breaks and zero days were not affecting continuity of care of the patient's as well as our training. It required several meetings (and coffee!) before we finally agreed on a template that ticked all boxes. I felt the better communication, listening and responding in a friendly manner was the key to success."

Response analysis:

This response is detailed, gives an example that can occur in day to day life and offers solutions. The candidate has shown capabilities to handle the situation and reach an all happy options. It also conveys empathy as the candidate has stood firm for his colleagues showing strengths of his character. It is interesting, how cleverly he has sneaked in important issues like EWTD, patient safety etc.

Overall:

Do not be afraid to state when asked about issues that you think can be taken as a weakness. It is perfectly natural to be in situations where you can disagree with others. If you are not, it can be a sign of weakness. They are not interested in knowing if you have ever been in difficult situation. They want to know how do you deal with these issues? Do you know how to handle difficult people and how to deal with problems? In addition, you also need to convey that conflict is bad for team working, leads to low morale, lack of confidence in leadership and eventually impact patient care (in NHS setting). Be honest, be natural, be yourself. Give real life examples, see how they can potentially impact patient care and come up with a solution.

117. Do you motivate people? How?

Do not be shy and undersell yourself. This is your opportunity to highlight your strengths, what you are good in and what you have achieved. Be careful though. You should not come across as arrogant and not appear to be bragging. Give examples if you can.

Bad Response:

"I motivate people by leading by example. I am a hard-working goal orientated person, I always make sure I am on-time, people can rely on me. I read a lot and pass any information on to people around me. I therefore believe that by doing what I am doing people can see that I am doing a good job and like to emulate me."

Response Analysis:

This is nothing but 'bragging'. The candidate does not give an example of how they motivate, who they motivate, why it is important and it just a very short explanation.

Good Response:

"Motivation is important and there are lots of opportunities that we feel inspired by – such as other people who have done something and we would like to replicate their experience. It could be something as simple as doing an act – e.g. creating a nice topiary in the garden or being a fast clinician, who is able to solve problems, diagnose quickly. It could be an example where someone is able to produce lots and lots of papers and publish in prestigious journals. I believe I have learned from experts during my training and my short time as a Locum Consultant; I feel that I motivate people because I work hard and that when I am on time people also feel that they should be on time in order to avoid wasting time. Similarly, when I am teaching, it is a good activity and not only people who are teaching and gaining from it – even the teacher is learning. Therefore, people like to stay updated.

Another example I could give is when I am presenting at Grand Round I tend to prepare very well; I work with my junior to get the slides perfected, to give them some practice; this means they have learned and done a good job. Not only will this improve the quality of Grand Round and teaching activities, it will also produce good quality doctors for the future which will be productive for people in person as well as for the organisation. I believe I motivate by continuing to work hard where other people can learn from it and emulate."

Response Analysis:

This is a lengthy response; it could possibly be reduced by about 2/3rds but it does give a situation where people get motivated in different ways. Therefore, in summary, it is a reasonably good example. It could have been made better by trimming down the contents and relating it with some form of patient care – e.g. a better way of talking about punctuality; This improves patient care because of ward round or that the clinic gets started on time, we finish on time and jobs can be continued in a timely manner; it also improves patient flow through the hospital and reduces backlog and impact on other issues such as A&E breach time and patients end up being on the appropriate ward because of the better flow. This is therefore just another way of bringing about other NHS issues in your response.

Overall:

This is again a question which tests your personality and is testing how you deal with different kind of situations, life situations and whether you have what it takes to be a consultant who can lead, who can motivate and inspire people to take bigger aspirations. There is going to be no right or wrong answer as long as you give something which could be improved upon for which you can give examples.

118. When did you argue with your colleague? Why?

This is again testing your handling of conflict. Interpersonal skills are important. You will be working with other consultant/team members within the department. In this question, you are asked "not about why" but "how you managed" the conflict with colleague. Situational conflict due to task or processes can be managed but interpersonal conflicts are very difficult and often leave scars. It is no use saying you have not been in conflict situation as it will show that you do not stand up or hold firm or simply appear spineless! It is safe to give an example where the disagreement as on goal or project rather than making it look like personality clash.

Bad Response:

"I try to avoid situations where I may need to disagree with a colleague. I am not very good at arguing. Arguments can cause team break-downs. The last time I remember arguing with someone was when there was some leave planning which was needed as both of us wanted to have leave during the school holidays, we had entered an arrangement where one of us would go and the other consultant would remain to provide Trust cover. Unfortunately, because of a number of issues both of us wanted to be away for the Christmas period. I felt that I had not taken any leave around the Christmas holiday period for the last few years whereas my counterpart felt that because he had applied for the leave before I did he should have been allowed the time off. Eventually, our manager looked at our previous leave plan and who was away at which time and came up with a mutual agreement."

Response analysis:

It is not good to say that you avoid a situation because arguments can happen over simple things such as who is paying the bill for a meal – as both parties would like to pay. It could be a pleasant argument or it could be something that can turn into something a bit nasty. The question needs to be understood appropriately so that it can be answered with some substance in it. The example given here is quite a good example but it just shows the handling of the whole issue means that there is no team working spirit, there is no understanding of the role of a consultant, there is no understanding between the two consultants and neither of the two consultants were willing to see from the service point of view, from the policy point of view and they had totally disregarded previously agreed policies and protocols. Involvement of the managers in such a trivial matter also shows that both parties were unable to decide by just discussing and sorting out the matter between themselves.

Good Response:

"Argument is something that happens when two parties do not agree on a common point. It is can happen over trivial issues and escalate into a really big problem. When I was on call as consultant surgeon, the previous day's surgery was still happening which meant that when I was on-call on that day and emergency surgery needed to be done I had to wait for the previous day's surgery to finish. When I looked at the reasoning it was mainly due to the shortage of nurse cover so some of the night surgery was spilling into day. When I spoke to the theatre co-ordinator, she felt that I was trying to criticise the service whereas she was doing her best to run the theatre safely. I had to be slightly firm and say that I was not trying to criticise anyone, I was just trying to point out a gap and that we need to work together. As a result of this we looked at the time when the surgery was delayed or the night surgery was conducted the next day. We identified a patient safety issue and then went to the managers to get some extra nursing support during the night or early hours of the morning. This way, although we had an argument we were able to close it amicably without any hard feeling between us and improve patient care and achieved better flow."

Response analysis:

This response shows maturity; it shows that while an argument can happen as long as they end up in a healthy dialogue between two people, as long as the understanding exists and it leads to a good outcome as a result of that it is acceptable. The argument is also given with a good example which raises a patient safety issue as well as talks about briefly on clinical governance. An all-out good response which will leave a good impression.

Overall

A question which appears probing, that challenges you is usually good to see whether you are showing maturity, whether you have the capability to handle difficult situations. In situations like that it is very easy just to given an example and walk away; always include an example, try to bring some aspect – such as a clinical aspect – or something which leads to changes in policies or some protocol development. This will show not only that you have the ability to find a problem but that you can come up with solutions as well.

119. Do you think people trust you? Why?

The ability to trust is extremely important whilst working within NHS. NHS holds lot of personally identifiable information that and people don't always like everyone to know about their health issues. People should be able to confide in you. Probity is one of the main attributes within the GMC's good medical practice framework. This is an opportunity to shown your awareness, hence that you follow, your knowledge on issues surrounding trust/probity.

Bad Response:

"I think people trust me because they tell me lots of things that they would not tell anyone else. They wouldn't tell me if they didn't trust me would they. For example, recently I was having coffee in the restaurant when my next-door neighbour – who was passing through after having come to the hospital for an appointment - saw me and came to me and told me all about his impending divorce because he was going through cancer treatment. I thought that was pretty bad because family shouldn't split because of the stress of an illness. He wouldn't have trust me with something as private and personal such as a divorce or sickness."

Response Analysis:

This is a very bad response; the candidate has no idea what trust is about. The candidate does not have any insight into giving correct examples. Also, the opportunity to bring out the Caldecott Guidance Data Protection Act within the NHS is also missed.

Good Response:

"I feel that people trust me because they approach me many times asking for some advice and solutions – more so when they are stuck in situations where they need some way out. I have come across this in personal situations when people are going through difficult life situations or even in their professional life; my colleagues, juniors or healthcare people have asked me if they can take my advice. People trust me because they know that what they discuss will stay with me. As a Clinician it is extremely important that we safeguard the data because data protection is very high and we need to ensure that we do not breach. The NHS Trusts have a Caldecott Guidance to ensure that these aspects of patient care are strictly followed. In addition, the newly implemented GDPR is again a directive which reminds us about data protection and breach. Therefore, people's trust is again an extension of a similar trust that people put their faith and because I have been in a situation where I have not divulged secrets of other people makes me feel that people trust me. Another example of this is a situation where a colleague was thinking of changing jobs but he did not want other people to know, hence he came to me to seek advice on how he should go about it; my advice resulted in that person getting a job for which he was very thankful."

Response Analysis:

This is a good response; it is slightly lengthy and could be trimmed up. It gives an example, it mentions an example which is actually topical, it also talks about the Caldecott Guardianship and links the date protection and trust with NHS policies.

Overall:

As always, understanding questions is important and then linking something relevant to working within NHS is the key when responding to this question. No point saying, people give me their passwords to bank accounts or facebook!

120. Do you think your patients respect you? Why is that?

This is a continuation of the theme from previous question and the opportunity to reflect on similar attributes with a slightly different phrasing.

Bad Response:

"I think my patients do respect me because of the manner in which I approach them; I also explain in non-medical terms complex conditions to them and I always have them at the centre of my consultation. I also think that they naturally would respect a doctor - but you have to gain the respect from them."

Response Analysis:

While this is not such a bad response because the candidate does give reasons which he explains, follows the process and explains in simple linguistic terms - a slight error is that he has not given *why* and elaborated by giving examples.

Good Response:

"I believe my patients respect me because when I see them in clinic they are looking forward to attending the clinic not only because they are going to be managed for their long-term condition but they appear to be genuinely happy to see me. Often, they have requested to the clinic nurse that they would particularly like to see me (this may be added to the notes by the nurse). As I am only a Locum Consultant this is quite rewarding as most patients usually prefer to see the substantive consultant. I also often receive thankyou notes and cards from patients and patient feedback - which is included as part of my revalidation process - has been exemplary and I have had comments which make me feel very valued. I believe that this is because I am nice to them, I am clinically competent and I speak to them in a language that they understand. If they are not able to understand I will make sure that they have all the necessary information in the form of leaflets or any support material which we can provide. When they contact my PA for any extra information I am always available to them within the remit of my clinical work."

Response Analysis:

This is a good detailed response; it gives the reasoning, it gives examples, in addition it brings in some of the issues where the follow-on questions can be asked – e.g. GMC, good medical practice and revalidation.

Overall:

Respect is not given but earned. This is your opportunity to showcase your positive attributes, your strengths. Think of something patients may have written in your patient feedback surveys.

121.   Can you describe a time you showed leadership?

Leadership is a key quality in a doctor. The important thing is to show that with this experience you had to demonstrate qualities such as initiative, decisiveness, organisational abilities and the ability to manage, guide and motivate others. It may be that you have not had any leadership roles, however, these experiences can be small. If you have ever taken the lead in organising a social event or group activity, an audit – then this can be used as an example. Describe the situation, how you came to be in a leading role, the steps you took to keep things running smoothly, and the result – for example, a successful event or crisis averted.

When answering this question, it is helpful to think of good qualities in a leader and weave them into your answer. Remember that managing a team doesn't necessarily make you a great leader. It's important to choose a story that demonstrates true leadership- stepping up to guide or motivate or take initiative, ideally in challenging circumstances. Do not be afraid to sell yourself!

Bad Response:

"I do not often take on the leadership role. I prefer to work as a team member and work together to achieve a collective goal. I'm never in charge so I never really get an opportunity to show leadership."

Response Analysis:

Although it is essential that doctors act as team members, they also pay a dual role as team leaders due to the multidisciplinary nature of healthcare. Above answer does not give any example of leadership and is inadequate. It is clear that the candidate does not realise the importance of leadership in the role of a doctor.

Good Response A:

"I am a Charity Officer currently and had to organise the Charity Fair to raise money for the Urology equipment. I scheduled a meeting for the full team to discuss ideas but discovered that four people had dropped out. We had to divide the responsibilities between the remaining team members as a result, people were overworked and morale suffered. I baked for each weekly meeting to demonstrate my appreciation for all of their hard work during a challenging time. I also ensured that I asked them for ideas on how to be more efficient. I made it clear that no idea was stupid and that it was a safe environment for making suggestions. Performance improved and we all worked together to make the Charity Fair a huge success and we raised sufficient funds to get the equipment we wanted."

Good Response B:

"After having a string of lost CCG bids, I noticed that morale in the team was getting low. To try and counteract this, I tried to be as positive as possible and encourage my team-mates to come to a brain storming session to discuss and to make sure we all knew what was expected of us and what was needed to get to the goals. We arranged this outside of the workplace to avoid distraction. I think this was important in stopping some of my team-mates from choosing to abstain from meetings and was one of the reasons why we were successful in getting our bid. I think being able to help organise and motivate team members is important in my role as consultant."

Response Analysis:

The answer shows many key qualities needed in a leader. By baking, the candidate shows that they understand the importance of motivating team members and showing appreciation for their work. The candidate also shows great listening and communication skills.

Overall:

A good answer will demonstrate knowledge of the qualities seen in a good leader such as communication skills, motivating others and inspiring trust. A better answer may relate the skills shown to what they have seen in clinical practice and give examples.

122. Do you think it's better to lead from the front or from the back?

This question may be asked to test your ability to argue and defend a point and stimulate further discussion so that the interviewers can get a better understating of your personality. It is reasonable to pick either of the options, however, it would be wise to consider both in your answer. Where possible, try to include examples of leadership you've seen or experienced (not necessarily in a healthcare setting) and analyse the good and bad points about them and how that influences your decision. You may wish to take a more neutral stance and suggest that leadership is dependent on the goal and team so needs to be tailored to them rather than a particular style. This idea also lends itself to the notion that leadership is a more fluid concept than simply 'from the front' or 'from the back'.

Bad Response:

"I think leadership is almost always better from the front – setting a good example and explaining what is expected but being able to look back to support members of the team that need it. When doing SpR rotation, this is that style of leadership I saw from one of the consultants who all the juniors liked and respected. They said he was nice to work for as they all know what he expected of them but he was approachable to ask for help if needed."

Response Analysis:

This response isn't terrible; it's just narrow-minded and would almost certainly be challenged by the interviewers with a counter example. Discussing personal experiences would be helpful here too, particularly as during your training and early career you should have witnessed many different leadership styles but it is developing your own that is important.

Good Response:

"I would argue that leadership is specific to the situation and team it is applied to and, therefore, a good leader will adapt their style accordingly. I saw a good example of this during my SpR rotation. The consultant very much led 'from the front' during the ward round and all the juniors said that this was helpful as they knew exactly what they needed to do for all the patients that day. However, at a different time, I saw my consultant lead rather more 'from the back' when he was encouraging his juniors to take the lead in consultations during a clinic session. He also allowed us a free hand when we were planning an audit project.

In situations where I have led, I have also experienced that the style of leadership needs to be adapted to the team I'm leading. For example, in the audit project that I worked with the foundation year doctors, I let them develop the data collection sheet and analyse the data, this gave them the freedom to explore different dimensions in the project. This suits the group of peers I'm working with and also shows us as a united team. I think one must have the flexibility to change the style and this should be dependent on team members and the team dynamics, project, skill mix and goal."

Response Analysis:

This response includes both clinical and personal experiences of leadership and demonstrates a good depth of thought into the subject. The neutral stance allows you to put more arguments forward for both styles and shows you're not blinkered by one experience but open to new ideas. When discussing the leadership style of others, it's good to ask the members of the team what the style is like and whether it works for them, as in this response where you say you spoke to the junior doctors. Of course, your own observations are valid and good to talk about too.

Overall:

Leadership is a big part of medicine and this question is a great opportunity for you to demonstrate that you are aware of leadership, different styles and are already developing your own. Personal examples of either experiences being led or leading are great to include. This is an opportunity to show off your team working. Bring out your audit/QIP work if this has not been discussed!"

123. Would you describe yourself as a leader or a follower? Is it better for doctors to be a leader or a follower?

This question really gets at the idea that a healthy balance between these two personality traits is highly desirable in a good doctor. Leadership skills are absolutely essential in being able to coordinate a potentially large team of highly educated and skilled individuals in the most efficient and effective way possible. However, being a "follower" in the sense of being part of a team led by another member of staff is an intrinsic part of being a doctor. Throughout your training right up to consultancy (and commonly even during this period), being part of a team and following instructions is pivotal to ensuring the best possible healthcare for your patients.

This is the kind of question that promotes an immediate knee-jerk response ('leader!') from many candidates, but is actually asking for a deeper analysis of the roles within the interdisciplinary team that doctors work in. A balanced answer is the best approach to this loaded question!

Bad Response:

"I am a leader because doctors lead their team. I have a very strong personality that has been cultivated from my experiences in leading my group during the SpR training days when I was in charge of leave planning, audit project and was the president of the doctor's mess. I enjoy executing my vision of how a task should be completed and am proud of my ruthless attitude in ensuring that my team complete the job in hand the way I want. I rarely get questioned or challenged, and therefore, I believe that I make an excellent leader, and would be a very decisive doctor."

Response Analysis:

Though it is good that the candidate cites occasions where he has led a team, his explanation of his role is very worrying. He puts far too much emphasis on his personal vision and strongly implies that he doesn't consider the views of his team, but just forces them into executing his plan. Doctors should confer with their team to come to a consensus for a treatment plan given that often "more heads are better than one" and also will build better team morale by considering their views.

This view leaves little scope for the doctor to be humble and learn from others. No one can know everything, so the team members rely on each other to make sure the patient receives the best care possible. For example, nurses tend to know more about how the patient is doing on a day-to-day basis, and are often confided in by the patient when they don't want to interrupt the doctor or 'waste their time'.

Good Response:

"I would say that I have a healthy mixture of these two traits. When I was working in the rota redesign group, I effectively sought a consensus of opinion on our group member's views. Having every member of the team contributing to the plan led to a collaborative attitude within the team and helped me to fine tune our approach leading to a team-based decision. This was invariably very appropriate. Likewise, I am a good member of my local care home's staff and ensure that I best apply the plan implemented by the management for the care of patients whilst also offering feedback from my experiences as to where things could be improved.

The doctor should be both a leader and a follower depending on the situation. The job involves taking on responsibility and learning to organise and lead a team. However, the doctor is also a follower – always looking to learn from others and better themselves. Having the integrity to recognise and actively work on our failings is very important, so whilst the doctor should try their best and be confident in their abilities, they should also have the humility to learn from their juniors as well as their seniors.

Overall, I would argue that the doctors should be able to make a seamless transition between a leader and a follower to provide the best care for their patients."

Response Analysis:

This response *uses a small project on rota redesign as a* parallel for the everyday decisions that need to be made by teams of doctors. It shows that the candidate has cultivated crucial team-working skills as both a leader and a follower and accurately assesses the doctor's role in the multidisciplinary team, recognising the importance of learning from everyone around you regardless of hierarchy. It also acknowledges that the doctor should gain confidence in their abilities and take on responsibilities. This dual nature is essential for doctors, so being able to recognise it before beginning medical school shows a valuable insight into the true nature of the profession.

The final part of the response throws a bit of a curve-ball to the interviewer – medicine should always be patient-focused, but whilst discussing hierarchy and roles in the multidisciplinary team, the patient is often forgotten. By invoking the patient, the candidate shows they can think outside of the medical team and focus on what is really important.

Overall:

This question attempts to elucidate a reflex response based on the old paternalistic view of doctors as leaders. A thoughtful and balanced answer to the question can show a very realistic understanding of how a medical team works and the role of a doctor, which are essential qualities in a medical student. Thinking of the patient in this context demonstrates a high level of empathy and an attitude that is patient-focused.

It is essential that you identify an experience that you've had which demonstrates you as having a balanced approach to leadership. Leadership is an essential quality in doctors, however, the interview answer must not accidentally sway too far the other way and suggest the candidate is arrogant and doesn't consider the opinions of the rest of his team. Likewise, you should appreciate that for large chunks of your career now, you will be a senior doctor or manager, and therefore, should have a healthy attitude to 'following' too.

124.   Tell me something you have done that you are proud of.

This is a simple question with many potential pitfalls. Many will use this opportunity to list all their achievements, often without adding any further depth to their responses and failing to use this opportunity to highlight the qualities they have that would make good future doctors. This question aims to test a candidate's ability to self-analyse. Do not be afraid of picking an achievement that you're worried may seem boastful. Remember, the main point of the question is not to focus on things that you have done but rather the skills you learnt from them.

Bad Response:

"I am most proud of my publications in prestigious journals. "Publish or perish" is my philosophy. So, I am very happy and proud of my publications. I was also recognised in the local newspaper which was a very rewarding experience. I was delighted to make my family proud, but even more so, I was pleased that my hard work and determination paid off."

Response Analysis:

This answer, unfortunately, lacks any real depth. The candidate failed to explore the skills that they gained from the experience but rather focused on the superficial details. The candidate also needed to highlight more qualities that they need to demonstrate as a consultant. The candidate should have chosen a broader response to develop a more comprehensive answer.

Good Response:

"One of the most memorable moments that I am proud of was presenting my research in the main stream sessions of an international conference and win the award of the best presentation. It was an honour, but I like to think of it as a culmination of efforts by my team (audit, research, statistical support team) that contributed to the project. It was a great experience and really showed me how effective team working leads to outcome. I also developed my communication skills, an essential attribute in reaching common goals. Successful completion of a project requires consistent hard work, a quality that is core to being a successful doctor,

I was also a part of the organising yearly cricket match between consultant and registrars. This was great fun and helped to develop my sense of teamwork and accountability in a competitive environment- attributes that I firmly believe apply to the world of medicine. All in all, I believe being recognised for the hard work was a great experience and I feel proud for myself and my team. This gave me a lot of confidence moving forward."

Response Analysis:

This answer is a good example of being able to take an achievement and break it down into its component skills and qualities. Not only does the candidate highlight their ability to self-analyse, but they are also able to relate their skills back to your role as a consultant.

Overall:

Think of something you have done which incorporates a lot of different qualities, then break them down to discuss individually. It is important that you expand on each individual thing and relate them back to your role as consultant.

125. In what way will you contribute to this organisation if you were appointed?

The interviewer wants to see that you have considered your future life in your new place of work and that you are a balanced individual with a variety of interests that predisposes you to be a well-rounded individual. Your answer should be enthusiastic and passionate. You could talk about your clinical work, any extracurricular activities you would consider or anything that you are passionate about and is also available in the new organisation or in its vicinity. It could be something you have never tried before, or any skills you already have that you want to bring to the new organisation (and become an asset). If you have any ambitions of taking up specific roles of responsibility, it would be worth mentioning them in your answer, as well as if you have any ideas of things you would like to discover and explore or start up.

Bad Response:
"When I get this job, I will work exceptionally hard as a consultant. I will aim to achieve clinical excellence and put the trust on the map of xxx speciality by contributing heavily and making the organisation well known."

Response Analysis:
This answer does not give the impression that the candidate will gain much on a personal or developmental level; it does not show a willingness to get involved. The candidate is very focused on his/her role to an unhealthy extent and also demonstrates arrogance in their answer. The candidate shows very little interest in extracurricular pursuits and appears to have a limited awareness. The candidate appears unprepared to be a consultant and it does not seem as though he/she will make the most or contribute to patient care.

Good Response:
"I would love to live in a city which will be a very interesting experience for me as I have lived in rural areas all my life. I would be interested in getting involved in supporting homeless people or those with disabilities in the city. I am very keen to stand up as an ambassador for the homeless by supporting the neighbouring communities. I would love to take part in a team sport such as hockey as I can use my organisational skills from immediate past where I used to organise hockey matches between juniors and consultants. I feel I would gain some really useful skills from the experience. I would also use my SIM training and develop SIM training for the junior doctors which I believe the trust is planning to develop."

Response Analysis:
The response is very personal, which makes it stand out to the interviewer as well as marking it as an honest and respectable answer. The answer is not overly ambitious and realises that limitations may be placed on the candidate. Nevertheless, the candidate demonstrates motivation to try new things and a willingness to help others. It shows that he/she can see past the clinical role of the consultant. Candidate leave the interviewers thinking that you have read the job description and have a gone a step further to discover future plans (SIM trainings).

Overall:
Aim to show the interviewer that you are passionate, have a lot to offer to the trust in multiple ways than just as a clinician, and that you are excited about your new role. Being pro-active is a good trait which shows that you are an independent and capable individual.

126. Name some of the difficulties involved in leading a team, how did you make a difference?

In whatever job you do in the future, it is very likely that you will be working as part of a team. This question is looking for examples in the past when you have worked as a team, but more importantly, the challenges that the team experienced and what you did about those challenges. It is perfectly fine that you had problems working with a team in the past, but the interviewer really wants to see your response to these challenges. This does not have to be related to a medical team (although this can only help the answer) but should show skills desirable in a doctor.

Being a good doctor means more than simply being a good clinician. In their day-to-day role, not only are doctors expected to provide clinical care, but they are also expected to provide leadership. The interviewer knows that you are capable of leading, but wants you to prove it to them. The way to answer this question is to provide them with a strong example of when you led a team successfully.

Bad Response:
"I do not often lead teams so this question is a little difficult for me. I think I tend to follow the team leader more often, but if no progress is made then I do step up. For example, we were involved in a group presentation and the 'leader' wasn't really leading, so I had a discussion with the other members and it was decided that I should become the leader for this presentation. I was quite uncomfortable with the whole situation but I didn't really have a choice. We managed to get the presentation together after I became the team leader. In this way, I think I did do a good job of leading the team."

Response Analysis:
This answer lacks confidence and assertiveness. These are skills that good leaders should demonstrate when leading their teams. The candidate perhaps did not use the best example of leading from the front as they had not volunteered to be the leader but were coerced into the position. The answer could have been improved by expanding further on how the candidate thinks they did as a leader; did they motivate their peers after morale was low, did they re-assign tasks to people? Example of taking over from other leader as he was "not up to scratch" is not one to use in interview setting though it does show assertiveness but can be perceived as challenging behaviour and not a trait some managers like to have.

Good Response:
"I have developed my teamwork skills but it has not been without challenges. Poor communication within the team, lack of diversity and poor leadership are some common issues faced by dysfunctional team or teams that underperform. When working in a group, sometimes personalities of the people can make team cohesion difficult. Skill mix and inappropriate task allocation can also cause difficulties. When I was leading the ERCP panel recently, we were unable to start our meetings in time as two team members were always late. I spoke to them and this was mainly due to having a clinic in community requiring travel. We changed the meeting day and the problem was resolved. Timely action and communication led the team together and we were able to develop our new ECP pathway."

Response Analysis:
This response is significantly better. The candidate is focused on what they did within a team rather than talking about how they led a team. The person also brings in a specific challenge that they faced in this team as well as a suitable way of dealing with the challenge.

Overall:
This question may throw a few people because it involves talking about a weakness or challenge, but do not be fooled. You should show your strengths by showing how you dealt with a particular challenge. This will be a common theme in questions that ask about challenges that you faced in the past. The main part of this question lies with how you worked within a team to create a positive impact; any challenges that you faced and how you dealt with them also increase the maturity of the response. Poor working conditions (lack of space, telephone lines, computers), confusion on the roles lead to conflict and wasted energy to resolve conflict within the team taking away the focus from goals and you could give examples to show these issues.

127. As a consultant, who do you think is the most important part of your team?

Teamwork is an important part of medicine, but this question also requires you to understand your own role in the team and the specialist services that members of the team can offer. You can approach this question in several different ways – for example, from the point of view of different situations or from the point of view of your grade. When structuring your response, you may wish to start by exploring exactly what the 'team' at the time or situation you're discussing would consist of, and then, having demonstrated you really understand how much of a multidisciplinary approach medicine is, you can comment on who you think would be the best important part.

Bad Response:
"I think the nurses would form the most important part of the team for me. They are the people who know their patients best and spend more time with them during the day than the doctors have the time for. I feel the nursing staff are very helpful to patients, junior doctors and families."

Response Analysis:
This response falls into the trap of speaking before the candidate fully structured their response. This question is so broad that you need to start by narrowing down the situation you are referring to, for example, a situation you have experience as a clinician is a good place to start. When preparing your answer to questions, also try to think about what holes the interviewers could pick in your argument. Here, they could ask you what would happen if there were no doctors, or why have so many doctors if nurses are the most important team members.

Good Response:
"This is a really tough question because medicine so often relies on the skills of a multidisciplinary team in order to work well. Therefore, everyone is, in a way, as important as each other. For example, as a surgeon, I know that surgery cannot happen without the correct patient, a skilled anaesthetist, an assistant, a team of scrub nurses, and so on. Even porters that bring the patient to theatre are important. Missing any one of those people or skills would have meant the theatre will not run properly (delayed or cancelled surgeries).

In some situations, one could argue that the patient is the most important member of the team as the majority of factors affecting their health will be experienced outside the hospital, so they are the one with the most power to make decisions and changes. However, in the case of neonates, not all patients can be educated by doctors in order to make decisions about their health. Overall, I would say there is no 'most important' member of the team provided all the necessary members are there and each situation is highly dependent on the specific patient and their health."

Response Analysis:
This response justifies your opinion well using an example to illustrate a situation common in medicine. Suggesting the patient is the most important person is unlikely to be a novel or exciting response for the interviewers, however, if you reason why you think so and highlight cases where this may not be the case, you have demonstrated a well-thought-through approach to the question. In this kind of question where there are multiple points and situations to consider, summarising your thoughts at the end of your response will demonstrate conviction and will be impressive.

Overall:
This question is definitely worth thinking about and structuring your ideas in advance of attending interviews. You can really impress with a well-thought-through reply that stands out from the 'nurses' and 'doctors' the interviewers will have heard a lot of. Any experience you have of teamwork can work well as an example to include in this question.

128. What is the biggest challenge you faced and how did you deal with it?

This question is aimed at trying to identify those candidates who have the personal attributes to thrive in this often challenging and stressful career. It is important that the example cited by the candidate has some kind of "moral to the story" that demonstrates these attributes. This is the sort of question where it pays to have thought about examples beforehand.

Bad Response:

"I was visiting a nursing home when an elderly lady fell on the floor. She was clearly very distressed and appeared to have suffered a fracture of the neck of the femur due to her obvious osteoporosis. Everyone in the room was very scared and didn't really know what to do as moving her may cause added pain. Finally, one of the care workers came and called an ambulance and put a blanket on her to keep her warm."

Response Analysis:

Though the candidate has indeed identified a challenging situation, they fail to demonstrate that they performed any sort of active role in overcoming the problem. The candidate has suggested a decent insight into what has medically happened to the elderly lady, but this is not what the question was asking. The candidate should ideally have themselves called for help, fetched the blankets and perhaps calmed the lady and everyone else in the room down. This demonstrates knowledge and an application of problem-solving skills, as opposed to merely watching others perform them. In addition, thinking about a fracture in an old female is not something that is challenging so it does not answer the question.

Good Response: (Outside medicine)

"I was captain of our football team (local club) and we went through a very bad run of results right at the start of the season. Team morale was very low and people were starting to have a go at each other on the pitch. This was having a huge knock-on effect on our relationships with each other and our teamwork. As captain, I had to analyse the situation closely and identify where things were going wrong. Unfortunately, this entailed dropping my best friend from the team and exerting my authority over my peers. Though this was an awkward situation, I feel I dealt with it maturely and my team respected me for that. Sure enough, the team's on-pitch success and morale improved."

Good Response: (Medicine)

"I was the registrar on call and my SHO called in sick This left us short staffed The ED was very busy and I was stuck in theatre. A female patient was brought to the ED who was bleeding heavily. I had to attend to her but was worried that I was delaying the surgery. I contacted the night matron and asked for help. We were able to get the ENT SHO to attend to the patient in ED and stabilise her whilst I managed the patient in theatre. This way with right team working, delegating the task to the right person I was able to managed two sick people."

Response Analysis:

Though the candidate chooses an apparently trivial matter (a football team), it is the principles that he garners from this experience that will interest the interviewers. He demonstrates that he has the leadership qualities to successfully improve team performance and is not afraid to make hard decisions for the good of the team overall. These problems are not dissimilar from those encountered by teams of doctors in ensuring the best possible patient care. The candidate would be well advised to then draw the parallel between their footballing situation and real-life medical team situations to solidify their point.

In the second example, the candidate has chosen a situation where he was torn between two sick people. He had shown his delegating abilities, his convincing power to get a doctor from a different firm. Consultants often are pulled in different directions and the ability to delegate is crucial. They also need to have the ability to know what to delegate and what to keep for themselves.

Overall:

Doctors occasionally face life or death situations. The interviewers will be impressed if you can identify the necessary problem-solving and leadership skills that are beneficial in your future role and show from a personal experience of any sort that you have these qualities.

129. Tell me one thing that you learnt about MDTs during your SpR training.

Multidisciplinary teams (MDTs) are an essential day-to-day component of any healthcare system. This question aims to ensure you understand the importance of the MDT in action and to highlight the skills needed to ensure the MDT operates at a high standard in every clinical scenario and setting. The other component of the question is to come up with an example from your work experience – this does not necessarily have to be a poignant, acute situation (where an organised MDT can mean the difference between life and death). Inter-professional communication is a core theme through all aspects of healthcare provision, from inpatient care through to community services.

Bad Response:

"I noticed how important MDTs are within the hospital setting as both doctors and nurses come together to provide a high level of patient care in a critical situation."

Response Analysis:

It is important to demonstrate an understanding that MDTs are applicable to all healthcare settings: primary through to quaternary care. This response fails to mention the key members of the MDT, which suggests a naiveté as to their importance. This answer needs to expand on the actual function of the MDT and what skills are involved in providing comprehensive care.

Good Response:

"One thing I identified is the importance of having a profound understanding of your individual role within the team and how this interconnect with other members' skills to provide a cohesive, quality intervention. Geriatric Medicine is a speciality that epitomises the importance of a well-polished MDT. By sitting in the MDT meetings early on in my training, I learned how the different roles contributed to the patient's pathway of care. It was impressive to see just how many different disciplines came together to help a single patient: doctors, nurses, occupational therapists, and physiotherapists. I was impressed with the communication within the team. Later on, in the training, I was leading these MDT meeting and was able to make final decisions. I believe the cohesive running of a team help better outcomes for patients and minimises stress which is imperative to a patient-centred approach."

Response Analysis:

This answer demonstrates a comprehensive understanding of the importance of inter-professional communication and its implications in the clinical setting. The answer is backed up by a detailed example from personal experience with the benefits of the MDT acknowledged and understood. Unlike the example of a bad response, this answer shows an understanding that the inter-professional team is not merely limited to doctors and nurses but involves multiple healthcare professionals. The learning points from this answer should be applicable to any situation/speciality e.g. Gastro intestinal MDT team, Thyroid/Urology or oncology MDTs.

Overall:

MDTs are a foundation to all healthcare provisions, so are important. The answer to this question needs to be a detailed example, rich enough to demonstrate an understanding of the breadth of input into an MDT and the importance of each individual role. It also needs to show that you understand that ensuring high-level patient care requires a cohesive and well-oiled team. Again, this is an opportunity to show off your team working, conflict resolution (different team member may have different approach on patient management) and communication skills.

130.   Tell me about a time when you felt saddened in your job?

This question wants to ensure you understand that as a consultant, you will encounter sadness and other emotional challenges on a regular basis. Think about your experiences, how you dealt with them, and how you can pass this to junior doctors.

Bad Response:

"Working as a consultant oncologist mean that often I have to tell patient that they have terminal disease and they are dying. Though I always ensure that this is not affected me personally, it is hard to remain detached all the time. I had a young female who was found to have metastatic breast cancer and I had to discuss the diagnosis prognosis and further treatment plan. It was very difficult and painful to do so as her first child, aged 2 years, was sitting next to her."

Response Analysis:

Whilst this response describes a clearly emotion-evoking scenario, the answer does not go into enough detail. This answer would be a wasted opportunity to demonstrate an understanding of life as a consultant and the qualities required to overcome its challenges.

Good Response:

"I was the on-call consultant and I was contacted by the ED nurse in-charge at the request of my SpR. She needed me in ED resuscitation room as the SpR wanted to me to decide on the CPR. I walked into the ED, few minute later. The CPR was in full swings. I was given the history of an out of hours cardiac arrest in a young 21-year-old boy. He was brought in to the hospital with CPR by the paramedics. The total CPR time was 40 minutes with no sign of life. This was young patients. On further probing, his brother had died a similar death 2 years ago (age 21). The parents were present with their third child age 19. I had to make the sad decision to stop CPR and inform the family of the death of the son. This was a moment where everyone in the room was in tear (nurses/doctors inclusive). I was able to stay calm and keep my composure but was very sad. We discuss this case in post CPR debrief as well as in the Schwartz round. Though I always ensure that work conditions do not affected me personally, it is hard to remain detached all the time. I have learned to keep myself composed and use debrief sessions and Schwartz rounds to learn and ensure that we always show compassion to make a difference in patient care as well as support staff in that process."

Response Analysis:

It is essential to recognise that you will often face sadness during your medical career, this is more challenging as a consultant. Whilst it may be tempting to act seemingly unaffected by something like this, it is more important to recognise and address these emotions. Relating the experience to becoming a better doctor gives a well-rounded and complete answer. It is important to think carefully about how you can relate your experiences to answer a question like this. The response is very emotive and the extent is obvious as the candidate has gone a step forward to discuss this in the Schwartz round. Think of the sad event as a challenge to be overcome and learned from.

Overall:

Don't be embarrassed to say that you were emotionally affected or brag that you don't get emotionally affected (you will come across a non-caring person that is not compassionate). It will show that you understand that being a doctor entail emotional scenario that even the consultants are not immune to. It shows that you have the ability to control your emotions and a strength of character. What is important is that you discuss how overcoming these emotions would actually makes you a better doctor.

187

131. Your junior doctor forgets to introduce medical student to the patient/ask their permission for medical student to observe the consultation. What would you do as consultant in charge when the ward matron raises this with you? What would you do if the patient does not want medical student in the room?

Medical students need to see patients and learn from the ward round. This question may be asked to assess how you react to the situation you may well be presented. Sometimes, the doctors forget to introduce medical students to the patient. Medical students are advised by the schools that they should introduce themselves so that the patients know that they are part of the team and feel comfortable during the consultation. The second part of the question also addresses another very common scenario.; not all patients feel comfortable when there is someone else in the room especially if discussing an intimate or personal topic.

Bad Response:

"Although I agree that it is important for the patient to be aware of who is going to be present, if the consultation continues then introducing medical student by interrupting the consultation may not be appropriate depending on the circumstance, especially if a sensitive matter is being discussed. Moreover, it is the doctor's responsibility to introduce the medical student and if the doctor does not introduce them it is probably for a good reason. Only if the patient asks "who they are the extra people" would I tell them."

Response Analysis:

Although it's easy to see the merit in this response, it is still not the best route to take. It is definitely important not to interrupt *during* the consultation, especially if the doctor is building a rapport with the patient so as to allow them to open up. However, the patient has a right to know who other persons are and why they need to be there. Normally, the doctor should introduce medical students but if they do not, it is absolutely upon medical students themselves to do so. Patients should consent to having medical students in the consultation. It also lacks an insight into why and does not answer the last part of the question.

Good response:

"Patient should know exactly who is part of the team. when the ward nurse raises this concern, firstly I would ensure that it is correct and is a regular occurrence rather than as a one off. I would ensure that when I am doing my ward round I introduce medical students, so that the junior doctors learn from this and follow pursuit. I would discuss with the junior doctor to do so to reduce such issues. I would also have leaflets displayed in ward areas highlighting that this is a teaching hospital and medical student would be seeing them or present in the ward round with team. This gives the patient an opportunity to let their views known so that we can take appropriate steps. If a patient object to presence of medical students, I would politely point out that teaching of medical student is important and continue with the ward round with medical student and rest of the team. If a patient strongly object, in that case, we would respect their decision. I would advise the junior doctor to request the medical student to step outside and join back for the next patient"

Response Analysis:

This is a much more empathetic response. It demonstrates an understanding of the relationship between a patient and a doctor and insight as to why the patient may feel uncomfortable with medical student being present in the consultation. The response addresses the question in three parts: what the problem is, why it might be a problem and an acceptable solution to the problem. This is the approach which should be taken in all situation-based questions.

Overall:

This question can be used to show your empathetic skills and demonstrate that you understand your role as an educator but keep patient's interests the foremost. You can also link this to the trust's values (keeping patients foremost, value you or whatever the trust values the trust has chosen)!

RESEARCH, TEACHING AND TRAINING

132. You have stated in your application that you are passionate about teaching. Teaching is a significant component of this job. Do you think problem-based learning is a better way of teaching?

This question is more likely to get asked in a job with significant teaching commitment or by the royal college representative in a follow up question. More so if your application/CV includes a lot of teaching from you. You should be aware that different medical schools each have a different format of delivering their programme. Some will deliver lectures and be classed as having the more 'traditional' approach, whilst many schools are now offering a problem-based learning (PBL) course where students are given regular cases to prepare. Students then meet with a facilitator to discuss the answer. With an increasing number of schools offering PBL style learning, this question is worth perfecting. Try and approach this by firstly demonstrating a good understanding of what PBL is. Then discuss situations where you have already facilitated some PBL and why it suited you. Finally, conclude that it is therefore suitable method of learning. If you are being interviewed for the teaching University job, you should already know whether the organisation follows tradition or PBL style. If the organisation does not follow PBL, you should have an argument up your sleeve for that too.

Bad Response:

"PBL would be good for me because I cannot imagine myself just delivering lectures all day. I don't think I would be able to concentrate for that long. I would rather facilitate a problem-based learning (PBL) as it stimulates discussion and learning from others. We give far too much information in lectures these days. I would rather give only the core knowledge which stimulates students to do some self-directed learning and supplement teaching."

Response Analysis:

Whilst the candidate has highlighted reasons why he/she would prefer PBL to a more traditional method of teaching, in that they would prefer to facilitate discussions in the group to get the answers to the problems. It may not be a good idea to suggest that he/she only wants to teach the minimum necessary to help students pass the exam.

Good Response:

"I think that teaching in PBL style, as used at this trust, would suit me. I have always found that I facilitate very well and deliver information best when I have been given PBL style to teach. PBL stimulates/encourages self-directed learning. I also really enjoy undertaking group work, and therefore, I think I would thoroughly enjoy facilitating and participating in group discussions. Lastly, PBL gives you the ethos and skills to teach yourself and continually update your knowledge, which is invaluable, as doctors must continually learn and teach."

Response Analysis:

The candidate is able to apply his/her current positive experience of PBL teaching to demonstrate its suitability to his/her learning style. Interviewers also really like to hear that learning in medicine is lifelong and that PBL gives you the skills to teach yourself.

Overall:

With many schools now offering PBL, it is important to know exactly how it benefits its students. If you want to go one step further, you may want to show that you have read up on its effectiveness by quoting a few studies- look up things like GenScope, or even Google PBL in the British Medical Journal. This will definitely impress the interviewers!

133. What is a clinical trial? Have you been involved in a research trial? Would you like to continue?

Research is integral to patient care. Clinical trials are an important part of the licensing process of a new drug. There are several stages of clinical trials, designed to assess safety and effectiveness of a drug. The clinical trial stage follows a series of other trials preceding it in order to provide an idea of safety for human testing. Before entering the clinical trial stage, a drug needs to be deemed safe for human use. To further ensure safety, reduced doses of the drug are usually used for early stage trials. Despite these steps, sometimes things go wrong in clinical trials and participants get hurt. Various institutions tightly regulate clinical trials.

Phases 1 – 3 happen before a drug is licensed. Phase 1 trials, involve the determination of safe doses, Phase 2 trials the determination of general effectiveness, and Phase 3 trials aim at comparing established treatments with new treatments to provide a judgement on superiority. It is important to note that not all drugs that enter Phase 1 trials will progress to Phase 3 and to licensing. Phase 4 happens after licensing and usually aims at determining long-term risks and benefits etc.

Bad Response:

"I would like to be involved in research. Clinical trial is important to get new drugs/procedures discovered for the benefit of patients. For example, in clinical trials, volunteers are given an experimental drug to determine its effectiveness in the treatment of a certain disease as well as its safety for use in humans. Human trials are superior to animal trials as they allow a judgement of the effectiveness of a drug in humans. After a drug has passed clinical trials, it is available to the general public in form of treatment. Through this process, we can progress quickly from drug formulation to use. Research is also an opportunity to get papers published."

Response Analysis:

This answer is too short and shows little understanding of research process. Whilst the general concept of clinical trials is correct, there are some errors regarding timescale as well as associated procedures and risks. Firstly, it takes about 10 years from the formulation of a drug to it entering the trial phase and even then, only a fraction of all drugs designed enter the human trial phase. Secondly, there are several levels of clinical trials before a drug can be licensed for safe human use and even then, more time will go by on additional licensing procedures before it is available for use in treatments. It is a very superficial in responding to the intent to continue in research role.

Good Response:

"Clinical trials represent an important milestone in the licensing process of new medications/procedures. They usually are preceded by extensive testing on cells, computer models, and animals to provide an idea of effectiveness and safety in mammals. Human clinical trials themselves are organised in different stages, depending on how close a drug is to licensing. Due to the nature of human testing, clinical trials of all phases are tightly regulated by governing bodies and the declaration of Helsinki as well as the Nuremberg Code.

I have been involved in clinical trials in my previous post as registrar and recruited for different trials (insert examples). I have also submitted (successfully) research application/proposals to be the principle investigator in (insert name) trial. I would like to continue to participate in research trials if possible."

Response Analysis:

This answer is a good one reflecting good knowledge of the process of clinical trials giving examiners a quick summary of how precisely clinical trials work in the different phases. Showing insight into this is important as the term "clinical trial" is often misunderstood. It further demonstrates a good understanding of the challenges of human testing and the responsibilities arising from using human test subjects. Candidate has also answered all three questions. Be prepared to be asked further questions on the ethical approval, Research and Development with the organisation. If you are interested in continuing research in the new job, you could/should have explored this in the pre-interview meetings and you can bring this here by stating something like "When I met the R&D team (Mr Smith) I know that there is an active research team and I would like to continue to participate."

Overall:

Due to the use of human test subjects, clinical trials are an important ethical issue. As they play a central role in the development of drugs and the very real prospect of doctors treating patients that either are part of a trial or have an interest in participating in trials, it is essential for doctors to understand how clinical trials work and what differentiates the distinctive stages. Remember that all new drugs go through the same rigorous process before becoming available to the public.

134. Should doctors interested in research stop doing clinical medicine?

This question tests your motivation to be a senior clinician and weather you have a greater knowledge of the healthcare and research field in general. It is possible to do both and many clinicians do research alongside their clinical practice, so if you're unsure on whether or not you are interested in research, then explaining that the two are not necessarily mutually exclusive may be impressive to the interviewers. Many consultants participate in research whilst keeping their clinical commitments.

Bad Response:

"It's true that with clinical research one has the potential to save many more lives overall, however, it lacks the patient contact that I really think I enjoy in medicine. I haven't done any research in the past but have closely observed the research methodology. I really think I am a clinician and I want to contribute to direct patient care. Furthermore, I believe I would enjoy teaching more than the research."

Response Analysis:

This response is quite negative towards clinical research and doesn't analyse the merits and demerits. It also does not give the impression that you're particularly informed about either job or certainly not how the two can occur together. Where you can, try to keep your answer focused on the question – this response does not talk about 'saving lives' after the first sentence. Research also contributes to life saving so it is incorrect to state that clinicians seeing patient are the only one that save lives.

Good Response:

"Medical research is certainly something I might be interested in, more so with the well-established research unit at the XXX trust. I have participated in research trials in the past and aware of the ethical principles and ethics R &D approval process. I'm planning to get involved in some local research projects. If I found an area I was particularly interested in, I would consider expanding my research role. To continue to do clinical work depends on the individual. Whilst some doctors are happy participating in research only, many (myself included) would like to have a mix of the two. The concept of 'saving lives' is not limited to the doctors/consultant. Lives can be saved in multitude of ways, including applying the knowledge gleaned from research. I think I would get great satisfaction from being on the front line of delivering that care and that is why I shall focus on providing clinical care"

If the trust you are applying to has a big research centre, you can include this in the answer by stating: *"This trust is known for the quality research work and if an opportunity came, I would consider involving myself in the clinical research whilst pursuing my career as consultant."*

If the trust you are applying to does not have research facilities, you can include this in the answer by stating: "I would like to pursue my interest and use my experience from previous research to set it up here."

Response Analysis:

This answer breaks down the question and addresses each aspect separately. Candidate understand the roles and responsibility of the consultant and is aware of research and it impact on life. Candidate is very honest and give his choices in a balanced way whilst keeping the option of participation in research if need arose or circumstances changed.

Overall:

Try not to fall into the trap of simply explaining why you don't want to do clinical research but take a step back and think about every part of the question. It's a good idea to be well informed about the opportunities to get involved in clinical research at the institution you are being interviewed at and during your training so that you can speak fluently about both the answer to their question and why you'd choose one over the other.

135.   If you could change your SpR training, what would you change?

Speciality training involves rotating through different hospitals, ability to learn quickly and adept to new ways of doing things. This provide a varied experience in different components of the training and maturity. The curricula are designed by specialists and is approved by GMC and relevant colleges. Changing anything would need to be thought through and will require approval.

Bad Response:

"Registrar training involves five-year period for higher specialist training and therefore it offers a breadth of experience. However, I found that as I went through this training process there are some areas that I favoured more than others. The whole idea in the NHS now is to make you a 'generalist' – a general Endocrinologist, a general Diabetologist, a general Physician. People always complain about the workload of general medicine in the training process, so if there is one thing that I would change actually, it would be to have more dedicated time for specialty training and less time doing nights and recovering from nights - therefore becoming a specialist in Diabetes and Endocrinology but still with a good knowledge of general medicine; I don't feel we need to do the volume of general internal medicine that we do in order to be good general physicians".

Response Analysis:

While the candidate does give a very good reason why the speciality training always suffers as a result of generalised training – in this case endocrinology - training suffered because of a heavy GIM commitment. The Trust and organisations are dealing with an increased unprecedented work load which is presented to A&E or ED with medical conditions which need to be managed within time pressure (avoid 4 and 12 ED breaches).   Good medical clinicians are important because they can reduce this pressure. While this response may go down very well in an academic centre or a tertiary referral centre, in a district general setting or where the jobs are dual accredited training it will not be an acceptable and in fact may reduce your chances of getting a job or even put the seeds in the mind of your future employer that you possibly are a candidate who is taking this as a stop-gap job and would leave at the earliest opportunity or would like to have a change in job plan to get out of GIM commitment. Therefore, tread very carefully. It also gives an impression that your training possibly has not been completely adequate because you have spent a lot of time on GIM - so they may have concerns regarding the possible lack of your endocrinology training – which you have yourself admitted to.

Good Response:

"I have had good training in a good mix of teaching university hospitals, tertiary centres and district general hospitals. I feel that I have had complete all round training covering different aspects of my work. If I could change a part of my training I would possibly consider if the training could be completed with less travel. If I could reduce my travel time, and have the same amount of work and training completed that would result in me focussing more on similar areas but without the extra hour of travel that I have had to undertake which means I would be working more and will be more aligned and readier so that patient care was improved".

Response Analysis:

This response is very appropriate. It addresses the issue faced by most trainees as they all have found themselves in this position. The candidate has very successfully, stayed clear of criticising the curriculum, any specific subject choices or any comparison between hospital set up (district vs academic). This shows maturity.

Overall:

In an interview setting, avoid criticising what you have chosen to! It will create doubt in their mind about your abilities and training.

136. Do you like teaching? How do you know you are a good teacher?

Teaching is an important component of being a consultant. Teaching opportunities are shrinking due to the EWTD and rota implications. Every contact with juniors must be used to the fullest to maximise learning.

Bad Response:

"I like teaching, I do it every day on the ward. I know that I am a good teacher because when I am teaching my audience are listening and ask me questions – that makes me believe that they do not sleep when I am trying to teach them and learn new skills."

Response analysis:

This is an inadequate response because it does not cover the question, there is no structure, it does not have a beginning, middle or summation. It only says that the candidate likes teaching, it doesn't give an example, there is no depth to this answer.

Good Response:

"I like teaching. Being a consultant, there are many opportunities and I use them well to ensure that I provide learning and make ward rounds/clinics a rewarding educational experience. In addition, I do on-the-job teaching for junior doctors, paramedics or health care professionals that are assigned to the firm. When I am doing clinics, again there is a teaching opportunity and I use different forms to share my knowledge and experience. I also like the formal lecture-based teaching where I have to do presentations and cover topics.

I believe I am a good teacher because of the feed-back I receive - I usually request feed-back from the course organisers. I reflect on any critical feed-back that I have received and learn from it. I frequently get asked to teach – more-so where exam teaching is concerned – so I therefore feel that I am a good teacher because of the demand that I put on myself – which would not happen if I was not a good teacher and people were not gaining from my input."

Response Analysis:

This is a slightly better response because it does give an example of the teaching activity the candidate has taken – although it still does not give enough input regarding the role of the consultant as a teacher, which could add extra depth to the question. This is otherwise a fine response.

Overall:

Consultant roles are expanding. There are now academic posts focusing more on the teaching components – more so if the job has a heavy teaching component. You could also use this question to shine through if the GMC survey of the organisation showed that teaching was not scoring very high in the junior doctors' feed-back. Again, if you did bring that into your response, this will show that you have applied good research. Therefore, the bad response or the good response could be improved by saying

"I like teaching as it is an integral part of the consultant post. We have to ensure that the team stay up to date and is able to provide an evidence based robust care to the patient so that patient journey is a smooth experience, risks are minimised because the doctors and team are up to date. The GMC survey for our organisation (which you are being interviewed for) show that junior doctors felt that there were no teaching opportunities or the majority of the job was service oriented rather than teaching and they were not able to get the teaching they desire. I believe we could improve on that and use my skill to teach because I have been a trained teacher, I have done on-the-job training and train the teacher training course so I believe I would be able to contribute".

137. What is your teaching style? What do you do when you are teaching a group with differences in knowledge base?

This is your opportunity to showcase your teaching skill, courses that you may have attended. Teaching is an important integral part of being a consultant. The Royal Colleges are recognising this and the facto that in a busy clinical job, teaching opportunities could be limited (not helped by EWTD). So, having a teaching diploma, certificate, on the job teaching or any form of validated teaching is important. If not, you can use the experiences and feedback you received to reflect when answering this question.

Bad Response:

"I like to teach and I like to teach any group of people. I can teach a small group, I can teach a certain number of people depending on their requirement and I can teach when I am doing a busy clinical ward round. I know when I am teaching a group of people which has a skill mix e.g. – a group of Registrar's where there will be a 1st year Registrar and final year Registrar. I need to know that because I would have checked with the course organiser. I would be aiming to ensure that everyone goes home with something they have learned and I will be targeting at middle level but would deliver something so that every member of the team feels more engaged and have learned from this."

Response Analysis:

Basically, this response just answers the question without adding any ground to it. Rather than giving details of the teaching style it talks about different opportunities, or different settings where the teaching takes place. When probed into the different teaching groups, there is again a paucity of the understanding.

Good Response:

"I believe my teaching style is quite fluid. I vary my teaching style based on the group of people I am teaching as well as the setting in which I am teaching. For example, if I am teaching during a busy post-take ward round setting I need to have a very quick skill transference technique so I use something approaching like 'elevator approach or 1-minute preceptor'. Basically, I am asking open ended question and, rather than waiting too long for them to reply (and feel bad if they don't know the answer), I will give them hints so that they can develop the answer. The advantage of this is that they do not feel challenged, put on the spot but feel comfortable as I have guided them through. On the other hand, when I am doing lecture based teaching or class room style teaching, in that case I would use my slides but I may break the monotony of a long lecture by making it more interactive, incorporating some group work exercises, splitting them into groups, come up with solutions etc. In essence, my teaching style is variable depending on the setting in that point in time.

If I am teaching a group where there is a different knowledge base I would prepare myself by having a brief from the course organiser and then I would then try to focus and target my knowledge so that people with less knowledge base feel that they have moved forward and the people at the high extreme of the knowledge base feel that they have been challenged to gain something from it. I would achieve this by introducing group work and assigning them in different groups so that each group goes between different levels of difficulties and different groups are asked to present back so that everyone learns from the experience."

Response Analysis:

The above response could be shortened but covers what is asked for. Consultants have teaching role is gradually evolving. They are asked to teach in different settings. Therefore, an effective learning or teaching style is the key because teaching opportunities are getting less and less with EWTD, the service and training battle that is on-going and the junior doctor's paucity on the rota because of time pressure, so we have to ensure that every teaching opportunity is used so that different teaching style are important. Candidate could use this to show how they have developed teaching skills (attending various courses, on –line modules, reading around, watching YouTube modules as well as doing the Accredited Train the Trainer course).

138. How do we teach these days when the junior doctors are off base ward so often (due to rota/leave)?

Be careful. This is not asking you to explain that it is getting difficult to teach but checking whether your attitude towards teaching and whether you would use the opportunities available.

Bad Response:

"The rota is not my problem; I don't think I have created this problem but we still need to deal with it; I therefore try to train the junior doctors when they are with me on the ward or when I am doing an episode in the theatre or on-call. It is finally up to them how to make best use of their learning because, at the end of the day, they are adults and they have to take some responsibility for their learning. If they don't listen to what I am teaching then they are the ones who are going to suffer."

Response Analysis:

This is such a bad response! It also shows that the candidate is not interested in teaching at all; he is not taking any ownership of the teaching; he is not taking responsibility or taking teaching business seriously – which is an important part of their job. It also comes across as a very brusque response whereby it appears that he does not care. It is not a good idea as some of the issues are not created by junior doctors, these are the issues that have come about because of the change in NHS reforms – for example the EWTD, modernising the medical care etc. Therefore, whilst there is a battle for maintaining a work social life balance it does impact on the training of the doctor and is important to use these training opportunities as much as we can.

Good Response:

"Getting a balance of junior doctor's training with service and training commitment is a battle which we have to fight almost every day. Being a consultant requires not only just the clinical aspect of the job but I have to ensure that we train the doctors of tomorrow efficiently so that we can produce good quality doctors. Not only will it improve the quality of the doctors, it will also reflect in the care that we provide; the patient flow will be better. Patient satisfaction would be better and they feel comfortable and safe. This will restore public's faith in the NHS.

*I make every use of contact with the junior doctors, when they are on the ward, doing procedures etc. I also make sure that the first few patients (at the start of the ward round) are discussed in detail and they have learned from the first few patients followed by a business ward round where my focus is on ensuring patient care. This has been a good mix. Although the latter part of the ward round might be a business ward round there are still things that junior doctors are learning; but by 'highlighting' that **that was your teaching** I have reinforced in them that they have received teaching because teaching happens without them sometimes realising that they have just been taught. It is important to tell them they have just been taught so that they remember this. This way the teaching that happens imperceptibly will possibly get seeded into the doctors head and will make much impact."*

Response Analysis:

Slightly lengthy – it could be improved by cutting down on a bit on 'fluff'. The doctor has however given a balanced view of the teaching, the trainer part, the teaching activity and has actually given an example about using the ward round and splitting the round into a business ward round so that the junior doctors learn.

Overall:

As we said earlier, teaching is important and consultants need to strike a balance between learning, educating, keeping themselves updated as well as updating their junior to ensure that the whole team is up to scratch. See also response to above question.

CLINICAL GOVERNANCE

139.   What is clinical governance? Why is it important?

Background:

Clinical governance is one of the most important principles in the NHS but you may not have been aware of its formal existence. It refers to the systematic approach used by NHS Trusts to maintain and improve the quality of patient care within the health service. Prior to the introduction of clinical governance, NHS Trusts were responsible only for the financial management of their organisation and it was the responsibility of individual health care professionals to maintain high standards of care. Nowadays, each trust (alongside the individual clinicians) is responsible for maintaining the highest possible standard of care and doing so in the safest possible manner. The best answers to this question will demonstrate how effective clinical governance is achieved and in doing so will explain its importance.

Bad Response:

"Clinical governance is the process by which NHS Trusts ensure that their health care provision is delivered in the most efficient way. In a time when cuts to healthcare budgets are commonplace, trusts have to find innovative means to reduce spending while still providing an appropriate level of care. The cornerstone of clinical governance is finding the most cost-effective methods to serve the local population."

Response Analysis:

This answer shows a lack of understanding of clinical governance. Clinical governance refers only to the process by which trusts ensure the highest standard of clinical care. Cost-effectiveness of treatments may form part of clinical governance but financial factors are not the focus of clinical governance. It should be noted that trusts are under increasing pressure to control spending but this is not the same as clinical governance.

Good Response:

"Clinical governance is the systematic approach used by NHS Trusts to maintain and improve the quality of patient care within the health service. It comprises several different components. The trust and clinicians are together responsible for continued professional development so that all professional knowledge is up to date. The trust must commit to clinical audit in which clinical practice is reviewed, altered and reassessed and also to make decisions surrounding clinical practice based on clinical effectiveness. Effectiveness can take into consideration things like value for money and QALYs. Trusts also commit to evidence-based medicine and to find ways to introduce new research into practice in a way that reduces the lag between new discoveries and a reduction in associated morbidities.

In order to ensure proper clinical governance is possible, trusts commit to collect high-quality data on their processes and to allow this data to be openly scrutinised in order that bad practice cannot continue unnoticed. Ultimately, clinical governance is important in creating systems in which bad practice is stamped out and excellent practice is able to flourish."

Response Analysis:

This is a very thorough answer which explains the mechanisms by which clinical governance is achieved. Crucially, this answer demonstrates an understanding that every mechanism is put in place with the top priority of achieving the highest standard of clinical care.

Overall:

Despite being a concept, you may not previously have been familiar with; clinical governance is very easy to get your head around. To summarise, clinical governance is about the NHS trust taking appropriate steps to provide 'right care to the patients, at the right time, by the right people in the right place'. This is done by ensuring that staff remain up-to-date, regular audits, implementing evidence-based medicine and learning from mistakes.

140. Why do we worry so much about Hospital-acquired infections?

Hospital-acquired infections are a big issue. This is due to several different factors. Firstly, there is the issue of antibiotic resistance which is greater in hospital-acquired infections. Hospital bugs become resistant to commonly used antibiotics due to the selection pressures exerted by the antimicrobial environment. Secondly, many patients in hospital have a dampened immune response as they are ill. This reduces their ability to fight off infections- making them more susceptible to severe and prolonged infections. Lastly, hospital-acquired infections have an important financial impact as well, as they increase the time spent in the hospital. A patient may be cured of their original disease, but then acquires an infection in the hospital prolonging hospital stay.

Bad Response:

"Hospital-acquired infections play a little role in a hospital setting as patients coming to the hospital are already ill anyway and treatment for an additional illness does not make much difference. Due to the availability of highly effective antimicrobial treatments, even the most persistent infections can be successfully treated. Whilst antibiotic resistance is a big issue in the community, it is less of an issue in the hospital as there are strong intravenous antibiotics available. In addition, hospital-acquired infections are relatively rare due to the strict cleaning procedures in place that prevent the spread of disease."

Response Analysis:

This answer is factually wrong. Hospital-acquired infections are of great worry. Whilst it is true that there are strict cleaning procedures in place to reduce the incidence of infection, they do not prevent all of them from occurring. In addition to that, hospital-acquired infections affect approximately 8% of all hospital admissions which represents quite a significant proportion of the patients. Also, whilst it is true that there are some antibiotics that can be used for some of the more resilient bugs, these pretty much represent the last resort and have quite significant side-effects for the patients.

Good Response:

"Hospital-acquired infections have to be taken seriously. They are an issue for multiple reasons. The most significant reason is the increased resistance to available treatments. Many of the bacteria responsible for hospital-acquired infections have developed a multitude of antibiotic resistance traits that allow them to evade many of the mainstay treatments. In addition to the resistance, many of the resistant organisms are more virulent, causing more severe disease. This may also be due to the general status of poor health that the patients in the hospital are in. Being sick reduces the immune system activity, not only making the patients more susceptible in general but also giving the disease a more acute and severe course. There are other reasons why hospital-acquired infections represent an issue. They include the financial strain of prolonged hospital stays as well as the associated worsening of the hospital infrastructure as more beds are being occupied for longer, making it more difficult to find room for new admissions. This can cause suboptimal bed flow and patients' move (out of ED) to the first bed that's becomes available and not the one that's is appropriate to them e.g. a heart failure patient can go to the respiratory ward instead of cardiology. The safari speciality ward than in turn leads to delayed speciality input creating a vicious cycle."

Response Analysis:

This is a good answer as it provides good insight into the issue surrounding the question. It also shows insight into the complexity of hospital care and what role hospital-acquired infections play in that context.

Overall:

This question deals with an important issue and with antibiotic resistance becoming an increasingly big problem, it is important to recognise the role of hospital-acquired infections in that context as well. Without research into new antibiotics proving increasingly challenging, this is a very important issue that needs to be addressed in order to ensure the future effectiveness of available treatments. With the high prevalence of hospital-acquired infections (8% of all admissions), it definitely is an important factor to recognise. This is an opportunity for you to bring in the hospital policy on isolation, barrier nursing, allowable Cl diff/MRSA rate of the hospital, infection prevention policies (bare below elbow) and the governance surrounding these issues.

141. Do you think you are a safe Doctor?

This question is checking whether you understand what a safe doctor is and the issues surrounding it. It is an opportunity for you to bring out good medical practice from General Medical Council; you can discuss EWTD because that has work/social life balance issues it also can bring in team working as well as your clinical competence or communication skills.

Bad Response:

"I am a safe doctor because I have had no problems so far in my life and I do not have any complaints; people are generally happy about me and I make sure that I do my clinics and ward rounds in a timely manner and instructions are appropriate".

Response Analysis:

While this response covers and touches on a few issues about patient care it is not a structured response; it is not looking at different aspects and an opportunity is missed to bring in the issues that could be raised here. It does say what the safety as a doctor means but has missed the opportunity to demonstrate that you are aware of challenges and processes to deal with them.

Good Response:

"I am a safe doctor. I have had good structured training; I have been doing this job for a number of years and I am quite diligent when it comes to patient care. I am punctual; I keep myself updated and participate in revalidation so that I am fit to practice. I have not been directly involved in any significant events or any Datix (a report was given to me at my appraisal). I read regularly and I read the reports that are regularly sent out by the Governance team on serious adverse events and route cause analyses. I also remain up to date with NPSA bulletins that identify and highlight any patient safety errors and I learn from that. As a result, I believe I am a safe doctor."

Response Analysis:

This response covers the majority of aspects; the clinical competencies as well as the training aspect, it also reflects on why it is important for a doctor to be safe and how this is assessed - Datix clinical errors, NPSA, Governance report, RCA etc. He has used the opportunity to pass on to the panel members to ask him any further questions to probe. This is going to be a rewarding experience for the candidate as he has brought in the subjects that he should feel comfortable with and at ease. Beware, if you are not sure what NPSA is or if you are not 100% sure of the processes of RCA, do not bring them into the interview.

Overall:

This is a simple question but it just shows that you are aware of what is involved and what it takes to be a doctor and take it further to be a safe doctor. This is an opportunity for you to show that you are aware of the changes, different agencies that govern patient safety and provide guidance on those aspects.

142. Do you think 360 ° assessments can be manipulated?

360° assessment is the process where the nominated people comment on different attributes of the person being assessed. GMC requires this to be undertaken as part of one revalidation cycle (every 5 years) but the trust may require it every three years. The author herself felt that on the first assessment when a comment was made that the author could be sharp, it led her to change her communication on phone and it has been a very positive experience since.

Bad Response:

"360 ° Assessments is a process where we give out forms to people – usually your friends and colleagues – to comment on your performance. I feel that as we are giving out forms ourselves there is a potential that this can be manipulated or biased so I don't feel that it brings any value".

Response Analysis:

The candidate has no idea what the 360° Assessment is, how it is performed; in fact, even to elude that he would be using the forms to give to his friends and, hence, there might be a perceived property issue or issue where he can come across as unreliable or not trustworthy. Beware of this.

Good Response:

"360° Assessment is a tool to assess and identify any issues relevant to communication, commitment, probity etc. This is a tool that can help doctors to get rid of the 'blind spot' as sometimes what they feel is not a problem may be perceived as a problem by other people. As this assessment is taken by people nominated by the person themselves the assessment is quite reliable as it relies on the people who have had good contact with the person over a period of time. It does add value because responses have been useful for the Trust as well as for the person, because they would have identified something they were not aware of".

Response Analysis:

The candidate has given an example why the 360° Assessment is useful, helpful, how it can be useful in improving oneself. The candidate also gives some insight into how it adds value for both organisation as well as candidate.

MISCELLANEOUS

143. What is the difference between a good and a great doctor?

Different individuals have their own definition of what makes a doctor good or great. There are two ways to answer this: on one hand, you can use your own experiences as a doctor that you perceived as particularly great, or you can stay on a more theoretical level. Both pathways will require you to provide an explanation for your differentiation parameters.

Bad Response:

"A great doctor is simply better trained and qualified than a good doctor. In order to be a great doctor, you need to be close to the top in your field, if not the best in your field altogether. Only hard work and training will make it possible to reach the status of a great doctor as it is necessary to perfect all technical abilities to the extreme. Unless a doctor's medical skills are perfect, a doctor cannot call himself great."

Response Analysis:

This answer solely focuses on the technical skills of the doctor. It ignores that doctors need to be more than just very good at knowing the theory of their field. Medical care is a lot more complex than theoretical approaches. Not everybody that knows everything about their chosen field will make great doctors. This answer also ignores the distinction between good and great.

Good Response:

"First of all, it is important to stress that this differentiation is a very individual one. A doctor that seems great to some might not seem great to others. This is due to the fact that everybody has a different set of values when it comes to the definition of greatness in medical care. However, for me, being a good doctor requires the individual to know their subject and to be able to interact with their patients' satisfactorily. In order to be a great doctor, I believe that the doctors need to not only know his subject and be able to communicate it to others, he also needs to make people feel like he understands their needs and fears. If clinicians know that people can trust them to make the right decision for the care that not only will treat and cure them, but also respect all wishes and concerns wherever possible, then we can call him a great doctor."

Response Analysis:

This response is a good one as it appropriately reflects the complexity of the question. It also provides examples for the distinction between good and great and focuses on personal preferences. This makes the answer a lot more balanced and gives the interviewer a better impression of the candidate.

Overall:

This question is a challenging one as it reflects the most basic considerations of medical practice. We all strive to be great doctors to every patient we will ever have. Achieving this, however, is very challenging and requires a good balance of excellent theoretical knowledge and excellent people skills.

144. What do you think about the role of GPs in the NHS?

GPs play a vital role in the NHS. In a way, they provide a triage system for patients allocating them to the individual specialities through referrals if necessary. At the same time, GPs are increasingly becoming a bottleneck in the NHS as they have to deal with ever-growing patient loads and continuously reducing numbers of GPs. As waiting times for appointments increase, patients are more likely to seek help at A&Es, increasing an already enormous strain on these facilities even further.

This question is classic and belongs to a family of questions with variations; how important are nurses, or porters, or midwives in the NHS? It's important to have the facts right here explained with the role of GPs both in direct medical interventions but also in Clinical Commissioning Groups. It can't hurt to also throw in some anecdotes as well. It is also an opportunity to show work ethics by showing that you value the contribution from GPs.

Bad Response A:

"GPs are becoming increasingly irrelevant in the NHS. Waiting times have gotten so long that it is easier to simply go to A&E or call an ambulance when unwell. This is further encouraged by the NHS 111 service that gives advice to people. The main responsibility of GPs is to refer patients and to treat easy, chronic cases not requiring any specialist input. With the way medicine is developing, i.e. by becoming increasingly specialised, GPs often are far out of their depth anyway. Having to make an appointment with your GP to have specialist investigations is a nuisance to many patients as it prolongs the process unnecessarily."

Bad Response B:

"From my experience, GPs are the pillars of the NHS. They are the first line of interaction with patients so for many people, they are the public face of the NHS. GPs are effectively the first filter to further treatment. They are the ones who divert patients to specific departments via referrals to the hospital. It is up to them to decide that a patient is sick enough to warrant hospital attention, so they yield a great deal of influence over how patients get treated."

Response Analysis:

The candidate demonstrates a significant lack of awareness of the role of GPs in the NHS. Underestimating the importance of primary care in healthcare reflects very poorly on the candidate. GPs play a very important role in the delivery of care in the community and represent a necessary intermediate between specialist care and the patient. The candidate does, however, raise a relevant aspect of the reality of GP's roles in the NHS: there is too much demand for too few doctors.

The second response is incomplete. For the most part, the response is accurate. The comments about being the public face and first line of interaction are indeed correct, as is the idea of them being the means to accessing further treatment in hospitals. However, this response fails to acknowledge the relatively new role of GPs in clinical commissioning groups since the abolishment of Primary Care Trusts. The response is good but by failing to mention this, it shows a lack of awareness of the current state of the National Health Service.

Good Response A:

"GPs play an important role in the NHS. Originally conceived as a gateway and distributor of the patients between community and speciality care, GPs take a sort of triage function as well as providing care for non-specialist cases. GPs also are vital in ensuring the continuation of care beyond the hospital stage and are the main provider of health care in the community. They play a very diverse and complex role in the NHS. The general shortage of staff, however, has an impact on GPs as well. The lack of GPs overall makes it difficult for them to efficiently fulfil their roles. Long waiting times and general overload with patients contribute to the problem of high A&E presentations that could be avoided. All in all, GPs have not lost their importance, but like most other parts of our health service, they are spread increasingly thin making their job very difficult."

Good Response B:

"GPs are the public face of the NHS for a great number of patients, especially those who don't go onto secondary care. They effectively operate as the first point of contact for almost all patients in the NHS and fulfil the basic healthcare requirements for many patients. Beyond straightforward ailments, they are also the means by which patients interact with many other NHS services since GPs – by means of referrals – are the ones who direct patients with specific ailments to secondary care. GPs are effectively the ones who conduct initial investigations for patients to accurately target them to the correct treatment. On top of all this, GPs have also become the ones who determine what services are offered by the local NHS trust via Clinical Commissioning Groups since Primary Care Trusts with dedicated managers ceased to exist. The idea behind this is that, theoretically, GPs know best as to what services would suit their patients, but whether this works in practice is open to debate. Personally, it seems like we're asking a lot of GPs given their already heavy workload."

Response Analysis:

This answer attempts to not only outline the role of GPs in the NHS but also tries to provide insight into the challenges experienced by GPs and the consequences this has for the whole of the NHS. This is important as it demonstrates the candidate's ability to develop an argument and then apply it to a different situation. It also shows that the candidate has spent some time thinking about the issue and is also up to date with current issues surrounding the healthcare service.

The second response is better with a larger and more detailed overview of the roles and importance of a GP in the current state of the NHS. As in the bad response, this response covers the work of a GP as the first point of contact, but it goes further and touches on the role of CCGs. By mentioning both CCGs and PCTs, it shows that the candidate has engaged in current affairs and is aware of problems in our healthcare system – a trait often neglected by many candidates. Although you should also be wary of coming off as too politically charged. If your interviewer doesn't agree with you, that can be awkward.

Overall:

This question is an important one as the role of GPs in the NHS is a complex and very important one because they represent the first instance of patient contact. Also, since most applicants will have had some form of work experience in a GP practice, it can reasonably be expected that they have some understanding of the GP's role in the healthcare system. If being asked this question, a direct reference to first-hand experiences will result in a more complete answer.

This is no doubt a broad question, but it's important to try and get as much in as you can with sufficient detail. This question presents an opportunity to show off your extended reading and is a perfect chance to show that you've engaged with materials that many candidates often neglect. Doing well on questions like these will help you to stand out.

Top Tip: GP are the gatekeepers and fund holders. Criticising them in the interview setting will not be a good idea. On the other hand, recognising their contribution will portray you as someone that valued others and is a good team player.

145.   What are the biggest challenges facing doctors today?

You can choose what you feel comfortable and knowledgeable in to give a satisfactory answer about your chosen challenge. It could be something like financial pressures on the NHS, resources, shortage of doctors and nurses, chronic diseases or issues that affect training, e.g. European working time directive (EWTD). A good candidate will offer justifications for their answer, including why the problem is so severe and why it will affect most doctors. A recent good example could be the new doctors' contract or seven days service plan and its impact on the NHS. You could use an article from recent press as an opportunity to show your keenness to continue to learn and to keep updated on issues that affect patient care. Read around them to prepare a good argument. Some examples to choose from might include: smoking ban in public areas or the obesity epidemic. You could also cite some examples or challenges faced by your speciality e.g. out of hospital stroke thrombolysis, diabetes epidemic and prevention, fracture neck of femur and best practice tariff compliance etc.

Bad Response A:

"Obesity is the biggest problem facing doctors because it can make people ill in so many different ways."

Response Analysis:

The candidate has identified an important issue but hasn't developed their point sufficiently. This is a fantastic opportunity to showcase your subject knowledge, advances in your area (bariatric surgery) and demonstrate that you have a good understanding of the difficulties of being a doctor currently. The problem chosen is also very good as it involves great communication skills and empathy. This answer would be better if you expanded on the extended implications of obesity, e.g. the financial & socio-economic costs of the additional disease burden due to diabetes/cancer. This can be combined with a new change in guidelines or NSF (diabetes) where disease prevention is emphasised or the specific use of equipment required for investigations (MRI) or operating table. Discussing these in your answer make you look good as well as well read. You also come across someone that is aware of different issues and goes a step further to resolve the problem or aware of the problems so is prepared for them.

Good Response A:

"I would say the current obesity epidemic is perhaps the greatest challenge facing UK doctors today. This is because it is affecting a huge proportion of our population and impairs so many aspects of a person's health and healthcare management. Obesity often causes hormonal problems, such as Type II diabetes as well as cardiovascular problems, joint problems and many more. Therefore, obese patients often have to be seen by many doctors as they often have multiple co-morbidities, which complicate their treatment. Also, surgery in obese patients is much riskier than on slim patients. Indeed, the growing number of instances where patients have been too obese to fit on normal operating tables shows the sheer logistical difficulties for doctors treating an obese population."

Response Analysis:

This is a much better response that identifies multiple facets of obesity that cause problems and then expands on each of them. The candidate makes good use of their knowledge, e.g. the link between obesity and diabetes. It acknowledges the broader implications of obesity on a population basis and its contribution to morbidity.

Bad Response B:

"Doctors face challenges in many ways. They have to read a lot and remember a lot but there is not enough time to do that. The training period is appropriate but the actual training time is short and the juniors always seem to be on call or on away days for various reasons. I think training the juniors in the current the structure of the training programme is a big challenge."

Response analysis:

This is not such a bad response but it is lacking in giving details and offering some insights into it. Without more, it leaves an impression that the candidate will not be able to use various windows of opportunity to train juniors (on call). This response can be improved further as shown in good response.

Good response B:

"I think training the juniors in the current the structure of the training programme is a big challenge. The doctors working hours are impacted heavily with the EWTD and striking this balance of working time and teaching time to provide training is the biggest challenge. Whilst EWTD is good to ensure that the doctors have a good work-life balance. It also means that the compensatory time (that must be taken) limits training opportunities for doctors. The continuity of care is reduced and learning opportunity are small. This potentially can lead to longer length of stay of the patients (decision to discharge happen more on days of consultant ward round) and increased risk of hospital acquired infection etc. It is important for us to make use of every contact with the trainees (e.g. using bed site teaching, using 1-minute preceptor, ensuring they are well engaged in their portfolios etc) to educate future doctors"

Response analysis:

This is a better response. Still bit short but essentially gives the issues, explores its impact and offers some insights on how to resolve. Be prepared to be asked about EWTD in detail, infection rates of the trust you are being interviewed, CQC rating and Dr Foster MRSA numbers or about career progression of trainee doctors. You may also get quizzed in follow on question re length of stay and strategy to reduce it.

Overall:

You should draw on your experience and reading when answering. In terms of challenges facing doctors in the UK, some good things to think about are the problems from the growing obesity epidemic and the difficulties of having an ageing population. If you're thinking of problems facing doctors on a more global scale, some big problems that are worth thinking about may include the dangers of multi-drug resistant bacteria and the limits they put on the use of antibiotics.

146.   What is the most important disease?

This is a great opportunity for you to bring in any challenges that your speciality is facing, an opportunity to show that you are staying UpToDate (reading relevant literature). Give a good answer here to shows that you an expert in your field, tried to read beyond getting yourself signed off at PYA! Showing this sort of commitment is key in showing the interviewers that you have the appetite for this tough job that you will be doing for life. Generally, I'd advise approaching this answer as saying what you find particularly fascinating about a particular disease. Choose something from your relevant area.

Bad Response:

"In my view, necrotising fasciitis is very important as I find it amazing that bacteria can cause so much tissue destruction so rapidly. It just shows the power of insignificant organism that can cause chaos."

Response Analysis:

On the face of it, this is an okay response. The candidate has identified quite a niche disease (candidate is a Microbiologist) and has made a slightly profound point of the bacterial burden not necessarily correlating with the extent of subsequent tissue destruction. However, they fail to really justify why they this disease is important. They should have explained in greater detail that the toxins generated by the bacteria that cause the destruction and possibly link this to some recent relevant research they have read about in relation to diagnosis/treatment of the disease. It just requires better justification that reflects some insight into the underlying pathogenesis. An opportunity to discuss Cl Difficle and MRSA bacteraemia in the trust, root cause analysis has been missed. This would have made the panel to believe that you are genuinely interested in the job and have taken efforts to know about the issue facing the organisation and hence ready for challenges.

Good Response:

"I think Parkinson's disease is very important. This is because of the fascinatingly mysterious underlying pathophysiological processes that lead to the wide array of symptoms and, additionally, the different dimensions of treatment intervention that are currently being researched. For example, we can either try and directly modulate the pathological beta oscillations in the basal ganglia with deep brain stimulation or we could consider trying to directly replace the dying nerve fibres with stem cells. Considering the aging local population in the area I feel I could continue my interest and develop a Parkinson's service."

Response Analysis:

This is a good response as it shows that the candidate has genuinely thought and read fairly widely about a particular disease that they have identified as interesting. This is further followed up with suggestions to use the experience and develop services further directly benefitting the local population. The extra detail regarding the different methods of treatment suggests that this is a candidate who is caring, keen on innovations and to look way beyond this for their own interest. Also see how cleverly the demographic details about "aging population in the area" is sneaked in. This demonstrate candidate's keenness and that he has done a good background research for the job.

Overall:

These are the sorts of questions can catch out candidates who haven't done extra reading around their subject. Interviewers won't expect extensive knowledge at all, but merely want a taste of your keenness for medicine. Hence, going into detail about a particular disease is a good way of doing this. Also, if you're going for Oxbridge, then the extra scientific details will show your flare for this aspect of their course.

147.   What have you read recently?

This is a very broad question and it gives you the scope to tell the interviewers something about yourself. Make very good use of a question like this as you can bring in something that will impress the interviewers- there will not be many questions that allow you to say whatever you want, but this is one of them.

Bad Response A:

"The last book I read was War and Peace by Leon Trotsky; it was a fantastic tale of the Napoleonic wars and really highlighted to me the importance of medicine. To further my medical knowledge, I read the Journal of Thoracic Surgery and the Journal of Underwater Physiology. I really liked the latest article where they talked about... oh I've forgotten what they talked about but it was very good. Finally, I read about the Junior Doctor Strikes in the Daily Mail this morning."

Bad Response B:

"I recently read about a new 15-minute test for cognitive decline, which requires only a list of instructions and a piece of paper and a pen. It said it might increase the rate of diagnosis for Alzheimer's disease and other forms of dementia which would be good."

Response Analysis:

Firstly, War and Peace is written by Leo Tolstoy and not Leon Trotsky. Secondly, the candidate forgets the name of the article that they read in one of their research journals. Both of these errors suggest that the candidate has not actually read these and is simply lying their way through the interview. If you are going to pretend that you have read a book/journal, make sure you know some of the key ideas and can talk about them confidently. Secondly, the candidate is quite vague in both answers. In the first response, the candidate vaguely mentions that War and Peace somehow relate to medicine and then completely skips over the issue of Junior Doctor Strikes – a great opportunity to show your understanding of the new junior doctor contract. This suggests a lack of interest or unfamiliarity. Answers should always try to provide specific examples and justification. Finally, avoid mentioning tabloid newspapers!

Good Response A:

"The last fiction book I read was War and Peace by Leo Tolstoy, it was very interesting to see the difference in how the doctors treated their patients in that era compared to modern times. In terms of medical reading, I like reading BMJ. I recently read the recent changes in the stroke management and new advances in the stroke technology with interventional thrombectomy being trialled. This can potentially reduce the devastating impact stroke can have on people personal social and professional lives. Finally, I keep up to date with current issues by reading the Telegraph. Today's front page was on the recent strike by Junior Doctors so it was especially relevant to my interests."

Good Response B:

"I am a voracious reader. The latest article I read about was an article on dementia. This article was about, a new 15-minute test for cognitive decline, which requires only a list of instructions and a piece of paper and a pen. This test is intended to direct people at risk of Alzheimer's disease and other forms of dementia towards primary care. While widespread use of this may be very effective at increasing the rate of diagnosis of these conditions, it did occur to me that its application could be potentially harmful. There is a stigma and fear associated with these conditions that would make false positives particularly harmful. Also, an early diagnosis for a very slow cognitive decline may simply prolong the time for people to worry about their condition without having any treatment options."

Response Analysis:

In response A, the subject is very similar to the previous one but there are some key differences. Firstly, notice that the candidate provides a useful detail about War and Peace. It is perfectly acceptable to mention non-medical books in this answer. In both responses, the candidate mentions an article and some form of medical reading; note that although a major journal is cited, and you may get probed on a specific article published recently e.g. hospitals on edge or a major

NHS initiative or criticism of that! Finally, the candidate mentions a reputed newspaper and provides some detail on a relevant article.

Overall:

This question is very useful from the candidate's perspective. It allows them to shape the flow of the interview and lead the interviewer in a certain direction, e.g. by mentioning the Junior Doctor strikes, the interviewer may pick up on this and ask for your opinion- if you anticipated this and had already prepared a response (but of course make it seem spontaneous), the interviewers will be very impressed. This question will also give the interviewer a good idea of your cultural knowledge- are you one of those people who just read journals or your speciality related topics or do you read widely for interest?

It is important to research some contemporary news stories and read around them to know both sides of the coin. Reading beyond the original article to further investigate the topic and offering some small level of criticism/appraisal are good ways to demonstrate your interest/abilities as you may get asked about an article or controversial health bill/paper in the news e.g. cancer from a new drug, fracture risk with a diabetes drug or new miracle cure that makes life better for people with multiple sclerosis and your views on it. It would look good if you can give both sides of the argument on the article and come up with your own views. Remember, you may not know the views of your interviewer so there is a risk that your opinion might be opposite to theirs. Be perceptive, and if challenged on your view, explain it with a good argument (your background reading should have prepared you for that). Your invitation letter usually should give you the panel members (and if not, you can ring the HR department to ask who is interviewing you. A search on interviewers can help you in knowing their views, interests or publications. You can use this in your answers.

Suggested reading:

- ➤ Journals relevant to your speciality
- ➤ NICE guidance relevant to your speciality
- ➤ Some reputed journal covering multiple speciality so that you are aware of what's happening as it may impact your speciality: BMJ, The Lancet
- ➤ Changes within the NHS: Hospital journal, BMA newsletter, relevant college newsletter (you can subscribe to them for free)
- ➤ Be aware of any brewing or ongoing controversy in your speciality/wider medical field

148. If you could interview one person in the world, who would it be?

This question is not to try and trip you up or test your situational judgment but is essentially trying to find out more about you as a person. It's often asked towards the end of the interview and is a chance for you to speak about something you are passionate about, stand out, and make yourself a memorable candidate.

A lot of people will think the interviewer expects them to give an answer that is a famous scientific or medical figure, but this is by no means necessary. If you do not know very much/have just memorised some facts about them, it is likely to come across as clichéd. As long as you do not say someone and only provide very superficial reasons (no reality TV stars), you can potentially talk about anyone you like. Someone who inspires you is best as they are likely to be someone who has done something worthy of note, and worthy of interviewing.

Bad Response:

"I would interview the Prime Minister to see just what it's like to run the country and how he plans on managing the healthcare system. I would also see what foreign policy is like with other countries and what the Prime Minister's plans are regarding immigration. I would also discuss the world economy and whether or not it looks like the country is going to approach another economic downturn and how we would deal with that in terms of budget cuts."

Response Analysis:

This is likely one of the most overused answers. For one, there are *plenty* of available interviews to watch where these questions have been addressed, and also, there is no passion or feeling in this response whatsoever. The questions are vague and non-specific and thus likely to elicit similar answers. This is a very forgettable answer and the candidate has wasted the opportunity to show a bit of their personality to the interviewer.

Good Response:

"If I could interview one person in the world, it would be David Attenborough. Nature documentaries are something many people think of as boring, but he is incredibly engaging and never dull to watch and always genuinely passionate about what he does. I haven't had the chance to travel very much – it would be fascinating to be able to talk to someone who has explored such a broad range of places in the world. Aside from narrating nature documentaries, I'm sure he has many a story to tell about his experiences while he was exploring. He actually inspired me to try out wilderness medicine and to travel abroad on my elective, should I get the chance. He also has such an iconic voice – it would be quite something to be able to hear it in person!"

Response Analysis:

The candidate is speaking passionately about someone which they mention inspires them and whom they would genuinely like to meet. They also reveal a bit about themselves here in that they are excited by the prospect of travel and exploring, and enjoys watching documentaries depicting other parts of the world. This turns them from just another application form into a 'three-dimensional' person, making a welcome change from what may well be very fixed or rehearsed answers to previous questions. The answer is enthusiastic and, therefore, much more memorable than the previous answer, making them stand out in the eyes of the interviewer.

Overall:

This is not a trick question! Don't just tell the interviewer what you think they want to hear – give a genuine response and it will seem more natural and memorable. Avoid giving a superficial (e.g. a movie star) or clichéd (e.g. the Prime Minister) response. Talking about someone you genuinely want to meet is likely to be a lot more engaging and memorable.

149. What do you think is more important, spending money on hospital beds or on community care? Why?

One of the biggest challenges in hospitals these days is the discharge of medically fit patients into the community. This is particularly relevant for the elderly that are not able to care for themselves but have no medical conditions requiring hospital care. As they cannot be discharged into an unsafe environment, it is not uncommon for patients to spend a long time in the hospital, even though there is no medical need for them to do so. This binds important hospital resources, is very expensive for the health service, and also puts the patients at risk of acquiring further morbidities, including but not limited to infections by multi-drug resistant pathogens.

Bad Response:

"Hospitals are more important than community care. Waiting times in A&E are ever increasing and this is in large part due to the overall lack of hospital beds. The provision of more hospital beds is essential in alleviating this. This is particularly true as the patients presenting to the hospital are generally ill and in need of actual medical care whereas the cases in the community are less relevant. Therefore, money should go to hospitals."

Response Analysis:

This answer fails to appreciate the connection between hospital care and community care resulting in vital shortcomings in the answer itself. It furthermore fails to appreciate the complexity of hospital admissions and presentations. Whilst it is true that some people presenting to A&E will be very unwell and needing hospital care, a proportion of people presenting will not. Effectively, it is not possible to judge one more important than the other as there is a very close interaction between both spheres.

Good Response:

"Availability of hospital beds represent a great challenge in the NHS. In the view of bursting A&E departments that are unable to find space for presenting patients, this message is particularly obvious. It would, however, be wrong to assume that a simple increase of hospital beds at the cost of community care will necessarily alleviate the problem. There is a very fluent exchange of patients between community care, in particular, care homes and hospitals. It is not uncommon for patients that are medically fit for discharge to remain in the hospital occupying beds simply because they have nowhere else to go. This, in turn, produces other issues such as increasing rates of hospital-acquired infections as well as an overall poorer long-term prognosis due to prolonged hospital stay. Not to mention the high cost associated with an occupied hospital bed. In the light of this, it is, therefore, important to spend money on the improvement of both factors: the amount of hospital beds available as well as community care."

Response Analysis:

This response is well-balanced and well-argued, providing a good overview of the complexity of the issue of hospital beds and community care. It gives a precise and justified answer and makes intrinsic sense. It also provides an additional perspective by addressing the consequences of unnecessarily prolonged hospital stays.

Overall:

A very relevant issue to be aware of, especially considering the overall limitations in availability of hospital beds in the UK in relation to the population (237/100 000 in 2011). In the prospect of ever shrinking social care budgets and increasing amounts of council budget cuts, it becomes an even more pressing issue. Furthermore, a good answer to this question demonstrates an understanding of the interaction of different levels of healthcare and the interface between these levels and the patients. Different healthcare environments have different requirements in regards to funding, but all are highly relevant for the overall delivery of care that in the end spans all levels of care provision.

150.   What do you do in your free time?

This is a very nice question that comes up occasionally. Remember, the consultant jobs are long term jobs and they would like to see the human side of you. The interviewers are seeing if you are "like them". Maybe they are short in their football/cricket team? Maybe they need someone to carry the torch in the upcoming sporting event? Your response allows them to see you outside of medical field and you should use it to your full advantage.

Bad Response:

"I absolutely love medicine and everything medicine related. I spent my free time reading journals or look for ongoing research to see if I can get involved in some. I have also recently become interested in astrophysics so I bought a telescope last week and have been looking for stars in the sky ever since. I play video games in my spare time; my favourite game is World of Warcraft."

Response Analysis:

They are really asking what you do for fun. Please note that reading journal is not an activity that would make you stand out. Whilst you may be trying to impress them it can backfire. Do not worry if your free time activity is not medicine related- they don't have to be. The second interest of astrophysics may be genuine but it has only lasted one week- try to have activities that you have been doing for an extended period of time so that you can show commitment. Finally, there is nothing wrong with playing video games but this does not add anything to your answer. Activity you bring up must add a desirable quality to you as a candidate.

Good Response:

"Outside of medicine, I am very interested in astrology. I have been visiting my local fortune teller since the age of 14. Over the last ten years, I have really got to learn about the history behind this field. Although I myself do not really believe in this field, it is fascinating to look at other people's perspectives. I also really enjoy playing video games, specifically World of Warcraft. This game has been a real passion of mine so I have formed a World of Warcraft society. We are particularly interested in the graphics behind the video game, so each week, we analyse a portion of the computer code from the game and try to learn as much as possible from it. I think this has really led me to develop my programming skills which helped me create my own heart monitor application. This application allows users to track their heart rate over 30 minutes. We are now trialling this in marathon runners."

Response Analysis:

This response is significantly better as each pastime activity adds something to the candidate's skill set. Although astrology might seem like a ludicrous activity, many patients you see in hospital will rely partially on alternative forms of medicine. The candidate states that it is interesting to see other people's perspectives so this will be particularly useful for these patients. Just like the bad response, the candidate has an interest in video games, however, this time, they have formed a society. This shows both initiative and teamwork skills. Secondly, they learn programming in this society which can only be an advantage in an ever more digital world. Finally, they link these skills to a medical application which ties off the answer very nicely.

Overall:

The question might seem very innocent at first, however, it is very easy to mess it up. You must ensure that each of your extracurricular activities adds a positive characteristic to your profile. They do not have to be medically related but the skills that you gain from them should be applicable to medicine.

151. What do you enjoy most about your hobby?

This question is an opportunity to demonstrate that you are a multi-dimensional person. Doctors tend to be well-rounded people and often have other pursuits outside of medicine. When answering this question, focus less on what you have achieved through your hobby and more on how you have developed and how that can relate to a career in medicine.

Bad Response:

"I play the piano and the saxophone to a high standard. The thing I enjoy most is playing in the church choir where we get to try out lots of different music genres and also perform on a regular basis. I have played in the band for many years and am now the 1st saxophone."

Response Analysis:

This response does answer the question, but it also wastes the opportunity to show off achievements, skills, and knowledge. The answer is too superficial and should instead delve into what has been gained from playing in the choir, and whether or not this could be useful for the future. Also, only one element of playing musical instruments is discussed, which is a shame as the others could have demonstrated other qualities.

Good Response:

"My main hobby is music; I have played the piano and the saxophone for many. This has taken years of dedication, practice and commitment. This hard work has taught me to persevere and see something through to the end, because eventually, I would master the piece I was struggling with and would then really enjoy playing it. The sense of achievement and accomplishment is great. Music is something that can be appreciated by many, so I'm incredibly lucky to have been given the opportunity to perform many times which has brought my friends and family together and really heightened my confidence. I also joined the hospital radio, which truly developed my sense of teamwork. However, I play 1st saxophone, so I also have to lead the other saxophonists whilst listening attentively to ensure we all stayed in time and tune together. I think all of these skills I've been lucky enough to gain from something I enjoy so much will really help me to become a good consultant."

Response Analysis:

This response picks one hobby – music, and breaks it down into its different elements which allows for a much more complex answer. This can be done whatever your hobby – e.g. if you are interested in sports you can talk about training, matches, coaching other people etc. For each element, think of something you have learnt from it that you think might be an important quality in a doctor. Although this may sound like a simple question on the surface, it can be explored much deeper to demonstrate that you understand what it takes to make a good doctor. It clearly highlights some of the transferable skills that can be developed in music. The answer doesn't seem to be forced.

Overall:

Pick a broad hobby such as music, sports, or performing arts, and break it down into its individual components. You can draw on what you have gained and learnt while taking part in your hobby and how this can apply to medicine. It is important that you actually answer the question and demonstrate how much you enjoy your hobby!

152. Do you think you will have time to continue your hobby when you start as a consultant?

Being a consultant is an extremely demanding and challenging job with a large workload and plentiful patient contact hours. This means that time management is imperative for success. It does not mean that your life should involve solely your work and nothing else- this is not a healthy balance to have. Many consultants may think that the job is mainly focused on patient care or the academic side only, in reality, this is not true. Trusts recognise the need for consultants to have balanced lifestyles because hobbies are a good stress relief and enable them to develop skills such as teamwork and perseverance which will be beneficial to their future careers. Continuing a hobby demonstrates good time management skills, which is an important skill in many parts of life.

Bad Response:

"Although I currently have a few hobbies, I understand that the workload as Consultant Neurologist will be highly demanding, therefore, I might not be able to continue them. I would like to bring my guitar in case I get some free time when I am not working, and maybe play some sports. However, I know that the contact hours will be long so I may not have much free time when I take this post. At the end of the day, I have trained hard to be where I want to be and if I get time outside of that to continue a hobby that will be great, but if not, it won't be the end of the world!"

Response Analysis:

This response suggests that the candidate would be happy to just focus on their job and have no life outside of that showing poor time management skills. It is also worrying that the candidate is happy to give up all hobbies, potentially leaving them with no methods of managing stress which can be high at some points during the challenging job as a consultant. Therefore, the candidate may find it hard to cope with the stresses if they do not do anything outside of their studies.

Good Response:

"I fully understand and am expecting consultant job to be highly demanding and challenging, with busy time schedule, lots of work may need be done outside of normal working hours. Therefore, I am likely to have less free time available to me than when I was a registrar. I enjoy Football, play the guitar, and being part of the charities committee, all of which have helped me to develop valuable skills such as teamwork which will be beneficial in my future role as consultant. Doing lots of activities has also helped me to improve my time management skills, which is directly transferable to my career as consultant. Therefore, although perhaps I will not be able to continue all of the hobbies I currently have, I certainly will not stop them all to spend my time solely focused on job. Using my good time management skills, I would definitely like to keep up playing football but I am also keen to try something new. I strongly believe that to succeed in my future role and career, hobbies play an important part in maintaining a healthy and balanced lifestyle that will lead to success."

Response Analysis:

The candidate comes across as passionate about their hobbies and will likely use them in a positive way to benefit rather than hinder their career. The interviewers will be keen to meet well-rounded individuals who are able to manage their time well and develop important life skills which will be necessary during their future career in medicine. It is good that the candidate has recognised that being consultant is about learning life skills and becoming well-rounded as an individual.

Overall:

Although academia is obviously an extremely important part of the medical degree, it is important to have hobbies outside of your studies. Not only does this demonstrate good time management skills, but also hobbies are often a crucial method for managing the stress of such a challenging course. The trusts want to ensure that you are able to deal with this stress, and will also be keen for candidates to get involved with other aspects of life, thus make a positive impact on the community.

153. What does lifelong learning mean to you?

Background Analysis:

Life as a consultant inevitably requires a commitment to lifelong learning. Medicine is such a fast-moving field that even the most experienced doctors are required to work to keep up-to-date on recent developments in research, technology and clinical guidelines. This process, termed 'continuing professional development', is not just good practice but a formal requirement throughout a medical career. Consultants need to keep themselves clinically updated and follow good medical practice. They must demonstrate that they are up to date with modern practices.

Bad Response:

"Lifelong learning is something you are supposed to do in medicine to make sure that, as medicine advances, you know exactly what the perfect treatment for every patient is. For example, if you learn all the guidelines from NICE, the National Institute for Health and Care Excellence, then you will know what is best for all your patients."

Response Analysis:

While this candidate shows that they do appreciate that there is a need for lifelong learning in a medical career, there are significant problems with this answer. They have not shown why Consultant need to learn though they don't need to pass any exams any more. They also show very little understanding of what form this learning takes. There is substantially more to it than simply memorising guidelines. In addition, be careful when using terms such as 'the perfect treatment' as this may be taken to suggest that the candidate has an unrealistic understanding of what medicine is really like and can achieve – medicine remains an imperfect science, where sometimes doctors have to accept that there is no perfect treatment.

Good Response:

"To me, lifelong learning is a critical part of what it means to be a doctor. As well as the learning requirements that doctors are required to go through throughout their careers, such as building portfolios of their skills and undergoing revalidation, I think there is also a much more personal element to lifelong learning. I think it is about honing your clinical practice to try and be the best doctor you can possibly be. This is not just by making sure you are as up-to-date as possible with medical advances and guidelines, but also by reflecting on your own practice to think how you can improve it. It is also an essential requirement to stay updated and retain the licence to practice. This makes clinical care more evidence based and minimises error and care become more governance safe."

Response Analysis:

This candidate has demonstrated a good understanding of some of the elements of continuing professional development while also introducing a thoughtful and more personal response about what lifelong learning means to them. The candidate also shows a realistic understanding that it is not possible to be completely up-to-date with everything in the medical field, but that it is important to do our best to keep on top of the important things. As always, notice the clever inclusion of some buzz word (good medical practice, governance, revalidation).

Overall:

If you are someone who really enjoys learning new things, then this is the perfect kind of question to talk about that and how you have shown/experienced that in the past. It will reinforce the impression that you really are committed to a career where staying UpToDate is a must. Furthermore, continuing professional development is a very popular concept in the medical community and a requirement by GMC.

INTERVIEW PRESENTATIONS

Why are presentations used?

Medical Consultant interviews are getting more and more competitive. There are several dimensions to this role requiring presentations. Many times, when we have corporate meetings or a business plan which is presented, consultants may be required to present to a group of people. With an IT, surge most of this work is now done Power Point presentation.

In addition the panel would also like to know you and know whether you are someone who gets anxious, or whether you have a fear of public speaking, whether you have what it takes to deliver and whether you can speak coherently without feeling under pressure and whether you would be able to hold a meeting where people will have an interest in your presentation, what you are going to say and keep the interest alive and engage the audience. In addition, they may also want to hear your views about a certain topic.

Most of the time the candidates are given a topic to present so that they can have a coherent view. This is the opportunity for the candidate to come up with a problem, a possible solution as well as convey to the panel that they are a good speaker and can engage an audience in what they are doing.

What is this testing?

As discussed above, this is testing the following:

➢ Your presentation skills.
➢ Your comfort level with IT and Technology.
➢ Whether you are able to incorporate new changes – for example: use of animation, graphics, linking slides with audio visual aids.
➢ Checking whether you are able to communicate your thoughts, your presentation style as well as your problem solution abilities.

How to prepare for presentation?

Most people will have their own style after having had a structured training they would have developed their own strategies to make a presentation and deliver it. Following section give you some tips. These are just for advice only; feel free to experiment and follow your own style.

Know the topic:

You will be given the topic a few weeks before or at the time of invite for interview. In some cases or for senior post, it may be given at the time of the interview and you are given a short time to prepare your slides.

Prepare your presentation:

Do some research around it and find out **why** this topic has been chosen by the specific organisation. If you know this, you can do this by gleaning the information at the time of the pre-interview visit, talking to different people working in the organisation, looking at public ally available meeting reports (the Trust's, Executive report, the Public reports, the Board meetings). All of this should give you an idea about the reason why a specific topic was chosen.

Scale of the problem:

Check if the problem is unique to the Trust or whether it is a generalised problem. Your solution would depend on whether it is unique. If it is specific to the problem, again, look at working policies, guidelines at the Trust level to see

what could be the reason that the Trust is specifically having. If it is general, then the problem is wide-spread and you can come up with generalised solutions.

Problems specific to the Trust: Solution

The solution would depend on what you have found. For example, if the Trust is having lots of ED breaches and although the problem is seen across the NHS, in this particular Trust the A&E does not have the capacity, they do not have enough minor patient holding areas, the solution could be to create more space. While on the surface it may look easy, getting a space, finding a building and getting all this done within a time frame would be challenging. Therefore, a solution might be to increase patient flow, increase the capacity in Outpatient clinic so that patients who are admitted or are waiting for assessment for a problem which could easily be handled in Outpatients can be sorted by 'hot clinics', use of services such as a Rapid Assessment service, Ambulatory Care services would be another way to reduce or decant A&E.

Once you have found out what the problem is, also look at what is happening in your field, how can you involve the new changes happening, and see if any of those can fit into the problem. In essence, be aware of new changes, new guidelines, any bigger initiative at Trust level or a country wise level.

If this problem is in breach of some major guidelines or recommendations, look at that aspect.

Basically, good research would help you in preparing your presentation. Once you have collected the material, do a rough draft, put all the information on a slide and then give them headings. It would be a good idea to have the slides as the main topic and, if you can give sub-headings, it would be useful because highlighting the problem, the magnitude of the problem, the impact of this on the current environment, how it affects the NHS, how it affects the specific organisation, what are the barriers to a resolution, what is the resolution and how the barriers can be overcome. Then, sum up. The summary should include just the three lines – citing the problem, the barriers, solutions and a way forward.

Therefore, ensure your suggested solution is SMART (**S**mart, **M**easurable, **A**chievable, **R**eproducible, **T**imed)

Some buzz word to include are; the PDSA cycle, use of patient surveys, patient feed-back, national audit guidelines, CHC report, data from Doctor Foster. Showing all of these things in your presentation will make your presentation stand out, it will show that you have given some thought about the presentation, the magnitude of the problem is looked at and it will just add value to your presentation.

Slides:

Keep things simple; have mini sub-sections to include a beginning, a middle and an end in your presentation. At the start, always have a powerful sentence in order to engage your panel members; this could be something like *"I am going to show you...*insert topic". Therefore, if you are given a topic e.g. 'We have staffing issues with the medical on-call rota, we do not have enough junior doctors – what are the solutions?' Your statement could be: *"Today I am going to show you the problems with the on-call rota and how we can resolve it."* This is a powerful statement you are making; they will try to listen to you. Try to come up with problems and why the problem is there. This is an opportunity for you to show that you understand the working of the NHS, you understand the law around the NHS, you understand the problems and the Governance issues; therefore, in this example, the shortage of junior doctors.

"The problem that we don't have enough junior doctors is that the EWTD puts restriction on how the junior doctors are used. We do need to make a balance between the training and the service component. We need to ensure that our doctors do remain up to date and they attend their mandatory training days and that they are fresh at work following their on-call weekends or on-call night; all of this adds to the problem. The solution to this could be something as simple as making the rota compliant, by recruiting more doctors, finding different ways e.g. overseas doctor recruitment, use of physician assistants so that   here is a skill mix, we can up-skill people to do the task where major clinical decisions are made by the Clinicians but some of the tasks can be delegated to a different group of people who are skilled in such an area. The hospital at night, or   example, is an example where the nurses are trained to carry out simple tasks such as cannula, blood gasses or even certify death. This frees up the junior doctors when they are busy at night as these tasks are performed by someone who does not need medical training but can carry out the task safely. Juniors doctors continue to see the patients who are sick, unwell and make clinical decisions."

You have then given a solution, suggested some ideas after which you can say:

"In order to improve or resolve the solution of the shortage of doctors on-call in the rota we need to ensure that we are Governance safe, we remain EWTD compliant by either recruiting people from different sources, up-skill our team or develop the rota so that it has minimal impact on continuity of care as well as not compromising doctors' training and clinical work".

This way, you have given a good run-down of the whole presentation, given them an example of a Problem, Solution and barriers to the solution.

Some simple tricks in slide preparation:
➢ Keep slides background dark with a light font
➢ Choose font size and keep to it: do not change style in same slide or slide to slide
➢ Avoid use of multiple drop-downs or flying slides, word drops
➢ Use of animation is acceptable but avoid use of too much animation during presentation. It should add rather than distract.
➢ Avoid sexual references or any personal kind of comment.
➢ Try to avoid any controversy that could bounce back or reflect badly on you.

Delivering the presentation

➢ Appear confident and calm and have a strong opening, clear middle and strong ending
➢ Keep to time: No point in having a glowing presentation but not to have the time to finish it; if you are given 10-minutes. Aim to finish it in 9 ½ minutes. You will need to prepare, present and practice in order to finish it in time.
➢ Do not talk for a long time, use short sentences.
➢ Use slides as cue and talk around it
➢ Make eye contact: Pause in between and maintain good eye contact with different panel members.
➢ Look for impact: When you have made a point try to look at the audience and the panel to see the impact. If they are shaking, nodding or smiling you know that you have won them over, but if you feel that they are distracted, just waiting for the presentation to be over, then perk up your presentation.
➢ Panels reaction: Do not worry if they are making notes, they might just be writing down a point so that they can quiz you on this.
➢ Ending your presentation: You will be asked questions towards the end so ensure you finish on time and leave with a question saying "Do you have any questions?". You will be asked questions as you may have said something that interests them – so be prepared for them.

Top tip: Read around the topic. Look for extent of the issue and solutions

---

Some don'ts (when presenting):

➢ Don't be nervous or anxious
➢ Avoid slang/jargons
➢ Do not keep talking about past: Talk about present/future
➢ Do not joke: it may not go down well and if it does not create a desired response you will get anxious!
➢ Avoid busy slide and do not read every word from the slide: they can see for themselves
➢ You should not be pacing around – unless you need to get out of people's view, in which case find yourself a comfortable position where you can look at the audience
➢ Keeps slides less wordy: use pictures if appropriate.

When delivering your presentation:

➢ Appear confident
➢ Your stance should be solid
➢ Your presentation is visible to you
➢ You should not turn back to look at the screen. Position yourself in such a way that you are able to see the slides on the computer in front of you
➢ Ensure you have previously used the projectors, you have used the slide forward or remove button etc and you are aware of its use so that any mishaps can be avoided i.e. accidental slide forward etc. If this happens during your presentation just say *"the slide has gone forwards, let's go back to the slide"* – rather than confusing the audience and getting nervous about it.

You should appear energetic during your presentation because the audience usually mirrors your energy level. If you appear very drawn out, bored etc, they will lose interest in your presentation very quickly. A good presentation is something that makes a strong, powerful statement; it has a beginning, it has body and it sums up.

The best presentations usually:
1. Tell them what you are going to show.
2. Tell them
3. Sum up by saying "I have just shown you this, this is the way forward" end by giving them the opportunity to ask questions.

Avoid time recording to automatically forward slides as you deliver your presentation. Whilst it can give you the liberty to stay away from the keyboard, a number of things can cause the slide and talk to become out of synch! You may be fast/slow because you are nervous or you may be stopped for a question and the Power Point *auto-play* will continue to play the slide which may make you nervous even more.

Another recommendation is to have some extra slides which may be relevant to the topic but that you keep them as a reserve; therefore, just in case there is a question you can say " *well, I was expecting this question so let me show you this slide"* – which will have your evidence, your thoughts and will just give a good impression because they can see that you are prepared, you have thought about it. You will therefore come across as a strong person. You can see more tips on making a winning presentation or getting a feedback on the presentation that you are doing by visiting www.medicalconsultantinterview.co.uk

FINAL ADVICE

1) **Don't be put off by what other candidates say** in the waiting room. Focus on yourself – you are all that matters. If you want to be in the zone, then I would recommend taking some headphones and your favourite music.

2) **Don't read up on multiple advanced topics in depth to the exclusion of others.** You should be able to give a balanced view and hence you should know both sides of the argument.

3) **Don't worry about being asked seemingly irrelevant questions.** Focus on being able to answer the common questions, e.g. "Why this job/this organisation" etc.

4) **Don't give up.** Faced with a situation where you are asked questions outside of your experience/knowledge, e.g. you're presented with complex scenarios, go back to the absolute basics and try to work things out using first principles. By doing this and thinking out loud, you allow the interviewer to see your logical train of thought, show them the experiences you have, draw from experiences and come up with some plausible explanations.

5) **Practice.** There is no substitute for hard work. Work your way through medical Consultant Interview questions.

On the Interview Day

- Get a good night's sleep before interview day
- Take a shower in the morning and dress at least smart-casual. It is probably safest to turn up in a suit
- Get there early so you aren't late or stressed out before the interview even starts
- Don't worry about other candidates; be nice of course, but you are there for you. Their impressions of how their interviews went have nothing to do with what the interviewers thought or how yours will go
- It's okay to be nervous – they know you're nervous and understand, but try to move past it and be in the moment to get the most out of the experience
- Try to convey to the interviewer that you are enjoying the interview

Some Dos:

- ✓ **DO** speak freely about what you are thinking and ask for clarifications
- ✓ **DO** take suggestions and listen for pointers from your interviewer
- ✓ **DO** try your best to get to the answer
- ✓ **DO** have confidence in yourself and the abilities that got you this far
- ✓ **DO** a dress rehearsal beforehand so that you can identify any clothing issues before the big day
- ✓ **DO** make many suggestions and have many ideas
- ✓ **DO** take your time in answering to make sure your words come out right
- ✓ **DO** be polite and honest with your interviewer
- ✓ **DO** prepare your answers by thinking about the questions above
- ✓ **DO** answer the question the interviewer asked
- ✓ **DO** think about strengths/experiences you may wish to highlight
- ✓ **DO** visit www.medicalconsultantinterview.co.uk for more interview questions
- ✓ **DO** consider attending an interview course: www.medicalconsultantinterview.co.uk

Some DON'Ts:

- ✗ **DON'T** be afraid to pause for a moment to gather your thoughts before answering a question. It shows confidence and will lead to a clearer answer
- ✗ **DON'T** rehearse scripted answers to be regurgitated
- ✗ **DON'T** answer the question you wanted them to ask – answer the one that they did!
- ✗ **DON'T** lie about things you have read/done (and if you already lied in your application, then read/do them before the interview!)

AFTER THE INTERVIEW

Its over. You have put in your best feet forward. You can't change anything now. You have the option to head home or wait for the HR to contact you. You can choose to wait to hear the outcome and receive feedback. Remember, it is very difficult to predict how an interview has gone so don't be discouraged if it feels like your interview didn't go well – you may have shown the interviewers exactly what they wanted to see even if it wasn't what you wanted to see. Indeed, many people who are given an offer after their interview had felt that it had not gone well at all. Once the interview is over, take a well-deserved rest and enjoy the fact that there's nothing left to do. Above all, smile.

Interview outcome

After the interview the possibility is that on the day of the interview a number of candidates will be interviewed so you have the option to wait, however sometimes the interview could last a long time and it may be quite late and you may have a journey to make. In those situations, the HR personnel from the panel will take your details and advise you that they will contact you by phone later on. If you need to leave, hopefully the HR personnel will inform you the next day or at a suitable time that you have been offered the job. In the unlikely situation that you have not been successful it is useful and strongly recommended that you take the name of the designated person who is giving you feed back.

Feedback: Not getting the job

Feedback is an essential part of the interview process where the panel members will designate a person - who is one of the panel members - to take it upon their self to give you the feedback on your interview. Sometimes the feedback could simply be in the form of 'The better candidates were available' or 'You just did not make it'. If it because you were not competent enough or you couldn't 'make it' because the other candidates were brighter, it might be useful to probe the feedback provider to ask what you could do better next time.

We strongly advise you to ask specifically whether it was a clinical issue i.e. your clinical experience not being sufficient, not matching the department needs (you should have sussed it out at the time of the pre-interview visit and from the job description though); or was it that they needed a more managerial/hands on person who could also be involved in management, did they require a senior person, did they require a more experienced person because the tasks or clinic etc. are more complex in nature, was it your interview skill – did you not perform well, were your answers too long, too short or lacked the depth.

Good feedback is essential as it is important to learn from the mistakes you made in this interview so that you do not make those mistakes again and again. If it is local it might be useful to take this feedback face to face but, understandably, this will require commitment and some travel and will not always be possible so set aside some time when the person providing feedback also has 10-15 minutes to give you the feedback to make it useful.

Important Links/websites

The list is not exhaustive and you should try to explore and get as much info as you can o prepare, plan and succeed in your interview.

Please visit www.medicalconsultantinterview.co.uk for more questions

➢ NICE: National Institute for Health and care Excellence: https://www.nice.org.uk
➢ GMC: general Medical Council: https://www.gmc-uk.org
➢ Conflict resolution: https://improvement.nhs.uk/resources/managing-conflict/
➢ CQC:Care Quality Commission: https://www.qcs.co.uk/
➢ CQUIN:https://www.england.nhs.uk/publication/commissioning-for-quality-and-innovation-cquin-guidance-for-2017-2019
➢ National Health Executive: http://www.nationalhealthexecutive.com
➢ NPSA: The National Patient Safety Agency: Now abolished
➢ BMA: British Medical Association: https://www.bma.org.uk
➢ MDU: Medical Defence Union: https://www.themdu.com
➢ MPS: Medical protection society: https://www.medicalprotection.org/uk
➢ Dr Foster: https://www.drfoster.com
➢ CEA: Clinical excellence award
➢ Francis enquiry: executive summary):
https://assets.publishing.service.gov.uk/government/uploads/system/uploads/attachment_data/file/279124/0947.pdf
➢ NHS Jobsite: https://www.jobsite.co.uk
➢ MMC: Modernising Medical Careers
➢ The Medicines and Healthcare products Regulatory Agency: http://gov.uk/mhra
➢ NHS Improvement: https://improvement.nhs.uk/resources/patient-safety-alerts/
➢ National Reporting & Learning System: email: patientsafetyhelpdesk@nrls.nhs.uk
➢ RCA: https://improvement.nhs.uk/documents/2156/root-cause-analysis-five-whys.pdf

Afterword

Remember that the route to success is your approach and practice. Don't fall into the trap that *"you can't prepare for consultant interviews"*– this could not be further from the truth. With targeted preparation and focused reading, you can dramatically boost your chances of getting that job you have worked so hard. Work hard, never give up, and do yourself justice.

Good luck!

Acknowledgements

Authors wish to thank Mrs Loraine Wilbourn for the assistance in the preparation of this manuscript. We also acknowledge valuable time given by Dr Shaughn Ude to fine tune some sections. I'm hopeful that future consultants will continue to benefit from this work for many years to come.

About MCI: Medical Consultant Interview

MCI is a consultancy that specialises in Medical Consultant Interviews. MCI is the brain child of Dr Ranjna Garg, Consultant Endocrinologist and Dr Anil K Agarwal Consultant Stroke with more than 25 years of experience as clinician, author and editor and Dr Rohan Agarwal CO-founder of UniAdmissions and author and editor of the Ultimate guide series.

We work with registrars and consultants to help them attain their dream jobs. To find out more about our support like intensive consultant interview courses check out **www.medicalconsultantinterview.co.uk**

Printed in Great Britain
by Amazon